TEMPORALITIES

Temporalities presents a concise critical introduction to the treatment of time throughout literature. Time and its passage represent one of the oldest and most complex philosophical subjects in art of all forms, and Russell West-Pavlov explains and interrogates the most important theories of temporality across a range of disciplines.

The author explores temporality's relationship with a diverse range of related concepts, including:

- historiography
- psychology
- gender
- economics
- postmodernism
- postcolonialism.

Russell West-Pavlov examines time as a crucial part of the critical theories of Newton, Freud, Ricoeur and Benjamin, and explores the treatment of time in a broad range of texts, ranging from the writings of St. Augustine and Sterne's *Tristram Shandy*, to Woolf's *Mrs Dalloway* and the poetry of Philip Larkin.

This comprehensive and accessible guide establishes temporality as an essential theme within literary and cultural studies today.

Russell West-Pavlov is Professor of English at the University of Pretoria, South Africa.

THE NEW CRITICAL IDIOM

SERIES EDITOR: JOHN DRAKAKIS, UNIVERSITY OF STIRLING

The New Critical Idiom is an invaluable series of introductory guides to today's critical terminology. Each book:

- provides a handy, explanatory guide to the use (and abuse) of the term;
- offers an original and distinctive overview by a leading literary and cultural critic;
- relates the term to the larger field of cultural representation.

With a strong emphasis on clarity, lively debate and the widest possible breadth of examples, *The New Critical Idiom* is an indispensable approach to key topics in literary studies.

Also available in this series:

The Author by Andrew Bennett
Autobiography – second edition by Linda Anderson
Adaptation and Appropriation by Julie Sanders
Allegory by Jeremy Tambling
Class by Gary Day
Colonialism/Postcolonialism – second edition by Ania Loomba
Comedy by Andrew Stott
Crime Fiction by John Scaggs
Culture/Metaculture by Francis Mulhern
Dialogue by Peter Womack
Difference by Mark Currie
Discourse – second edition by Sara Mills
Drama/Theatre/Performance by Simon Shepherd and Mick Wallis
Dramatic Monologue by Glennis Byron
Ecocriticism – second edition by Greg Garrard
Elegy by David Kennedy
Genders – second edition by David Glover and Cora Kaplan
Genre by John Frow
Gothic by Fred Botting
The Historical Novel by Jerome de Groot
Historicism – second edition by Paul Hamilton
Humanism – second edition by Tony Davies
Ideology – second edition by David Hawkes
Interdisciplinarity – second edition by Joe Moran

Intertextuality – second edition by Graham Allen
Irony by Claire Colebrook
Literature by Peter Widdowson
Lyric by Scott Brewster
Magic(al) Realism by Maggie Ann Bowers
Memory by Anne Whitehead
Metaphor by David Punter
Metre, Rhythm and Verse Form by Philip Hobsbaum
Mimesis by Matthew Potolsky
Modernism – second edition by Peter Childs
Myth – second edition by Laurence Coupe
Narrative by Paul Cobley
Parody by Simon Dentith
Pastoral by Terry Gifford
Performativity by James Loxley
The Postmodern by Simon Malpas
Realism by Pam Morris
Rhetoric by Jennifer Richards
Romance by Barbara Fuchs
Romanticism – second edition by Aidan Day
Science Fiction – second edition by Adam Roberts
Sexuality – second edition by Joseph Bristow
Stylistics by Richard Bradford
Subjectivity by Donald E. Hall
The Sublime by Philip Shaw
Travel Writing by Carl Thompson
The Unconscious by Antony Easthope

TEMPORALITIES

Russell West-Pavlov

Routledge
Taylor & Francis Group

LONDON AND NEW YORK

First published 2013
by Routledge
2 Park Square, Milton Park, Abingdon, Oxon OX14 4RN

Simultaneously published in the USA and Canada
by Routledge
711 Third Avenue, New York, NY 10017

Routledge is an imprint of the Taylor & Francis Group, an informa business

British Library Cataloguing in Publication Data
A catalogue record for this book is available from the British Library

Library of Congress Cataloging in Publication Data
West-Pavlov, Russell, 1964–
Temporalities / Russell West-Pavlov.
p. cm. – (The new critical idiom)
1. Literature–History and criticism–Theory, etc. 2. Time in literature. I. Title.
PN441.W4565 2012
809'.93384–dc23
2012014145

ISBN: 978-0-415-52073-7 (hbk)
ISBN: 978-0-415-52074-4 (pbk)
ISBN: 978-0-203-10687-7 (ebk)

Typeset in Garamond
by Taylor & Francis Books

Printed and bound in Great Britain by the MPG Books Group

CONTENTS

ACKNOWLEDGEMENTS

I wish to acknowledge the kindness and support of John Drakakis, who suggested a book on this topic when I had something else in mind, thus obliging me to enlarge my intellectual horizons in ways I could not have foreseen. I also wish to acknowledge the friendly and professional expertise of Niall Slater and Emma Hudson at Routledge.

I would like to thank my colleagues at the Free University of Berlin, Jens Elze, Andrew James Johnston, Cordula Lemke and Jennifer Wawrzinek, for their friendship during the initial phase of the writing of this book and beyond.

I wish to thank my marvellous colleagues at the University of Pretoria, Marc Botha, Molly Brown, Will Burger, Antony Goedhals, Patrick Lenahan, David Medalie, Stephan Mühr, Idette Noomé, Kulukhazi Soldati-Kahimbaara, Andries Visagie and Andries Wessels for the welcome they afforded me and my family in South Africa and for their unparalleled collegiality.

I owe a large debt of thanks to my international Australian colleagues, Andrew McCann, Philip Mead and Stephen Muecke, who have contributed to the making of this book in many diverse ways.

Finally, this project would not have taken on the texture it did without the everyday chaos of family life, shared with my wife Tatjana and our wonderfully noisy, messy, funny, creative and time-consuming children Joshua, Iva and Niklas.

SERIES EDITOR'S PREFACE

The New Critical Idiom is a series of introductory books which seeks to extend the lexicon of literary terms, in order to address the radical changes which have taken place in the study of literature during the last decades of the twentieth century. The aim is to provide clear, well-illustrated accounts of the full range of terminology currently in use, and to evolve histories of its changing usage.

The current state of the discipline of literary studies is one where there is considerable debate concerning basic questions of terminology. This involves, among other things, the boundaries which distinguish the literary from the non-literary; the position of literature within the larger sphere of culture; the relationship between literatures of different cultures; and questions concerning the relation of literary to other cultural forms within the context of interdisciplinary studies.

It is clear that the field of literary criticism and theory is a dynamic and heterogeneous one. The present need is for individual volumes on terms which combine clarity of exposition with an adventurousness of perspective and a breadth of application. Each volume will contain as part of its apparatus some indication of the direction in which the definition of particular terms is likely to move, as well as expanding the disciplinary boundaries within which some of these terms have been traditionally contained. This will involve some re-situation of terms within the larger field of cultural representation, and will introduce examples from the area of film and the modern media in addition to examples from a variety of literary texts.

INTRODUCTION

A 1953 poem by the British poet Philip Larkin asks the apparently simple but shockingly confounding question: 'What are days for?' It gives an equally simple but also unfathomable response: 'Days are where we live'. This apparent certainty is immediately undone by the irritated rhetorical question, 'Where can we live but days?' Such a riposte, of course, is not much of a solution. And so the poem has recourse, by way of conclusion, to merely sketching the dire consequences of asking questions that admit of no answers:

> Ah, solving that question
> Brings the priest and the doctor
> In their long coats
> Running over the fields.
>
> (Larkin 1988: 67)

Larkin's poem dramatizes the inscrutability of time, rendering it both more pedestrian by reducing it to 'days', but also more strange by the absence of any qualifier. He suggests that asking about the nature of time, one of the age-old questions of philosophy, may be a wrong-headed, Sisyphean endeavour: so much so that interrogating time's enigma may herald intimations of mortality, an impending sense of the end of one's days, or worse, may unseat reason. The raising of such imponderable questions is sanctioned by the authority of the church or by the threat of medical intervention. Larkin seems to be implying that the interrogation of such a fundamentally self-evident and thus unquestionable cornerstone of human existence may in some mysterious way constitute a threat great enough to trigger the immediate invocation of authority and repression.

Larkin's poem links two salient points: the self-evidence of time, manifest in the blank incomprehension aroused by this simplest of questions; and an only vaguely articulated threat which appears to respond to the question. This book seeks to link these two aspects by embarking upon an interrogation of the self-evident nature of time and of the coercive forces which may lurk behind the façade of common sense time. Common sense may be one of the most powerful instruments of ideology, allowing habits of thought to anchor 'false consciousness' deeply in our sense of what is natural, normal and invulnerable to scrutiny. And yet the questioning of common sense may be one of the most pressing of intellectual tasks, and time one of its most urgently beckoning sites of enquiry.

Characteristically for Larkin and his refusal of highbrow themes, the poem does not answer the question, but merely deflects it. The poem's own texture is baffling in its simplicity – but is equally baffled itself, whence the abruptness of its conclusion. It seeks to close down the interrogations it has raised, forcing the reader either to turn the page, moving on to the next poem, or to seek to go beyond its gruff dismissal of the very questions it throws up. The poem triggers what chaos theory calls a 'bifurcation': an unpredictable moment of decision, in which the various factors at work in a dynamic process act upon each other in apparently only marginally varying ways, but with significantly divergent consequences (Gleick 1988: 70–75; Bennett 2010: 7).

The interaction between these extracts from Larkin's poem, my discussion of them, and your reading of both the extracts and my comments are the constituent elements of a moment of 'bifurcation'. You may merely shrug your shoulders and hasten on to the next section of the introduction. Or you may begin to wonder what 'Days' (the poem) and 'days' (the temporal segments) are really all about. And that, in turn, may have quite various effects upon how you live your own days. This, I suggest in the book you have before you, is what time is 'for', to take up Larkin's turn of phrase. Time is neither for calibrating the progress of existence, nor for containing its forward movement ('where we live'). Rather, before and below any utilitarian 'for', time is the very dynamic of existence, the pulsating drive of the unceasing transformation of being itself.

'Time' is a term that at first glance may seem utterly common sense, indeed, banal, albeit rather abstract. Upon closer scrutiny, however, it transpires to be one of the oldest and most complex subjects of philosophical reflection, artistic representation and aesthetic **discourse**. It underpins virtually all aspects of everyday life, as even the term 'everyday' reveals. It is also riddled with issues of power and hegemony, and is at stake in much political struggle: calendars, for instance, were always the creations of political elites (whence the 'Gregorian' calendar, promulgated in 1582 by the Pope of the same name, becoming hegemonic in Europe in the seventeenth century and still in use today [Holford-Strevens 2005]). This makes time a fascinating, wide-ranging and central subject of enquiry for the humanities.

This book maps the ways in which 'time' has been constructed by technological, economic and geo-political forces over centuries, rather than simply being a natural given. In contrast to the absolute and **universal time**, abstract, transcendent, 'empty' and 'homogenous' (Benjamin 1999: 252), that we take for granted, this book posits multiple temporal regimes which are coeval with the dynamic processes of life itself. There is no 'time' outside of the multiple ongoing processes of material becoming, the constant transformations, often invisible, that make up the life of apparently inert things. Every 'thing' is in fact a process; all these processes, taken together, make up the world as the sum total of its immanent 'times'. Going beyond the facile opposition of 'human experience' of time vs. 'public' or **absolute time**, the book proposes that multiple temporalities inhabit but also exceed the human scale, with agency and processual transformation (immanent temporalities) inhering in all human and non-human processes of becoming. This notion of temporalities has consequences for a radical critique of the unsustainable world order in which we live.

TIME AS DILEMMA

Time is self-evident, it needs no explanation. Its passing is indexed all around us on wrist-watches, mobile phone screens, digital displays, timetables, in train delays, traffic jams, deadlines, clocking-on and clocking-off. Its internal structuring into past, present and future is embedded in language, in collective memory and public monuments, in learnt aspirations and bodily ageing. Yet time is intangible, invisible, colourless, odourless, soundless.

All of this is self-evident yet deeply problematic for us. The nature of the past is incessantly debated. Death and ageing are taboo topics in our youth-obsessed society. The future is represented for us in a plethora of consumer images, of things we can have or ways we can be as soon as we buy this or that product. But simultaneously, it is a source of anxiety as the global climate becomes increasingly unstable and financial crises and worldwide food shortages loom on the horizon as recurring events.

Definitions of time have been perennially unsatisfactory. Saint Augustine (1961: 264) famously complained, 'What, then, is time? I know well enough what it is, provided that nobody asks me; but if I am asked what it is and try to explain, I am baffled.' Time has been the object of countless scientific or philosophical definitions, from the Greek Presocratic philosophers onwards. It can be defined mythically, poetically ('Truth is the daughter of time'). It can be gestured at indexically, as in Heidegger, who claims it is where Being happens (in Larkin's approximation, 'days are where we live'). It can be enumerated ostensively, by its linguistic usages (we can win time, save time, spend time, waste time). John Wheeler defined time as 'that which stops everything happening at once' (qtd in Davies 1996: 53). It remains all-pervasive, yet elusive.

Time is both eminently common-sensical and highly abstract at once. In Thomas Mann's turn of phrase, it is 'a secret', 'insubstantial and all-powerful' (1975: 344; translation modified).[1] This paradoxical mixture of not-needing-to-be-discussed and not-being-able-to-be-discussed constitutes a double subterfuge which is one of the most effective conspiracies of modernity. For, as I will posit in this book, time is in fact both highly complex, anything but self-evident, and by the same token, entirely concrete. It demands stringent analysis even though it is close at hand, indeed quite tangible, literally so, at every moment. However, the combination of self-evidence and abstraction effectively keeps it safe from interrogation so as to leave a particular version of time intact and immune to critical scrutiny.

Following Butler's example for gender, this book will suggest that time is one of the great 'natural' givens of our culture, 'performatively constituted by the very "expressions"' – increasingly accurate temporal calibrations, universal time frameworks – 'that are said to be its results' (1990: 25). The very naturalness of time reposes upon its power to elide, from the outset, its construction in discourse and via the mediation of technology. It is this elision which endows it with an extraordinary potency in organizing social life and managing it in the interests of power relations. As Elizabeth Freeman (2007: 160) has suggested, 'temporality is a mode of implantation through which institutional forces come to seem like somatic facts. Schedules, calendars, time zones, even wristwatches are ways to inculcate ... forms of temporal experience that seem natural to those they privilege.' Time's attributes of linearity ('what is past is past'), universality, quantifiability and commodifiability ('time is money'), and finally contemporaneity and modernity ('newer is better') all work to structure human existence according to the restrictive but profitable mechanisms of late capitalism. Time in its common-sense meaning is the most everyday but also the most ubiquitous practical codification of contemporary capitalism in its self-presentation as our planetary destiny. This version of time is so insidious because it has managed to persuade us that it is coextensive with the very fabric of existence itself, despite the increasingly daunting evidence to the contrary: the destructive nature of capitalism, and its globally self-vitiating dynamic, is revealed by global climate instability, the fragility of global financial systems, and impending global food shortages.

The recent history of time since the Enlightenment has evinced a progressive narrowing of the spectrum of temporal modes. The gradual streamlining of temporality down to universal linear time as the self-evident calibration of human existence has repressed and elided other possible temporal structurings of individual and global existence. It inherently claims, 'There is no alternative!' Such elisions have culminated in many cases in the wholesale destruction of alternative encodings of existence and concomitant communal practices. For instance, the atemporal environmental ethos of the Australian indigenous nations prior to European conquest was declared to be that of a 'timeless' but 'dying' race and was almost completely eradicated by colonial violence and state management. However, like the Australian indigenous ethos of the land, alternative temporalities remain latent and active under the threshold of linear time and its all but ubiquitous stranglehold. Other temporalities persist or subsist as marginal, subaltern practices susceptible of resuscitation under favourable circumstances.

It is curious that in the era of now-waning American-dominated finance capital, time has largely disappeared from the agenda of philosophy and the social sciences. Up until the 1940s, it was one of the dominant themes in European philosophy (Heise 1997: 36). By the middle of the twentieth century, however, time had gone out of fashion:

> The novelists and poets gave it up under the entirely plausible assumption that it had been largely covered by Marcel Proust, Mann, Virginia Woolf, and T. S. Eliot and offered few further chances of literary advancement. The philosophers also dropped it on the grounds that although Bergson remained a dead letter, Heidegger was still publishing a posthumous volume a year on the topic. And as for the mountain of secondary literature in both disciplines, to scale it once again seemed a rather old-fashioned thing to do with your life.
>
> (Jameson 2003b: 695)

Where time continued to be studied, it was merely 'social time', without the concept of time being itself given very much critical attention (Gurvitch 1964; May and Thrift 2001: 2). In general, both time and space, regardless of whether they were the focus of study in any respective social sciences discipline, were treated apart from each other. In this way, the crucial Enlightenment separation of time and space remained intact in the polarized components of a conceptual dualism (May and Thrift 2001: 1–2).

By and large, however, time has been neglected by gender studies and cultural studies (Grosz 2005: 1). Only in the last couple of decades has time begun to come back into view in the sciences (Prigogine and Stengers 1984: 208). Recently, though, philosophers such as Wood (2001: xxxv) suggested that 'our century-long "linguistic turn" will be followed by a spiralling return to the focus and horizon of all our thought and experience'. This book seeks to make an accessible contribution to that re-emergence of temporality as a subject of study in the humanities.

NOT JUST A BOOK ABOUT TIME

But this is not merely a book 'about' time. Rather, like any other entity, this book is caught up in time. It has been published by a commercial publisher interested in filling a gap in the academic market before some other publisher does. It will have a certain shelf-life, moving from front-list to back-list, before becoming a digital re-print, with fluctuations in the curve of profits as it competes with other titles, before perhaps becoming a 'classic' or alternatively becoming 'outdated'. It will also be involved in other temporal structures such as the hierarchical progression (e.g. first, second, final year) of a university degree for which it will perhaps be on a prescribed reading list or in the bibliography of a research thesis. Perhaps you are reading it in haste, with a tutorial or an essay or examination deadline looming on the horizon. As these last examples show, the book is part of temporal regimes such as formal education leading to professional qualifications which act as filters for social and economic power, channelling subjects into other temporal regimes (Berger and Luckmann 1971: 41). Such regimes, however, are the mechanisms that society employs to contain, control, exploit or master something far more fluid: an infinite multiplicity of material flows-of-becoming which unfold, emerge, dissipate and are transformed into other flows that connect with each other, converge or diverge, ceaselessly. These flows make up the unruly multiple temporalities which underpin streamlined Enlightenment 'time' but are subject to its hegemony.

This book, then, is not 'about' time; it is caught up in time, but even more, it embodies time in its very materiality. With its cover, its slab-like dimensions, the relative rigidity of its paper, it gives every impression of being an inert object. But that thing-ness, however, may assume different temporalities: is it a nondescript hardcover edition, intended for library purchase, made to withstand the wear and tear of repeated perusal by generations of students? Or is it a flimsy paperback with a striking cover, designed more to catch the eye of the bookshop browser than to endure for many years? Or is it a digital reprint, a slightly blurred makeover of an out-of-print first edition in our age of ever shorter shelf-lives and accelerating product turnover times? Or perhaps even an e-book, whose existence is as ephemeral as the time it is called up onto the screen from which it is read?

The book itself may become dynamic, may change in the course of reading: its pages may become frayed in the process of turning, it may acquire coffee stains or telephone numbers, or have bus-tickets placed between its pages. The reader may underline or annotate it. In the process of bending back the spine pages may fall out and be reinserted, accidentally, in the wrong order. Thus, the book as material object is itself merely a temporary coalescence of a long transformative process of trees into wood-chips into paper and print, which at some stage in the future will disintegrate and be burnt, pulped, recycled and eventually return in some form to the natural environment. But its changes may be more than simply entropic, for, as De Landa observes, 'inorganic matter is much more variable and creative than we ever imagined' (1997: 16).

More radically, then, let us consider the book as a material process of transforming ideas, one whose history extends backwards through a myriad of intersecting trains of thought, converging, colliding, merging, moving apart again, now coming together in the three or four dimensions of a book. The readings and writings and ruminations which led up to the composition of this book were a bundle of flowing processes hardly susceptible of being pinned

5

down to any origin. They have coalesced briefly and come to rest
between the pages of this volume, but only until the moment it
is opened. Now, after this short hiatus or hibernation on a book-
store table, on a library shelf or in your rucksack, those strands of
thought will be reactivated in the process of reading, which, for
some theorists is akin to writing: as Barthes said, 'the modern
scriptor is born simultaneously with the text ... there is no other
time than that of the enunciation and every text is eternally written
here and now' (Barthes 1977: 145). But the times of reading will
be far more complicated than this: one may read, re-read, one
may flip back and forth between different sections, one may
interrupt one's reading to check a source in another text (as I have
just done in my writing, to search out the Barthes quotation), one
may begin with the chapter that interests one most, then go back to
the beginning. Reading may be like Sterne's writing, 'digressive ...
[and] progressive too – and at the same time' (1985: 95). The text
may develop its own set of connections: it may trigger off new trains
of thought in one's own system of ideas, excerpts may migrate into
essays, or be adapted for use in a seminar or a discussion. Via
these possible trajectories they will live their own unpredictable
'after-lives' (Benjamin 1999: 72). The text will be rendered productive by 'one's best readers whom one never meets, [who] often
appear asynchronously, in unforeseen futural moments, as new
modes and registers of reception ... appear' (Freeman 2007: 168).

All these dynamic processes of change: to ideas, to materials, to
words and ideas as materials, to the person affected by words,
ideas and materials, do not merely happen *in* time. More radically, as
change, as transformation, they *are* the dynamism of time itself.

It is for that reason that literature, as a particularly highly tex-
tured form of the dynamism of language in time, plays a privileged
role in this book. Literature offers a high-density instantiation of
the particular temporal strand in which this book most obviously
participates. For this reason the book foregrounds literary studies
from the outset, devoting specific chapters to historiography,
narrative and literary discourse. The privilege accorded to literary
studies follows Ricoeur's notion of '*narrative as the guardian of time*'
(1984–88: III, 241; translation modified), whose ultimate purchase,
however, Ricoeur himself questions. Ricoeur admits a central and

insoluble aporia – namely, that narrative, which appears to give us the only ultimate grasp of time ('there can be no time except narrated time' [ibid: III, 241; translation modified]),[2] is always exceeded by that which it seeks to encompass. Experienced time as narrated time will always be contained within an all-encompassing **cosmological time** and thus will remain unable to comprehend it.

Perhaps that very tension is one that literary texts, far from being undermined by such aporia, thrive upon and take as one of their constitutive elements:

> these tensions and aporias are the very fabric of the novel: the tensions between narrated time and the time of narration, chronology and plot, objective and subjective time, cosmological and phenomenological time, time as topic and time as technique, and the constative and performative layering of the novel's dealings with time make it the discourse in which the dynamics and dialectics of time are most faithfully and properly observed.
>
> (Currie 2007: 92–93)

Literature, then, is a fictive construct, an artifice which, in playful re-working of the putatively factual givens of reality, may point us to, indeed participate in the plethora of temporalities subsisting under the threshold of an all-embracing and coercive time.

For that reason, this book maintains Ricoeur's privilege *and* his scepticism. To the extent that we as human subjects mediate all our experience via language and narrative, time will always be narrated time; but to the extent that human subjects are merely one of many actors, human and non-human, peopling the world, human narrativity is only one of the possible manifestations of a plurality of temporalities. This book thus repositions language and narrativity as one immanent temporal strand of becoming among others. Language 'models' temporalities (Lotman 1977: 9) but does not transcend them. Rather, language is woven among the fabric of countless intertwined temporal strands, thus defusing the aporia identified by Ricoeur, generated as they are by the absolute status he accords to narrative.

Accordingly, the textual analyses in the book do not merely illustrate the philosophical or scientific theories I explain, but are explicitly intended as performative exemplifications of the dynamic processuality of immanent temporalities. The text in its dynamic interaction with critic and reader is understood as a generative material process, not an inert artefact. As a creative process, the text forges new relationships between human and non-human actors, establishing connectivities whose material effects make up the future vector of time.

TRAJECTORY OF THE BOOK

This book sketches the ways in which 'time' has been imagined by highly politicized forces over centuries, rather than simply being a natural given. In contrast to the absolute and universal time, it then proffers an alternative vision of multiple temporal flows which are coeval with the dynamism of life itself. This notion of temporalities entails a significant recalibration of the unsustainable global practices which make up contemporary society.

The book proceeds in successive stages of complexity. Chapter 1 opens by taking a straightforwardly expository approach to the linked concepts of absolute and universal time. It seeks thus to begin with the most putatively self-evident manifestations of temporality, demonstrating their historicity and contingence, before moving on in Chapter 2 to philosophical approaches which increasingly complicate the initial terms of reference. Next, the book sets temporalities in the context of a number of societal practices: historiography (Chapter 3), narrativity and discourse (Chapter 4), the business of living as gendered actors in society and the everyday 'inner' life of subjectivity (Chapter 5), and the economics of global capitalism (Chapter 6). Finally, it explores the nature of temporalities with reference to two salient paradigms within the contemporary humanities: postmodernism and postcolonialism (Chapters 7 and 8).

Thus, starting from the common-sense notion of time as the measurement of successive scales of micro- to macro-durations (minutes, days, years) with universal validity, the argument advances via successive levels of complexity. It demonstrates progressively the material and political entanglements in which temporalities have always been embroiled. It suggests a more intricate but also more immediate paradigm of temporalities subsisting within the interstices of absolute and universal time. This paradigm also eludes the deceptive polarities of chronological vs. social time, or public vs. subjective time. In each chapter the argument rehearses a shift of perspective away from an abstract and singular notion of 'time', whose prevalence is neither neutral or 'given'. The argument proposes instead in each instance a notion of multiple, interwoven, immanent temporalities inhabiting entities of many types rather than providing their medium or container. Its thesis includes but also goes beyond a weak notion of multiple levels of everyday, lifetime and large-scale time (e.g. Felski 2000: 17), to suggest a more complex concept of intertwining temporal strands of dynamic becoming. I build upon the work of scholars such as Bergson, DeLanda, Deleuze, Latour and Wood, which radically alters ideas about the nature of 'human being' and its place in the larger order of existence in the world. The present introduction thus provides:

- a brief history of *time* as a philosophical, social and scientific concept, from Antiquity, via the Enlightenment and the emergence of merchant, then industrial and finally global capitalism, through to the twentieth-century revolutions of Relativity, macro-level theories of the history of the universe and micro-level Quantum Theory;
- a critique of the still largely hegemonic Enlightenment complex of theories of *time*, drawing upon anthropological cultural relativism, the vitalist theories of James, Bergson and Deleuze/Guattari, and the larger framework of non-linear dynamics (or chaos theory) from the natural sciences, in order to construct a pluralist conceptualization of interwoven and transformational *temporalities*;
- a double programme of showing the influence of hegemonic notions (*time*) and sketching possibilities for critique and a positive programme of conceptual exploration (*temporalities*), across a wide range of subdisciplines broadly belonging to the domain of contemporary cultural studies, such as critical historiography, linguistic discourse analysis and narrative theory, psychoanalysis and theories of the subject, gender studies, culminating in two disciplinary case studies, those of postmodernism and postcolonialism.

1

TIME-KEEPING

As a modern reader, one may be a little perplexed to find Chaucer in *The Canterbury Tales* praising a rooster by the name of Chauntecleer for being a better timekeeper than the clocks he competed with: 'Wel sikerer [more accurate] was his crowyng in his logge | Than is a clokke or an abbey orlogge [clock tower]' (Chaucer 1974: 199). Chaucer assigned separate lines to the natural and mechanical timekeepers, thereby coupling and contrasting, hyperbolically, the chicken run and the abbey belfry: the competing temporal regimes dovetail and overlap in a late medieval Europe world where clocks, already beginning to preside over the market places and civic spaces, were none the less far from reliable. Chaucer, as a civil servant in the incipient system of proto-capitalist trade and exchange, was attuned to the time-keeping needs of early accounting and nascent logistics. Clearly his praise of Chauntecleer is parodic, but natural rhythms (night and day, work and rest, harvesting, sowing) are still hegemonic enough to make the comparison viable.

But what Chaucer's successive lines perform, and perhaps even drive, is the beginning of a slow but ineluctable separation of two linearities: that of calibrated chronometrical time, and that of a mode of temporality given by nature itself and part and parcel of natural processes and events. This chapter traces the increasing sophistication of the former modes of temporality (from time-keeping devices to the development of universal time), but also points up the attendant aporia which allow the latter to remain partially visible even today.

TIME-KEEPERS

The earliest time-keeping devices remained close to natural processes. They measured the passage of time using the dynamic movements of certain elements or heavenly bodies: water, sand, the sun. The water clock (the 'clepsydra') was the simplest time-keeping mechanism. It was merely a receptacle to gather water, with a small hole to reg-ulate the flow of liquid trickling in, and calibrations to measure the rising water level. It was sensitive to low temperatures though: a water clock was not much use when it froze. Nor could the flow of water be easily connected to other devices so as to trigger time-signals, except when the force of gravity and, for instance, the weight of buckets were employed to drive a calibrated measuring device, as in Chinese water clocks. Similar natural limitations hampered the utility of the sun dial, which was dependent upon good weather. In the northern latitudes, where cloud or haze could obscure the sun for weeks at a time, its utility was severely attenuated. Devices using sand, such as the hour glass, could measure the duration of a period of time, but could not integrate that to a calibrated scale of measured time.

These early time-keeping devices, which attained considerable sophistication in China or in the Islamic world, were supplanted in Europe by the emergence of the mechanical clock, driven first by a weight on a cable, then, in the 1400s, by a coiled spring whose progressive energy loss was compensated by a cable taken up by a conical fusée wheel (Cipolla 1978: 47–50). The invention of the spring, which enabled clocks to be made smaller, was accompanied by the invention of **escapement** mechanisms, which regulated the time-keeper. The weight on the cable was a solution to the question of how to drive the clock. But that solution in turn generated a further problem: the cable unwound faster and faster and faster until the weight hit the ground. Thus the initial problem of how to drive the clock was replaced by the problem of how to slow it down. This dilemma was resolved by a mechanism which came to be known as the 'escapement'. The escapement was a blocking-releasing mechanism that worked to brake the downward rush of the cable and weight. A stop-go-stop-go function interrupted the continuous unwinding of the cable and translated it into pulses of movement which could calibrate the passage of time; these pulses could be relayed to auditory or visual indicators (bells, the movements of hands on the dial) so as to give a measurement of time; in addition, the stop-go mechanism conserved and rationed the energy of the weight or spring (Landes 2000: 9–10). Escapement devices underwent numerous technical transformations from the fifteenth to nineteenth centuries, including the invention of the pendulum and the anchor escapement. As clocks became more sophisticated and more accurate, single hour hands were supplemented by minute and second hands.

Technical improvements to the clock were given impetus by the search for **longitude**, essential to accurate ocean navigation and thus a crucial element in Europe's global trading and colonizing expansion. **Latitude** could be ascertained fairly easily by measuring the angle of the north star relative to the horizon. Longitude, however, was more difficult to establish. The solution was to treat the Earth itself as a large clock, and to measure the difference between the time at the place at which the voyage had started and the time at the ship's current position. This technique necessitated time-keeping devices that were extremely accurate, but also small and robust enough to be used on a ship. The search for a reliable, accurate marine chronometer drove forward the technical advancement of clock-making for several centuries. Thus two important aspects of modern time consciousness (accuracy of calibration and the global reach of a single time scheme), though merely incipient, were from the outset intimately bound up with expanding imperial capitalism.

Improvements to the accuracy of clocks, concentrating on the elimination of friction and changes caused by temperature, continued into the nineteenth century with the invention of vacuum cases and the use of electricity as a drive source. Mechanical clocks, spring driven and escapement regulated, were superseded in the twentieth century by quartz and atomic clocks. By the 1970s, timers at the Olympic Games could be calibrated to a hundredth of a second. In the world of subatomic particles, the calibrations of time attained hundredths and thousandths of a second, with new subdivisions being invented, from the microsecond (104^{-6}) via the nanoseconds (104^{-9}) to the picosecond (104^{-12}). These clocks converted the phenomena being timed into vibrations (analogous to the oscillations of an escapement), the most stable and highest frequencies providing the most precise measuring devices ever made. In 1999 the US national Institute of Standards and Technology announced a new atomic clock that would serve as America's primary frequency standard, with error of no more than a second in twenty million years (Landes 2000: 5–6, 202).

The Western history of the clock as a mechanism for regulating social life begins in the medieval monasteries, where the cycle of offices punctuating work with prayer was marked by bells. The earliest clocks did not run continuously, but served as alarms, set to ring bells to wake the monks for the night prayer (Biarne 1984). Such bell-timers give us the word for 'clock' (from German 'Glocke' or Flemish 'clokke'). The monasteries, however, were not merely places of prayer (*ora*), they were also places of work (*labora*). They were highly complex economic units, where organization and discipline, regulated by clocks, guaranteed productivity (Mumford 1963: 12–18). Likewise, clocks and bells were widespread in medieval towns (Thrift 1988), as a large number of commercial and technical processes needed to be coordinated there, necessitating timekeepers and time signals audible to the entire community. The textile industry, Europe's first major large-scale industry, depended upon the coordination of a large number of production processes, and various sorts of manufacturing: paid labour in the factories (heating the vats, etc.) remunerated by the day, and small workshop workers producing by the piece (Le Goff 1980: 35–36). Such tendencies increased exponentially as the industrial revolution gained in momentum and scope, driving the development of time technologies in conjunction with the quadruple processes of commerce, navigation, colonization and warfare.

The development of time-keeping devices had wide-reaching implications for European perceptions of reality. The new mechanical clock was a radical innovation, not so much because of its accuracy, but for two linked reasons: its potential for miniaturization, and the impetus it lent to the abstraction of time.

First, clocks, initially located in centrally visible public places such as a cathedrals or bell-towers, became increasingly smaller, portable and cheaper. They were replicated and dispersed among more intimate domains of life: in workshops, in private homes, in bedrooms, and finally in pockets or on the wrist. Accompanying this increasingly complete saturation of the spaces of everyday life by timepieces, was an ever more pervasive awareness of time, becoming part of the very structures of consciousness of modern European subjectivity. Time-keepers increasingly became prosthetic extensions of the body and calibrated temporality a 'second nature'. Mere time obedience, imposed from a central time-giver in a central place, often associated with royalty or civic authority, gave way to time discipline: 'Punctuality comes from within, not without. It is the mechanical clock which made possible, for better or for worse, a civilization attentive to the passage of time, hence to productivity and performance' (Landes 2000: 6). Indicative of this time consciousness, for instance, was the inverted progression from watch dials numbering the minutes at five minute intervals, then at 15, and finally, in the twentieth century, not at all, symptomatic of rising public familiarity with the notion of calibrated time (ibid: 140).

Second, clocks detached time-measurement from natural elements and processes. Mumford (1963: 15) observes that '[b]y its essential nature, [the clock] dissociated time from human events', to which Landes (2000: 14) adds, 'and human events from nature'. Time was released from a system of natural analogies. It no longer literally flowed or trickled, but was indexed, not embodied, by the clock, which stood for time itself. Time emerged as an entity dissociated from the natural world (Burkhardt 1997: 43). The development of the escapement system, which translated the force of gravity into a series of stop-go movements, effectively divided time up into mechanical segments: lock, release, lock, release, audibly perceptible in the tick-tock rhythm and visually evident in the staccato movement of the second hand. The flow of continuous time was now controlled by virtue of being broken up into ever smaller segments, which could be translated into abstract arithmetic values. The expression of 'telling' the time is related to the German 'zählen' [counting] in the sense of our 'bank-teller'; the digital clock, reduced to pure numbers, is the ultimate embodiment of this process. Time became susceptible of calculation. Rather than being a flow in which all things were caught up, it became manipulable as an abstract, atomized quantity. Co-extensive with the appearance of clocks in cities in the fourteenth and fifteenth centuries was a rising preoccupation with time as a scarcity, with the shortness of life, counterbalanced by progeny and fame, and the busy-ness of merchant life (whence business) as a mode of proactive combat against time (Quinones 1972: 25).

In the process, the concept of time separated from the machine which generated it, becoming an imaginary and ideal concept, released from the gravity-bound problems of the clockwork mechanism. There slowly emerged a split between a perfect, ideal, transcendental, cosmic time-in-itself, and the imperfect, inaccurate clocks of everyday reality. Clockmaking was motivated, in part at least, by the dream of constantly improving technical skills until real clocks, freed of all friction, resistance, indeed of materiality, would become synchronized with the imaginary ideal clock of the cosmos. In parallel, the forms by which time was imagined underwent a transformation, from the mechanical analogy of circularity, still embodied in the circular clock-face, to the mathematical concept of the arrow-like vector. The circularity of erstwhile natural rhythms and later, of the movements of the spheres, gave way to linearity. Likewise, the idea of time flowing away behind the subject was transformed, coming to be imagined as progression along a series of time-coordinates, moving towards the future (Burkhardt 1997: 60–63).

For most of us, disembodied, abstract time, doubled by deeply internalized time-discipline, is experienced in everyday life down to the minute ('just a minute', 'I'm running five minutes late'). The micro-, nano- and picoseconds of physics remain far beyond our experiential horizon. Paradoxically, however, contemporary physics which explores these foreign lands of time calibration also eschews the very separation of time and the natural world increasingly established by clock-time and legitimized by

Newton's 'absolute time'. By 1910 Einstein was assuming that 'anything passing periodically through identical phases' functioned as a clock Thus, 'if the clock were nothing but an atom, then time would be marked by its oscillations' (qtd in Galison 2003: 266). Modern physics has gone a step further, suggesting that time *is* the oscillations of certain particles. Quantum physics assumes that time is part of a space–time continuum. Time, like other phenomena such as light, is composed of a flow of minute particles known as quanta (Landes 2000: 428n7). These quanta are infinitely minute, estimated by Heisenberg and Levy at 10^{-26} and 10^{-24} of a second respectively (Le Lionnais 1959: 91). Time, according to this quanta-particle-flow theory, is not separate from events and from nature, but constitutes its most minute physical fabric. The infinitely abstract temporal calibrations of modern physics bring us full circle, back to the point where modern time-keeping began, that is, the separation of time from nature, space and place.

At the very opening of Virginia Woolf's *Mrs Dalloway* (first published 1925), we are reminded, and this will be the first of many reiterated instances throughout the novel, of time: 'Big Ben strikes. There! Out it boomed. First a warning, musical; then the hour, irrevocable. The leaden circles dissolved in the air' (1984: 6). The very plasticity of the image, hesitating between the deadening connotations of lead (the softest, most malleable of metals) and the implicit wave-form Woolf chooses as a **metaphor** for time-signal rhythms, recalls a forgotten materiality of time. This materiality links the various narrative strands of the novel's plot and their embodiment in the respective characters' consciousness. The materiality of the chimes also narrows the post-Enlightenment gap between time and physical processes. As Elias has pointed out, 'Clocks themselves are sequences of physical events' (1993: 1): clocks do not merely calibrate time, they also embody it in their own materiality.

The tangibility of the metaphor eschews the abstraction of modern time, thereby attenuating the apparent antagonism between time measurement ('Shredding and slicing, dividing and subdividing, the clocks ... nibbled at the June day') and the rhythms of existence: 'Like the pulse of a perfect heart, life struck straight through the streets' (Woolf 1984: 91, 50). This quasi-synthesis in turn allows the remarkable flexibility of interior, mnemonic time for which the novel is known: Mrs Dalloway's thoughts and memories roam over half a century of experience, moving backwards and forwards in utter anachrony.

But one other aspect of time is also foregrounded by Woolf's use of Big Ben's chimes as a regular time signal. Not only does it work to unify the disparate characters and their various paths through London, but also it emblematizes, despite Mrs Dalloway's idiosyncratic mnemonic time-roaming, the world standardization of time. The 'leaden circles' evoke global civic time, 'time ratified by Greenwich' (ibid: 93) — but the 'leaden' quality of the chimes also indexes the residual contextual 'heaviness' which always adheres to and encumbers universal time.

UNIVERSAL TIME

Up to this point we have concentrated upon the clock as a mobile entity imposing, via its own mechanical logic, a particular sort of time oddly separated from events and even further from nature. This disembodied time is paradoxical. On the one hand it is made mobile by its abstraction. On the other, the mechanical measuring devices which index this disembodied time allow it to seep into the very smallest nooks and crannies of individual life, saturating little by little global society in the entirety of its localities. Together, the apparently contradictory aspects of abstraction, miniaturization and invasive quotidian ubiquity have contributed to the cementing of universal time in global consciousness.

The nineteenth century saw the intensification of industrialization and of national economies, but within these national systems there was frequently little coherence between regional time areas, let alone along the borders between nations (Giddens 1990: 18). These discrepancies between regional time increasingly posed a problem for rapidly growing global capitalism and its tendency to 'nestle everywhere, settle everywhere, establish connexions everywhere' (Marx and Engels 1983: 83). At the local American level, for instance, major railway accidents with numerous fatal casualties were caused from the 1850s on by the discrepant time schemes used by various railway companies (Galison 2003: 104–5). This prompted the American railway companies to take the initiative in 1883 of synchronizing the various local times, and articulating them in five gigantic time zones extending from 'Pacific time' on the west coast to 'Atlantic time' on the east coast, with all of them taking **Greenwich Mean Time** as their standard. Greenwich Mean Time had become statute law in Britain in 1880, and was voted four years later at an International Meridian Conference in Washington DC to become the world time standard.

Other nations were following suit and standardizing their multiple local times. Russia set its clocks to unified, if multi-zoned, time in 1888; Sweden did so as well at about the same time, also following Greenwich Mean Time (plus one hour). This increasing articulation of unified regional time zones with one another and with Greenwich Mean Time was made possible by the development of telegraph communication, which allowed the widespread transmission of electronic time signals from the 1860s onwards, initially at local level, with metropolitan centres such as Cambridge, Massachusetts or Bern, Switzerland establishing the starting points for what rapidly became nationally coordinated time systems. Telegraph communication of time signals rapidly superseded short-lived attempts, in Vienna and Paris, to establish networks of coordinated clocks by means of steam-driven compressed air. By the last quarter of the nineteenth century, networks of coordinated time signals, transmitted via a capillary system of telegraph wires, from central time-keeping devices to local clocks in railway stations, churches, and numerous civic buildings, imposed a unified and all-pervasive sense of time. Like electric power, gas and sewage systems, unified civic time transformed collective-subjective experience of everyday life. Civic populations were alert to clock synchronization or its failure: when the pneumatic systems in use in Paris and Vienna in the 1870s produced fifteen-second discrepancies, the delays were quickly noticed by astronomers, engineers, and even the public (Galison 2003: 107, 92–98).

Such programmes of time synchronization were not restricted to European or American urban centres or nations, but rapidly took on a global dimension. From the 1850s to the 1890s, the

Americans and the French in particular undertook an immense programme of ever-expanding projects to map accurately longitudes around the world: first between Europe and the Americas, both north and south, via undersea telegraph cables, then continuing on to map the entire Americas and large parts of East Asia.

The technology of spacetime communication took a further leap forward with the introduction of radio technology, and the pioneering of long-distance communication of radio signals between Newfoundland and Ireland, and around Europe. The French began sending radio time signals from the Eiffel tower in 1909, finally synchronizing with Greenwich Mean Time in 1911. In 1912 France, under the aegis of Poincaré, hosted the International Conference on Time to agree upon uniform methods of determining and maintaining accurate time signals to be transmitted around the world. The combination of time signals and spatial positioning technology continued to be refined and perfected, particularly for military purposes, as for example in the intercontinental LORAN (Long Range Navigation) system designed for the US Navy in the Pacific theatre during the Second World War.

The culmination of such technical innovations is today's US$10 billion **GPS** system familiar to most of us via our mobile phones, our car-borne navigation systems, or internet mapping platforms which give the exact latitude-longitude coordinates of any feature of the built or natural environment. GPS works with twenty-four satellites orbiting the earth whose onboard clocks send time signals at regular intervals. Any receiver on the earth triangulates against four satellites (at any one point in time, at any one point on the earth, five satellites are always in view), measuring the time of their arrival relative to a measurement of latitude-longitude which is no longer mapped onto the curved 'two-dimensional' surface of the earth, but includes the three dimensions of the planet's near-space environs. Readings of positions on the Earth's surface are yielded with an accuracy of about fifteen metres (Galison 2003: 285–87).

There are two apparently contradictory conclusions which one can draw from this very brief history of the development of coordinated universal time. On the one hand, universal time tends to suppress local differences as it draws the entire globe into a single unitary temporal system. On the other hand, the greater the sophistication of the temporal measuring devices implemented to measure time within this single system, the greater are the discrepancies which emerge in the interstices of the system itself.

HOMOGENIZATION OR RELATIVITY?

The increasing coordination of clocks around the globe eradicated local times (of which there were 300 in the US in 1860 and even more in France until around 1900) (Cowan 1958: 45; Kern 1983: 13), pulling all times into a single global network of increasingly precisely synchronized time zones all keyed to Greenwich. The role of logistics, that is, the accurate planning of the transport of goods, and the tracking of their movement, was the driving force in the spread of time synchronization (Thrift 2008: 93, 95; Hanley, ed. 2004): the train timetable was 'a time-space ordering device' permitting 'the complex coordination of trains and their passengers and freight across large tracts of time-space' (Giddens 1990: 19–20). Other modern developments such as colonial expansion, increasingly industrialized war (the American Civil War and the Franco–Prussian War were significant in this respect), and the mass transport of populations by rail, con- tributed a large impetus to these processes. Advanced industrial capitalism homogenized different places, rigidly dovetailing a reduced number of local time zones into a global system. Global time thus realized, in an entirely pragmatic manner, Newton's notion of absolute time, which in his formulation 'flows uni- formly, without regard to anything external' (Newton 1966: 6; translation modified). Whereas in earlier societies, time had been connected to *place*, or locale, the new global network of standar- dized, synchronized time tore place and time apart, recombining them in a network of empty, abstract *space* denuded of local par- ticularities (Giddens 1990: 17–20). The various time zones retained their specificities, but only to the extent that they were arranged in an overarching, logical order so that temporal trans- lation became an easy matter: 'the severing of time from space provides the basis for their recombination in relation to social activity', comments Giddens (1990: 19–20). Local times were subsumed into global time, just as capitalism demanded the easy translation of all commodities and processes into the global currency of money (albeit with its own local variations) as a universal medium of exchange.

Paradoxically, however, although universal time established time as a place-independent system which erases differences between places and reduces friction in their articulation with one another, the very process of connecting disparate places to one another produces a plethora of contradictions. As Giddens comments, 'The separation of time from space ... like all trends of development ... has dialectical features, provoking opposing characteristics' (1990: 19). Historically this was clearly so. Even as the railway network in Britain expanded, bringing with it a standardized time system, anomalies abounded. By the 1870s, for instance, it was possible to travel in an hour from London to Cambridge – but the further journey to a smaller East Anglian town across the Fens might easily take a day (May and Thrift 2001: 17).

The contemporary end result of such developments in transport, means of communication and time-keeping technologies is universal time, or UT, a phenomenon which bristles with discrepancies. UT is by no means as coherent a measure as it appears at first sight. First of all, UT0 is calculated from midnight, on the basis of the prime meridian, itself displaced by several metres from the brass line at Greenwich that supposedly marks it. This UT0 must be calculated against the actual rotation of the Earth, which is not entirely uniform, as a result of the shifting of the poles and what is known as 'Chandler wobble', to produce UT1, the astronomical and navigational standard. This must be further corrected to take into account seasonal oscillations (UT2). Neither UT0, UT1, nor UT2 are as accurate as **atomic time** (TAI), which, based upon the radiation cycles of Caesium 133 (slightly more than 9 000 000 000 cycles per second), provides the most accurate time-measurement. Other UTs proliferate: universal coordinated time (UTC) has been the time used as the global standard since 2006 and usually referred to by the name of GMT; and **delta time** (ΔT, the difference between UT1 and TAI) is used by astronomers to calculate planetary positions (Holford-Strevens 2005: 15–16).

More paradoxically, however, in the production of a single global time system, time and place increasingly collapse into each other, and abolish each other as absolute. Newtonian time makes assumption about a single, universal framework of time, in which events happen sequentially, or, if they are simultaneous, occur in synchronicity within a single framework. Einstein pointed out very empirically in his 1905 paper that the synchronicity of simultaneous events was posited upon synchronization of clocks. And for the clocks in question to be synchronized, a signal had to be sent from one clock to another and then back again for them to be coordinated with each other. The synchronization of a system of spatially dispersed clocks had to take into account the small delay in signal-transmission. That delay might at first glance be negligible, until the precision of the clocks outpaced the transmission delay, or the distances traversed became great enough for the delay itself to become a significant factor. In other words, a perfectly empirical example demonstrated that there was no single time framework: time became matter of relations between different spaces, and these relations had to be established by a procedure which took into account differences in the space–time continuum rather than assuming they were irrelevant. Multiple times had to be read back into universal time, though their era-dication had been the basis of its constitution; now it transpired that discrepancies between local times were no less essential to its smooth functioning. This is one aspect of what would become Einstein's theory of **relativity**, which suggested that a universal, place-independent linear time, as formulated by Newton, was a pragmatic fiction valid only in a limited range of circumstances.

Einstein had argued that 'every reference body ... has its own particular time; unless we are told the reference-body to which the statement of time refers, there is no meaning in a statement of the time of an event' (2001: 28). For Einstein, time was not an objective given, but a consequence of the act of time-measurement. Time only existed when measured, and measurements varied according to the relative motion of the measuring body and the body measured (Kern 1983: 18–19). Such anomalies in time–space calculation became central in the functioning of the satel-lite-based GPS system which embodies early twenty-first century state-of-the-art global measurement of time. The twenty-four GPS satellites orbit the earth at 12,500 miles per hour. The cumulative differences between these moving time-measurement platforms and the moving earth, in accordance with Einstein's principles of relativity, mean that the satellite clocks run slow (relative to the earth) by seven millionths of a second per day. The positions of the satellites and their articulation against a plethora of points on the earth, all constantly moving at high speed relative to one another, must be programmed into the satellites' time calculations. In addition, general relativity, that is the influence of gravitational fields on the passage of time and its measurement, has to be factored into the corrections: eleven thousand miles in space, a weaker gravitational field means that the satellite clocks run fast (relative to the earth's surface) by 45-millionths of a second per day. Together, these factors necessitate a correction of 38-millionths of a second per day (that is, 38,000-billionths) in a GPS system whose margin of accuracy had to be within 50-billionths of a second per day (Galison 2003: 288).

The re-emerging significance of relativity within the progressive refinement and precision of temporal measurement may look like a perversion of 'absolute time' or 'return of the repressed', but in actual fact merely reflects the changing face of scientific method. Pre-Newtonian temporalities evinced a high degree of place-related specificity. They were superseded by an apparently place-independent modern temporality (emphatically in the singular). Modern temporality was in turn superseded by the respective temporalities of infinitely small orders (for instance subatomic processes) which in turn have been used to model temporalities of a very great order (for instance the history of the universe, the Big Bang, etc.). These latter temporalities are irrevocably plural, evincing multifarious and often perplexing spatial dimensions, in which time(s) has (or have) once again come to adhere to space(s) in modern physics' concept of '**spacetime**'.

At the very same period Einstein was elaborating his successive theories of relativity, Joseph Conrad fictionalized, in *The Secret Agent* (first published 1907), an attempt by an anarchist group to blow up the Greenwich Observatory. Clearly what grabs Conrad's imagination is the Quixotic futility of attempting to destroy by physical detonation something as abstract as Greenwich Mean Time. Precisely that impossibility is what Conrad's anarchists wish to achieve: namely, an attack on modern society's 'sacrosanct fetish ... science'. Such an act of terrorism, Conrad's Mr Vladimir says, 'must be purely destructive', indicating the aim of making 'a clean sweep of the whole of social creation' (1983: 31–32). The science of temporality, Conrad understands, is the central pillar of modernity, progress, and the expansion of Europe. What must be attacked is the abstraction of time itself, the separation of time from space, as the very operation that has driven Western progress: 'how to get that appallingly abstract notion into the heads of the middle classes ... ?' Mr Vladimir continues:

> The attack must have all the shocking senselessness of gratuitous blasphemy. Since bombs are your means of expression, it would be really telling if one could throw a bomb into pure mathematics. But that is impossible. ... The blowing up of the first meridian is bound to raise a howl of execration.
>
> (Conrad 1983: 35)

Conrad's fiction does not merely evince an acute sense of the relevance of time for modern culture. It is also remarkably prescient, prefiguring the primarily symbolic logic, for instance, of the 9/11 terrorist attacks on the twin towers of the World Trade Center in 2001. The object attacked provides a visible civic embodiment of something intangible which can only be understood in the production of global effects it engenders. This is an entirely relativistic notion: global time does not exist except in the phenomenon of its production. That production is pervaded by contradictions and irregularities, from local perversions of the system through to its own constitutive relativity. To what extent, however, those irregularities may accumulate to such an extent that they render the global system incoherent and bring it 'out of synch', to use a most apposite slang expression, is debatable (see Chapters 6 and 7 later).

Perhaps that is why, in Conrad's rendition of the terrorist attack on the prime meridian, symbolic violence is directed at the wrong targets. It is not one of the novel's anarchists, but instead Mr Verloc's 'retarded' brother-in-law Stevie who is given the task of carrying the bomb. Stevie, who spends his '*spare time* ... drawing circles with compass and pencil on a piece of paper' (1983: 10; emphasis added), recalling Woolf's leaden circles, causes no damage to GMT. The device detonates 'too soon' (ibid: 202) and the boy dies in the otherwise ineffectual blast. His very failure is circumscribed by the temporality it is his mission to destroy: '*Fifteen minutes* would have been enough for the veriest fool to deposit the engine [bomb] and walk away. But Stevie had stumbled within *five minutes* of being left to himself' (ibid: 229–30; emphasis added). In this way, the terrorists merely re-inscribe the universalizing temporality of modernity they seek to attack when their bomb kills a 'retarded' boy. For Stevie is one of those marginalized by the increasing time-competence demanded of industrial labour (Ryan and Thomas 1980: 99–102), and hence is relegated to boot polishing: 'there was ... *no future* in such work' (Conrad 1983: 10; emphasis added). To that extent, their victims, those subjects whose temporalities cannot be profitably subsumed to the global time of capitalism, are the same. Roughly contemporaneous to Einstein's theories, Conrad's fiction indexes the abstraction of universal time, its waning symbolic legitimacy, but also, para-doxically, the manner in which its hegemony continues unabated despite the evident contradictions in its interstices. The real 'secret agent' of Conrad's tale is perhaps the multiplicity of tem-poralities of non-human objects and processes themselves, gestured at tentatively by the stymied agency of the broken-down horses upon whom Stevie takes pity (1983: 9, 165–68). Those temporal agents are ones that not even Conrad takes entirely seriously, but he populates his novel with them almost despite himself. Marginal though they may be, they none the less continue to exert an influence, albeit generally unacknowledged, in every subsequent reading. Those agents and their temporalities are the subject, in turn, of this book.

2

PHILOSOPHIES OF TIME

In one of his most famous sayings, Saint Augustine worried, 'What, then, is time? I know well enough what it is, provided that nobody asks me; but if I am asked what it is and try to explain, I am baffled' (1961: 264). His puzzlement has been translated and retranslated and passed down over centuries, itself constituting a reiterated, and thus temporal, expression of our immanent experience of time, and of the sheer impossibility of speaking of time from anywhere but within its lived texture. Time eludes language, definition, understanding, yet is all-pervasive in our experience. This, perhaps, is the central dilemma of temporality that the present book investigates: how to understand something which informs the most intimate fabric of our experience, whose dynamic we cannot escape, and whose underlying identity we perhaps persist in misapprehending even as its constitutes us?

The previous chapter sketched a drama played out from the early modern period to the postmodern age, in which the flow of time was calibrated by increasingly accurate time-pieces, and its elusive character supposedly pinned down by a system of quantifying measurement. Yet that drama also highlighted the slipperiness of time and the refusal of time-keeping devices or systems to agree among themselves. What is evinced in this temporal *agon* of measurement and immeasurability is the age-old attempt to grasp the nature of time, to encompass it within the limited parameters of human understanding. By the same token, however, time itself appears to generate and erode that understanding, perhaps, as I will intimate in the final sections of this chapter, not because it is beyond human experience, but because it is identical with the very dynamism of life itself.

This chapter begins with an account of the Presocratic philosophers' sense of time as change, overlapping in many ways the notions of immanent, multiple temporalities with which the chapter concludes. It then reviews a series of temporal knots: the Christian tension between time and eternity; the early modern struggle against devouring time; the Enlightenment notion of absolute time and its complication by theories of relativity; and the attempts by phenomenology to replace absolute time by an 'internal', subjective time that, however, dwindles in importance as multiple human/non-human temporalities come into view.

CHANGE VS. STABILITY

From classical antiquity onwards, the conceptualization of time has taken the form of a confrontation with the notions of change and impermanence. The ancient Greek philosopher Heraclitus (c. 500 BC) imagined time by using ideas of water and fire. These images made time coeval with transformation and change. Famously, he remarked that 'Everything is in perpetual flux like a river' (Kirk, Raven and Schofield 1983: 195).

However, temporal flux came to be associated with mortality and imperfection. Thus Saint Augustine in the *City of God* notes that

> from the moment a man begins to exist in this body which is destined to die, he is involved in a process whose end is death. For this is the end to which the life of continual change is all the time directed, if indeed we can give the name of life to this passage towards death.
>
> (Augustine 1972: 518)

Augustine associates change with death and decay, and for that reason rejects time as change. Ever since, philosophy has 'feared time itself', in the phrasing of Virginia Woolf (1984: 28), attempting to confront or banish the problem of time as change, to 'control | All accidents' in the Romantic poet Wordsworth's phrasing in *The Prelude* (1990: 444). The twentieth-century French philosopher Merleau-Ponty observes that 'It is indeed the dream of philosophers to be able to conceive an eternity of life, lying beyond permanence and change, in which time's productivity is preeminently contained' (2002: 482). This is why later Presocratic philosophers such as Parmenides and Zeno argue that time and change are illusory, seeking to discredit the ideas of transformation advocated by Heraclitus (Fraser 1990: 14–18; Prigogine 2003: 9). Parmenides posits an unchanging reality, in which continuity is real, against the non-existence of the present and the future as instances of change. He imagines this unchanging reality like a perfect sphere, the same everywhere. Zeno, in turn, proffers a number of paradoxes which imagine the infinite divisibility of movement into units of time. His parable of the arrow which never reaches its target depends upon the idea that a given movement, taking place in a given period of time, can be divided into smaller and smaller units which themselves are instants of immobility. Zeno's attempts to reduce time to units of constancy is paralleled by Democritus' idea of empty space filled with minimal units, that is, atoms (Mainzer 2002: 20). Later eighteenth-century philosophers such as David Hume, in his *Treatise of Human Nature* (first published 1738) continue this attempt to reduce time to units of immobility:

> It is a property inseparable from time, and which in a manner constitutes its essence, that each of its parts succeeds another, and that none of them, however contiguous, can ever be coexistent … every moment must be distinct from, and posterior or antecedent to another. It is certain then, that time, as it exists, must be composed of indivisible moments.
>
> (Hume 1961: I, 38)

Hume breaks down time into units as a way of bringing its flow to a halt. For him a blurring of the distinction between moments reintroduces fluidity and thus inaccuracy into the measurable progression of time. But, as Lucas objects, 'Time and change are close bedfellows – they are so related as concepts that, perhaps, it is hard to think them apart' (2005: 2).

Greek philosophers such as Plato and Aristotle identify change and movement with an inferior ontological state. Plato in the *Timaeus* claims that the universe, with its temporal structures, e.g. the rotations of the stars, is an imperfect image of eternity (Plato 1952: 77). Aristotle criticizes the Platonic separation of an eternal and ideal world from the temporal cosmos, and proposes in its place a system of temporal modes (real, possible, necessary), arguing that material and form make up reality. Material, substantial mass and volume, is the real in which form follows its potential and becomes actualized. The transition from potential to reality constitutes movement; time, in turn, is the measurable aspect of this movement: 'Time is ... that by which movement can be numerically estimated' (Aristotle 1952: I, 387). Aristotle attempts thus to reconcile immobility (the present instant as a snapshot in the continuous process of movement from potential to actualization) and continuity. In the process, however, time is banished to the status of mere unreal measurement of the real movements of nature.

Aristotle's notions are suggestive, despite their denigration of time as unreality, for they provide an alternative to attempts to purge time of change. Aristotle thus prefigures, with a difference, contemporary conceptions of time as a dynamic process of ceaseless transformation. From the modal shift potential-to-real, it is only a small conceptual jump to the modal shift virtual-to-actual, as Kwinter suggests:

> This so-called emergence and evolution of form ... will follow the dynamic and uncertain process that characterizes a schema that links a virtual component to an actual one. ... unlike the previous schema where the 'possible' had no reality (before emerging), here the virtual, though it may yet have no actuality, is nonetheless fully real. It exists, one might say, as a *free* difference or singularity, not yet combined with other differences into a complex or salient form. What this means is that the virtual does not have to be realized, but only actualized (activated and integrated); its adventure involves a developmental

passage from one state to another. The virtual is gathered, selected – let us say *incarnated* – it passes from one moment-event (or complex) in order to emerge – differently, uniquely – within another.

(Kwinter 2003: 8)

In this contemporary conception of time as the unending passage of dynamic processes from virtual to actual, we discover a concept of life as a positive term without a negative. Time is the immanent process of transformation which, because it moves from one state of being to another, eschews negative terms such as imperfection or mortality. It is 'a process of morphing, of formation and deformation, that is to say, of the becoming otherwise of things in motion as they enter into strange conjunctions with one another' (Bennett 2010: 118). Nothing ends, or dies, it simply changes. And mutability itself is thus no longer an index of death; on the contrary, it is the hallmark of life itself.

TIME VS. ETERNITY

If, since the Renaissance and even prior to that, 'the true terror of Time's nature [has been] its changeability' (Quinones 1972: 430), then, it would seem that much of modernity's cultural production consists of attempts to overcome time. The late nineteenth-century American writer Thoreau appears to be embarked upon such a project when, fleeing from a New World enslavement to progress, in which man 'has no time to be anything but a machine', he says: 'Time is but the stream I go a-fishing in. I drink at it, but while I drink I see the sandy bottom and detect how shallow it is. Its thin current slides away, but eternity remains' (1906: 4, 85). The shallow flow of progress is revoked for a residual, protosecular notion of eternity.

Such a polarity has a long pedigree. Early Christianity posed a notion of human time in opposition to God's eternity. Augustine posits that God created time along with the universe, and thus necessarily had to be outside time himself. He rejects Aristotle's equation of time with movement, arguing that movement presupposed that time preceded it (Augustine 1961: 262–63, 272–73). Similarly, the medieval philosopher Boethius places God's knowledge of the world as a whole outside of and encompassing time, in which the successive moments of time are 'copresent in a single *perception*' (Ricoeur 1984–88: I, 159–60).

Medieval theories of temporality underwent numerous transformations, particularly after the caesura of the twelfth century (Le Goff 1980: 30–34). In general, however, they envisaged an interlocking of time and eternity. The Dutch seventeenth-century philosopher Spinoza provides a late summary of these notions: 'It is the nature of reason to perceive things under a certain form of eternity' (1996: 60): history is thus gathered up into a logic outside of itself: 'Time ultimately carried the Christian towards God' (Bloch qtd in Le Goff 1980: 32). For medieval people, time was thus experienced in a fatalistic mode, in which mortality, constantly present from birth onwards, was offset by the hope of salvation. The spread of Protestantism, the accelerating development of early capitalism which encouraged it, and increasingly sophisticated technological means for taking control of the natural environment encouraged a less fatalistic view of the individual's place in time.

In contrast to the medieval religious attitude of resignation and acceptance of change, cushioned by the assurance of a divine order of things, the early modern period saw a mounting sense of threat in the face of time's aggressive aspect, countered by a militant response on the part of humans: 'the sense of time as an urgent pressure was coincidental with the rise of bourgeois society and the middle class ... time figures prominently in the formation of middle-class values. It suggests an external world of real limitations, against which one must make provisions if he is to be spared an unsatisfactory reckoning' (Quinones 1972: 14–16, 349). Thus the English seventeenth-century poet Andrew Marvell instantiates the *carpe diem* topos by imagining 'Time's winged Charriot hurrying near' and, even more terrifyingly, 'his slow-chapt pow'r' (Marvell 1969: 21), playing upon the Latin adage *Tempus edax rerum* (time as an 'eater up of all things' in Golding's 1567 translation of Ovid's *Metamorphoses* [qtd in Stürzl 1965: 70]) – but poses the permanence of poetic agency, however counter-intuitively, against time. Within a predominantly Christian framework, the Elizabethan dramatist Christopher Marlowe imagines in *Dr Faustus* (c. 1590) the eponymous upstart figure who dares to revolt against the divine temporal dispensation, seizing forbidden knowledge in an attempt to escape the God-given limits of human life. Faustus comes too early, failing in his attempt to 'seize the day': 'The time is come', says Lucifer, in the final act. 'The clock strikes eleven', according to the stage directions, and Faustus reflects, 'Ah Faustus, | Now hast thou but one bare hour to live, | And then thou must be damned perpetually' (Marlowe 1985: 331, 336 [5.2.6, 5.2.143–45]). Eternity resurges as a form of punishment even more terrifying than the ravages of time.

Marvell's implementation of the topos of devouring time is a significant marker of a secular moment in which humanity enters into a struggle against time, and, increasingly better equipped with the technological means to control nature and make its existence safer and more comfortable, appropriates time for itself. This modern narrative of the mastery of time has, however, a sting in the tail. By the nineteenth century, capitalism had brought about a complete equation of time and money (see Chapter 6). In a grotesque moment of reversal, Marx imagines capitalism itself supplanting time as the devourer of all things:

> It is now no longer the labourer that employs the means of production, but the means of production that employ the labourer. Instead of being consumed by him as material elements of his productive activity, they devour him as the ferment necessary to their own lifeprocess, and the lifeprocess of capital consists only in its movement as value constantly expanding, constantly multiplying itself.
>
> (Marx 1976: 425; translation modified)[1]

What this paradoxical development assumes, however, is a form of time fully emancipated, on the one hand from divine dictates, and on the other from the restraints of the natural world. This emancipation of time, no longer subordinated to its other, eternity, and confirmed in its mastery over human subjects (Zoll, ed., 1988), signals the advent of our own experience of modernity.

ABSOLUTE TIME

In the introductory lines of her novel *Middlemarch* (first published 1871–72), George Eliot imagines Time as a scientist conducting 'varying experiments' on 'man ... that mysterious mixture' (1991: 3). This personified Time is a distant, omniscient figure, somewhat akin to the godlike 'heterodiegetic' (or so-called 'authorial') narrator who utters these opening words, removed from the action of which it is none the less the undisputed master and whose scope is encompassed by its command. In structural terms, Eliot's figure is an anthropomorphic allegory for what, by the nineteenth century had become a hegemonic notion of absolute time. This notion had been most succinctly formulated by Isaac Newton towards the end of the seventeenth century and was the conceptual bedrock of Enlightenment scientific experimentation.

Newton's famous formulation in *Philosophiae naturalis principia mathematica* runs, 'Absolute, true, and mathematical time, of itself and from its own nature, flows uniformly, without regard to anything external' (Newton 1966, I: 6; translation modified). Three points are salient within Newton's formulation. First, time is 'absolute' and 'true' – that is, it constitutes an epistemological authority and guarantor of truth as that which is real, although, oddly enough, Newton conceded that it was not empirically verifiable. Second, it flows 'uniformly', evenly, without the fluctuations in velocity that can be seen in the movement of things; indeed, it is the steady, 'mathematical' measurable standard by which those very fluctuations in speed can be judged and calibrated. Third, it is separated from the things it allows us to measure, somehow disentangled from the objects and events of life itself. Though this is the last part of Newton's definition, it may be taken as the precondition of the others. Newton peels time away from the world of which it gives an objective and judicious measure. The 'objective structure of the time relation' (Reichenbach 1951: 144) is a reified, albeit dynamic, structure. Time appears to flow around things, between them or even through them, but it is clearly not of them. Time must be separate from things and events in order to be absolute.

This transformation of time emerges in distinction to an earlier Biblical or sacred notion of temporality, still residually evident, for instance in the work of British antiquarians, for whom linear history was inaugurated by seminal biblical events (Piggot 1989: 37–40, 54–59). This Biblical chronology had to be abandoned [because] it did not contain the *right kind of Time*. It was Time relying upon significant events, mythical and historical, and as such it was chronicle as well as chronology. As a sequence of events ... it did not allow for Time to be a variable independent of the event it marks. Hence it could not become part of the Cartesian system of spacetime coordinates allowing the scientist to plot a multitude of *uneventful* data over neutral time, unless it was first naturalized, i.e. separated from events meaningful to mankind.

(Fabian 1983: 13)

Within this abstracted notion of time, 'simultaneity is ... transverse, cross-time, marked not by prefiguring and fulfilment' as in the interlocking of time and eternity, but by mere 'temporal coincidence ... measured by clock and calendar' (Anderson 1991: 24).

Because time is now separated from the events which occur in it, it becomes a receptacle untainted by that which it contains: 'empty' and 'homogeneous' in the celebrated formulation of Walter Benjamin (1999: 252). Why must this time be empty? Like space, it is reduced to a container, so that events can fill it. These events are 'reified', that is, without any trace of adhesiveness either to time or to each other. Homogeneity, in turn, installs a new form of translatability allowing different events to be connected to each other in a manner which reduces them to the same language, eschewing complex, interplanar relationships. Homogeneity permits a plethora of different events of differing durations, scales, speeds, to be evenly reified within an abstract framework of time. The virtue of **reification** is that the framework, unaffected by that which it contains, can posit an even speed of temporal progress.

Abstract time takes the tangibility out of time, makes it a mere invisible container in which concrete things, or visible events have their place or take place. Abstract, absolute time can be compared to Carter's image of history as 'theatre', in which 'the historian is an impartial onlooker' (1987: xv), endowed with 'a thetic consciousness *of* time which stands above it and embraces it' (Merleau-Ponty 2002: 482); in other words, time is imagined as something which can be seen from outside, objectified by the viewer's distance. The notion of history as a diorama allows us to imagine what it would be like to stand in the place of time itself, separated from events, arranging them in sequential order like dominos or counters on a table to create a logical sequence of cause and effect.

This place outside of events, objective and neutral, allows one to take their measure precisely because one is not *in media res*, embedded in their complexity. Absolute, abstract time is the very concept which allows the measurement of the speed of events and their linear causality to be posited. Not surprisingly, this place outside of time resembles almost exactly the position of the omniscient narrator outside the events recounted by the realist novel, as in the example from Eliot's *Middlemarch* quoted above. The god-like, heterodiegetic (or so-called 'authorial') narrator's position outside and above the novel's events is what gives them their sheen of real-world autonomy. This narrative position works to naturalize and popularize a version of time formulated well before, but in more arcane terms, by Newton the scientist. But that heterodiegetic position remains no less part of a fiction it pretends to stand above, just as absolute time itself comes to be seen as a no less partial account of the physical universe.

RELATIVE TIME

Newton's absolute time served the demands of industrial and scientific progress perfectly well for two centuries, but the emergent modern physics and mathematics of the late nineteenth century, represented by the Austrian and German mathematicians and physicists Mach, Reimann and Planck, increasingly revealed the limits of what had been regarded hitherto as a universal set of laws. Einstein's theories of relativity finally put paid to absolute time at the beginning of the twentieth century.

Newton's absolute time reposed upon the separation of time from place, that is, from specific localities, thereby allowing it to become universal (Giddens 1990: 17–21). The universality of absolute time was a specifically modern product with a limited shelf life. A long-standing literary mystery exemplifies this. From the end of the seventeenth century onwards, critics have remarked upon the temporal incoherence of many of Shakespeare's dramas.

Othello, for instance, appears to posit two conflicting time-schemes, one very rapid, but contradicted by a plethora of indices suggesting a much longer temporal duration (Bradley 1905: 423–29). Numerous ingenious theories were devised to resolve this dilemma, but a simple explanation may be the existence of several calendar systems in Shakespeare's Europe: an older Julian calendar which was still used in England and the more accurate Gregorian calendar of 1582 promulgated from Rome but eschewed in many countries for political-religious reasons (Holford-Strevens 2005: 33–43). The co-existence of two discrepant calendars until as late as 1700 caused temporal anomalies quite familiar to early modern travellers: an Englishman crossing the Channel to France knew that he would arrive there a year before the date of his departure. The **story**-world of *Othello* tacitly evinces a similar anomaly – namely, the discrepancy between the Julian calendar still in use in Cyprus and the Venetians' own local calendar, *More Veneto* – a discrepancy which generates the conflicting time schemes of the play (Sohmer 2002).

With Newton's absolute time, which was formulated at the period in which the Gregorian calendar became accepted in most of Europe,[2] time was extracted from its adherence to place; it became an abstract medium quite separate, for example, from the concrete embodiments of time in day and night or the seasons. (By the same token, space itself, long disciplined by the universal abstractions of Euclidean geometry, was increasingly defined as a neutral receptacle for the things and events which it contained; space, however, was understood as not being inflected or distorted by the local peculiarities of the specific places which exemplified it.) Two centuries later, in his Dublin epic *Ulysses* (first published 1922), Joyce playfully abolished this homogeneity of calendar time, happily reenacting a collision of discrepant local or culture-specific time schemes:

> the twelfth day of May of the bissextile year one thousand nine hundred and four of the Christian era (Jewish era five thousand six hundred and sixty-four, mohammedan era one thousand three hundred and twenty-two), golden number 5, epact 13, solar cycle 9, dominical letters C B, Roman indication 2, Julian period 6617, MXMIV.
>
> (Joyce 1969: 589).[3]

Flouting temporal homogeneity with characteristically flamboyant bravado, Joyce accurately took the measure of an ambient sea-change in scientific understandings of time.

Only a decade before, in very similar vein, Einstein's theories of relativity had brought time and space back together once again. Minkowski, following Einstein, announced, 'Henceforth space by itself, and time by itself, are doomed to fade away into mere shadows, and only a kind of union of the two will preserve an independent reality' (1952: 75). Einstein's basic point was simple: time and space are not variables independent of one another, but reciprocally influence each other. As Minkowski quipped, 'No-one has yet observed a place except at a time, nor yet a time except at a place' (qtd in Gray 1989: 186). What early modern travellers might have experienced prior to Newton's absolute time and the Gregorian calendar, once again emerged, in a different form, on Einstein's temporal horizon.

A very simple way of approaching relativity is to bear in mind the practical problems of time coordination (see Chapter 1). The only way to judge a clock's accuracy is by comparing it to another clock. That other clock, however, must by definition be somewhere else, be it a mere few centimetres away. The greater the distance to be covered by the time-signals used to coordinate clocks (say, between London and New York), the more the delay of transmission must be factored into the coordination process to erase possible errors. The greater the distance and the more precise the clocks, the more significant the spatial-temporal difference between specific places becomes (Galison 2003). Time is not independent of, but is influenced by the site of its measurement, and that site is always relative to other sites.

A second way of imagining relativity posits that clocks travelling at very great speeds do not remain constant in their time measurement, but produce what Einstein called 'time dilation'. Even more perplexingly, they change their speed relative to other clocks against which their speed is calibrated. Clocks travelling at very high speeds relative to one another and to stationary clocks accordingly read off divergent times. Einstein concluded that there is no objective time which can be measured by a time-keeping instrument, but that time is a product of the act of measuring determined by its position and speed relative to other devices' positions and speeds. Depending on its respective speed, each measuring instrument will have its 'local' time: 'Every reference body has its own particular time' (Einstein, quoted in Kern 1983: 19). We are 'obliged to define time in such a way that the rate of a clock depends upon where the clock may be' (Einstein 1952a: 117).

A third way of envisaging relativity arose out of observations of the manner in which light rays were bent as they passed through the sun's gravitational field (Einstein 1952b: 99). As Einstein posited that the speed of light was an absolutely unvarying given, apparently different elapsed trajectory times must have arisen from an altered trajectory of the light rays. Correspondingly, time measurement was shown to be influenced by gravitational forces: clocks down a mine, that is, closer to the Earth's centre of gravity, will run slower. A black hole, a collapsed star with an extremely dense gravitational field, will tend to 'suck' time into itself altogether.

Einstein's theories of relativity banished the illusion of the independence of space and time. Physics now speaks of 'spacetime' as a single term. 'Spacetime' is a hybrid dimension in which both space and time as relational variables together form a dynamic composite. Relativity doesn't contradict Newtonian time; it merely *relativizes* it, showing that time is dependent on place, speed, and the mode of comparison. Newtonian time works at the scales of visibility and the speeds available to empirical perception (Bohm 1965: 48–51). It fails to do its job, however, at very small spatial scales of measurement (subatomic proportions) or at very great scales (distances of light years); nor does it perform at very high speeds (the oscillation frequencies of very minute particles, or at the speed of light). Newtonian absolute time and Einsteinian relative spacetime appear to cohabit our world in a very relativistic manner: depending upon the particular pragmatic, axiological or epistemological framework that we happen to inhabit at a specific moment in time, we may use the one or the other. The two modes of understanding time complement each other antithetically (Plotnitsky 1994), or open on to each other (Bachelard 1966: 30–33) as radically incompatible, but nevertheless contiguous zones of time-understanding. Indeed, in the world of advanced finance capital they complement each other in particularly insidious ways: absolute time functions to elide the dynamic, immanent temporalities inherent in things themselves, colluding thereby in the reification of commodities; while relativistic spacetime underpins the flows of global financial speculation (see Chapter 6).

PHENOMENOLOGY

Well before Einstein, however, absolute time had already undergone sustained critique. The eighteenth-century philosopher Immanuel Kant, for example, contested that time was not an objectively existing entity in the universe but rather, that it was a subjective factor integral to perception itself. He claimed that time is 'nothing other than the inner form of sense itself', an 'a priori condition of all senses'. Kant granted that time was an empirical reality to the extent that it possessed 'objective validity in respect of all objects which allow of ever being given to our senses', but denied time 'all claim to absolute reality ... independent of any reference to the form of our sensible intuition' (2003: 78). In other words, time was a condition of possibility of perception of the world, and only because it framed perception could it mistakenly be ascribed to the external world itself. To this extent, Kant was the forerunner of modern phenomenological theories of temporality.

The phenomenological method emerged at the beginning of the twentieth century in an attempt to return to some sort of basic, fundamental knowledge. That knowledge was to bring philosophy back to things themselves as we perceive them in our consciousness. One of the great proponents of phenomenology was Edmund Husserl (1859–1938). His phenomenology of time focused upon the lived experience of time in 'inner consciousness' (1991). Time at its most fundamental level had to be experienced as subjective time, he claimed, following upon Kant's stipulation that time was one of the central *a priori* categories of knowledge or essential frameworks via which we could make sense of the world.

But phenomenology also signalled a rejection of abstract absolute time, and its mundane correlative, so-called 'public' time increasingly at odds with 'private' or interior time. At the end of the nineteenth century, middle-class intellectuals registered increasing levels of conflict between the regulated patterns of industrial and bureaucratic production (as in Taylorism, a forerunner of today's managerial science which pioneered techniques of analysing and timing production procedures so as to shorten production time and raise outputs) and the rhythms of personal life. The latter were privileged by discourses such as psychology and sociology, with philosophy also springing into the breach.

Husserl's phenomenology of time reposed upon a rejection of the notion of time as a sequence of present moments, a series of atomized 'nows'. Rather, in much the same sense as the French and American philosophers Bergson and James at the end of the nineteenth century, he insisted upon a present which was longer and more complex in its structure than a mere instant of perception: the present is 'no knife-edge, but a saddle-back, with a certain breadth of its own on which we sit perched and from which we look in two directions into time' (James 1890: I, 609). Famously using the image of a melody which we do not perceive as a series of isolated notes, but as preceding and succeeding musical elements linked to each other, Husserl (1991: 11–12) claimed that the present moment contained in itself residual traces of what had immediately gone before ('retensions'), and anticipations of what was immediately to come ('protensions'). As retensions drift further into the past, they fade into 'recollections' and then 'memory'. The past must diminish in intensity in this manner so as to avoid an overload of impressions (Kern 1983: 44), an experiential saturation of the sort parodically imagined in Borges' short story 'Funes the memorious' (1976: 87–95). Conversely, 'protensions' inhabiting the present anticipate more distant hopes and expectations which will soon come into close range. Husserl's present can be described as horizontally 'thick' because 'within the present we find both past and future' (Dostal 1993: 146). It is also vertically thick: every long, graduated present of retention-present-protension is overlaid by others already fading away into 'memory' or emerging out of 'hope': 'As time passes, each present (this [horizontally] "thick" present with three dimensions internal to it) is retained in the succeeding moment – retensionally' (ibid: 147).

Husserl thus claims that subjectivity is essentially temporal in nature. Husserl goes so far as to suggest that time *is* subjectivity. This poses the problem of an excessively 'egological' notion of time, which Husserl attempts to resolve by positing a pre-subjective, 'permanent standing now', thus bringing him back to something resembling Newton's absolute time, exterior to things and beings. Husserl's phenomenology thus never succeeds in resolving the dilemma of the Scylla and Charybdis of purely subjective and purely objective time.

Martin Heidegger (1889–1976) took up and radicalized Husserl's claims. Heidegger shifts the terms of the problem by suggesting that the *a priori* category of time as experience is not within the self but rather, that time is the condition of possibility of experience. Time, Heidegger says in *Being and Time* (first published 1927), is the very horizon of being. Being-in-the-world (*Dasein*, literally, 'being-there') is historical, temporal being. Time is thus neither subjective nor objective, but the condition of possibility of both subjects and objects. Time is 'the only standpoint from which Dasein, if it can do this at all, tacitly understands and interprets something like Being' (Heidegger 1962: 39). Time provides the only possible 'horizon for the understanding of being' (ibid: 39; translations modified).[4] Time in itself does not exist; it provides the conditions of possibility for existence and its apprehension. This is a radical reworking of Kant's position. If Kant had dictated that subjectivity underlay temporality, Heidegger reversed this notion, claiming that temporality is the prerequisite for subjective experience (Hoy 2008: 262). There is no other place from which we can understand our temporal existence.

We have no choice in the matter. Being in time is not something about which we were consulted beforehand, in much the same way as no one asked us whether we wanted to be conceived and born. Heidegger calls this condition of involuntary being in the world 'thrownness' ('*Geworfenheit*'). Even more dramatically, our condition of being thrown into existence is one that is limited from the outset by a use-by date, that of our own death. Our mortality constitutes the negative framework in which life is to be lived. Our being in the world is a being-unto-death from the very moment we are born. However, 'thrownness' does not merely define the limitations of being. Because it pegs out the basic parameters of temporal existence, it also shows up the realms of possibility of being. Thus Heidegger opposes to 'thrownness'

('*Geworfenheit*') the notion of project-ion ('*Entwurf*'), which contains the same etymological root of 'throwing', but makes it into an active gesture. A 'project' sees the futurity of being, even when it is finally limited by death, and marked at every instant by the finality of mortality, as none the less open to what is to come ('*Zu-kunft*').

There are two dimensions to the open future horizon which Heidegger discovers within the 'thrownness' of being. The first is the necessity of accepting the condition of existence-unto-death. Everyday life is customarily organized so as to allow us to forget our mortality. It is not merely that we are in time – this would be a way of 'spatializing' time, making room for ourselves in it and accommodating it. Rather, the problem is that time, and mortality, runs through us (Safranski 1994: 197). One aspect of project-ion ('*Entwurf*') is that the bleak temporality of existence doomed-to-death demands that we actively make our destiny. This brings Heidegger back to the present. The positive form that such a project might take is therefore that of the 'moment' ('*Augenblick*'). The flip side of the 'time of being' is the 'being of time', its crystallization in what Benjamin would call a 'perilous critical moment' (Benjamin 2002: 463). Like many other early twentieth-century thinkers for whom history had become 'a nightmare' from which they were 'trying to awake' (Joyce 1969: 40), Heidegger embraced the idea of the moment as an epiphanic instant of decision. His theory of the moment is decisionist: what counts is the act, not the content, of the decision. In the philosophical framework set up by Heidegger, there is no transcendent sense to be given to temporal existence, so that by implication, there is no moral ground or guarantee for making such a decision. This would have fatal consequences for Heidegger himself when he embraced the Nazi cause during his short period as Rector of the University of Freiburg.

In the complicated relationships between past, present and future which make up temporality, Heidegger elaborates a non-subjective, non-objective fabric of time which supplants Husserl's tripartite interior time. Heidegger calls this tripartite relationship of past, present and future an 'ecstatic' structure. 'Ek-stase' means 'standing out', and each of these temporal modes can only be understood by standing outside it, that is from the vantage point of the others. We can only understand the future in contrast to our present ('thrownness') and our past (the 'facticity' of what has already happened) (Dostal 1993: 156). Temporal progress cannot be understood as a mere succession of moments, as if one could escape from the experience of time and regard those moments with some sort of God's-eye view. Rather, just as being can only be understood from within time, which we are condemned to inhabit, so too temporality can only be understood from within temporality. Thus each temporal dimension must be understood from another. In an extraordinarily dense formulation, Heidegger claims that

> Taking over thrownness ... is possible only in such a way that the futural Dasein can *be* its ownmost as-it-already-was – that is to say, its 'been'. Only in so far as Dasein *is* as an 'I am-having-*been*', can Dasein come towards itself futurally in such a way that it comes *back*.
> (Heidegger 1962: 373; translation modified)[5]

In a sense, as a being-unto-death living under the sign of death from the moment of one's birth ('one's ownmost "been"', an ingenious translators' pun on 'being'), the anticipation and fulfilment of one's coming pastness is the very fabric of life, but also provides the conditions of its possibilities. Death dominates our existence from the outset (futurity) as a constantly present negation (an anticipated pastness), yet by the same token, provides the outer boundary of our possibilities, and defines the open horizon of what potential we may fulfil (in the present).

What Bowie (1993: 23) calls a 'pattern of cross-stitching between times and tenses that ordinary usage often seems intent on keeping apart' is a vital perception of the genuinely interwoven nature of temporal existence, both its limitations and possibilities, and its complex interactions between past, present and future. The French philosopher Jean-Paul Sartre, for instance, who owes much to Heidegger's temporal phenomenology, fails to understand this complex temporal interweaving, seeing the past as a dead weight which can only be escaped from by making a courageous decision to take responsibility for one's own existence (2003: 130–92). Sartre replicates the duality of 'thrownness' and 'project', but neglects the manner in which the two are intimately bound up with one another in a facilitating and not merely a limiting manner (Giddens 1982: 37).

For all the importance of these phenomenological approaches to time, a number of criticisms must nevertheless be mounted against them. First, although they claim to return to the bare bones of experience, whether perceptual or existential, thus giving us access to what is presented to perception or experience, phenomenology is dogged by the perennial problems of absence which plague philosophies of time. The past and the future are by definition not present, and the present is that instant, constantly fading away, which lies between them. The present, then, is hardly present (Derrida 1973: 64). Granted, it can also be observed that the complex cross-stitching of tripartite time in Husserl and Heidegger resembles a Saussurean differential sign, defined by what it is not (e.g. /cat/ as opposed to /bat/ or /mat/); this determination of the present, the past, or the future by their respective others similarly mobilizes a complex interplay of present absences and absent presences (Dostal 1993: 147; Currie 2007: 74).

Second, the limitations and possibilities of time are imposed, for Heidegger, by the prospect of death. For both Husserl and Heidegger the modesty, or scepticism, of phenomenology lies in accepting the necessarily limited character of subjectivity as the sole location where temporality can be accounted for. This assumed presence-to-self, however limited its nature, may be equally aporetic, because it neglects other more primordial aspects of the temporality of subjectivity. Subjectivity is always preceded by an other which gives it existence: the mother, language, the environment. In Emmanuel Lévinas' radical ethics of alterity, temporality is abruptly snatched from a subject aware of its own mortality and re-assigned to an other who imposes an ethical responsibility upon the self. This responsibility is one I cannot choose: it precedes and exceeds my will or intention. I become a subject, so to speak, by becoming *subject* to an ethical relationship which calls me into existence (Lévinas 2006: 45–57). Lévinas stresses the 'anachronic' nature of the ethical relationship: it precedes any possible present, it comes out of a past which is before any possibility of remembering. This is a temporality of the 'imperative' which the world issues to us (Lingis 1998). Lévinas radically revises Heidegger's temporality as Being-unto-death, substituting for the end-orientation of human life the futurity of the unpredictable encounter with the other. The other always recedes from apprehension or comprehension by the self, thus opening up the future in a way that radically contradicts death's ever-present closure (Lévinas 1987: 79).

Third, the idea of 'lived time' (the inner, experiential time of phenomenology) is a tautology. Once we abandon the external, distant temporality of absolute time, an abstract time surrounding beings, measuring their continued existence but peeled away from them; it follows that all time is lived time, in the sense that time is nothing but the vibrant, pulsing dynamic of life itself: a time immanent to the constantly changing being of things. This time-in-things, however, is not merely that of humans, but of all life, whether animate or inanimate, organic or inorganic. Phenomenology's interior time, or the time of the subject's being-unto-death, is premised upon the very separation of humanity and nature on which modernity is spuriously predicated (Latour 1993) and which has wreaked such havoc on our natural environment. Phenomenology merely constitutes a pendulum swing from one extreme to the other, but retains the dual structure of Enlightenment time (i.e. subjective/experienced/human vs. objective/non-human). The notion of a temporality which is neither subjective nor objective, neither interior to the self nor exterior to it, but rather immanent to the life of all things, and thus also to objects *as subjects in their own right*, remains as yet out of sight.

IMMANENT TIME

What is the alternative? It may be simply to accept the notion which philosophies of time, for the most part, have resisted: that of time as change and transformation. We are used to the idea that the world is made of more or less solid substances. However, the closer we look at things, that is, at the scale of subatomic particles, the more we discover that they are in constant flux. All materials are made up of particles linked to each other in complex structures, which are not static, rigid or motionless but vibrating according to temperature:

> Inside the vibrating atoms the electrons are bound to the atomic nuclei by electric forces that try to keep them as close as possible, and they respond to this confinement by whirling around extremely fast. In the nuclei, finally, protons and neutrons are pressed into a minute volume by the strong nuclear forces, and consequently race about at unimaginable velocities.
>
> (Capra 1983: 78–79)

Indeed, even the constituent units of these subatomic structures are constantly undergoing change, oscillating between various states:

> Matter is not even energy, but a continual movement between states. A proton never remains a simple proton. It alternates between being a proton and a neutral pion on one hand, and being a neutron and a positive pion on the other. The identity of a sub-atomic particle is inextricable from its potentiality as a range of other particles.
>
> (Ashcroft 2001a: 115n7)

No less invisible to individual human perception, but at the other extreme on a scale of size, is the earth itself. Far from being a solid entity, the globe we inhabit is largely constituted of fluids in constant circulation, as De Landa points out:

> the thin rocky crust on which we live and which we call our land and home ... is ... a mere hardening within the greater system of underground lava flows, which, organizing themselves into large 'conveyor belts' (convective cells), are the main factor in the most salient and apparently durable structures of the crusty surface.
>
> (1997: 257–58)

Because 'the oceanic crust on which the continents are embedded is constantly being created and destroyed (by solidification and remelting)', the 'rocks and mountains that define the most stable and durable traits of our reality would merely represent a local slowing down of this flowing reality' (ibid: 258). The Earth itself is a dynamic process; however, it is a process so ponderous, and whose proportions so exceed our individual frame of reference, that we perceive it as a stable given.

In other words, at many different scales of perception, it becomes clear that matter does not 'exist', but rather, is caught in a constant process of change and transformation. If everything in the universe is in a state of constant flux, as Heraclitus claimed, then there is no 'separate' time outside the dynamic, processual becomings of things. That dynamic process is temporality itself. Temporality is not the environment of these processes, or the measuring stick to calibrate them, but rather, the processes themselves. All these processes make up the multiply variegated density of being, a tapestry of interwoven immanent 'temporalities'.

Time is not a container (in which things exist and events happen), nor is it even a fluid medium (like air or water). Rather, time is immanent to things: 'The force of time is not just a contingent characteristic of the living, but is the dynamic impetus that enables life to become, to always be in the process of becoming, something other than what it was' (Grosz 2005: 8). The idea that there is no time outside the life-processes of all beings was intimated by Wittgenstein when he claimed in his *Tractatus* (first published 1922) that 'The world is all that is the case' (Wittgenstein 1974: 5). Or in Clément Rosset's (1977) Lacanian language, time in things is the Real, the sum of all things which necessarily exceeds our representational capacities. It is a plenitude admitting of no lack, except in our own (lacunary) capacity to comprehend it (Rosset 1971). The American poet Amy Clampitt succinctly puts it in a poem entitled 'Nothing stays put': 'All that we know, that we're | made of, is motion' (1991: 78).

If we relinquish the notion of stable entities, we also have to relinquish the notion of clear-cut ends and beginnings. Thus every moment of final entropic collapse is also a moment of autopoesis, of self-creative activity, within another neighbouring system. Reconceptualizing things as processes, we must also reconceptualize the notion of temporality as made up of constant processes of transition from one state to another. Heise (1997: 28) has intimated that postmodern culture favours the notion of a '"rhythmic" time, which is co-extensive with and inseparable from the individual event'. However, the concept of the event maintains the atomizing structure of absolute time, and needs to be rendered even more dynamic so as to open it up to processual flows. Exemplifying this, Ashcroft has remarked that '[a]t the subatomic level there is no longer any distinction between what is – authentic being – and what happens. Matter, or particles, are continually created, annihilated, and created again' (Ashcroft 2001a: 107–8). This appears to fly in the face of reason until we examine the life of subatomic particles:

> Particles live much less than a millionth of a second ... When a particle called a negative pi meson collides with a proton, both pi meson and proton may be destroyed (or other processes occur) and if so, two new particles are created in their place: a neutral k meson and a lamda. Both of these particles decay spontaneously into two additional particles, two of which are the same particles with which we started.
>
> (Ashcroft 2001a: 114–15n7)

At a more accessible level of comprehension, the body, for instance, is constantly transforming itself – cells are being created and dying constantly, our skin completely renews itself at regular intervals. Things are thus caught in a constantly shifting equilibrium between autopoesis and entropy. We tend to think of death as the endpoint, but in terms of autopoesis, no process ever ends, but merely shades over into new processes of a different sort. Beginnings and ends are both strategies for containing change by establishing narratives that are either determined from the point of departure, or pre-programmed by the point of arrival. They do not, however, accurately reflect the ongoing processes of transformation, in which, to misquote T. S. Eliot's *Four Quartets* (1982: 177), in my end is my beginning. Entropy and death are merely instances of becoming-other rather than marking a definitive end-stop terminus. Death is *'what never ceases and never finishes happening in every becoming'* (Deleuze and Guattari 1983: 330).

Systemic overlap, that is, embedded systems and sub-systems which overlap with each other and evolve temporally into other systems, is the key to a positive, dynamic and immanent notion of temporalities. Temporalities and their multiple strands cannot be conceptualized without an accompanying sense of the ecologies of dynamic systems. There is no way of viewing these temporal strands from outside, as classical versions of absolute time sought to do. Rather, in accordance with Heidegger's *Dasein*, but without the omnipresence of death he insisted upon, we can only understand temporalities as an infinite fabric of processes in which we are ourselves involved:

> [T]he world is finally composed of systems so extensive, so dense, and so complex that it is no longer a question of representing them in their totality/globality ... but rather of engaging those systems at certain specific or local points along their lines of deployment or unfolding. It is as if today one were forced ... to accept the mobile and shifting nature of the phenomena that make up our social and political world, and by this same token, forced to discover within this slippery *glacis* of largely indistinct swells and flows, all the ledges, footholds, friction points – in short, all the subtle asperities that would permit us to navigate, and negotiate life, within it.
>
> (Kwinter 2003: 12)

Correspondingly, we must think of what might have been named 'time' as a gigantic, immensely complex, interrelating and overlapping network of dynamic processes, each with its own tempo, life-span, and diachronic-synchronic transitions with previous, simultaneous or neighbouring, and successor processes.[6]

Some of these processes will be invisible to human perception because they remain below the threshold of our conscious apprehension, or because what we see is changing so slowly that we see only an apparently stable object; others will be clearly visible. Likewise, some of these processes will be familiar as part of our human environment, making up a spectrum of plural social temporalities (Gurvitch 1964); some will be less familiar because they belong to our non-human environment. The human/non-human gulf is a distinction to be overcome (Latour 1993), because it has underwritten the modern global destruction of the environment: 'the image of dead or thoroughly instrumentalized matter feeds human hubris and our earth-destroying fantasies of conquest and consumption' (Bennett 2010: ix). What is needed in its place is a

sense of the immense heterogeneity of temporal processes immanent to the world and its various human and non-human (animal,
vegetable, mineral) inhabitants: 'Postmodern culture exposes
human time as just one among a multiplicity of temporal scales,
one that can no longer be considered the measure and standard of
continuity' (Heise 1997: 46). Thoreau's notion of 'all change' as 'a
miracle ... taking place every instant' (1906: 8) or what Virginia
Woolf called 'the question of things happening, normally, all the
time' (1980: II, 400), or Whitehead's notion of being as 'a continuous
stream of occurrence' (1920: 172), allude to this multiplicity. Our
own temporal existence is merely one strand within the complex
hybrid temporalities of things-in-process, a 'creative not-quite-human
force capable of producing the new' (Bennett 2010: 118).

We are accustomed to separating out time and the things that
occupy it or the events that happen in it. Things are reified and then
lodged in a linear-temporal continuum conceived as a measuring rod;
events are also reified into segmented cause–effect units. All these
processes of segmentation are a correlative of modernity's apogee:
namely, the tendency of capitalism to reify, quantify and translate
everything, including time itself, into units of exchange under
the universal currency of money (see Chapter 6). What we take to
be real things or events are merely reified, atomized slices of
dynamic processes which are then declared to be real, and their
native processes denigrated as mere impermanence and contingency:

> Now, life is an evolution. We condense a period of this evolution into
> a stable perspective which we call a form, and, when the change has
> become considerable enough to overcome the fortunate inertia of our
> perception, we say the body has changed its form. But in reality the body
> is changing at every moment; or rather, there is no form, since form is
> immobile and the reality is movement. What is real is the continual
> *change of* form: *form is only a snapshot view of a transition*. Therefore,
> here again, our perception manages to solidify into discontinuous
> images the fluid continuity of the real.
>
> (Bergson 1911: 302; translation modified)[7]

We must rewind this process, reverting from the notion of reified
things within segmented time to a notion of immanent time

embodied in the dynamic processes of becoming inherent in all beings. This counter-intuitive move reverses a historical progression in which fluid processes have been attributed 'end-stop' character-istics to make them appear as bounded entities within a segmented temporal environment. The sequence of re-conceptualization reverses the sequence of historical mystification.

This re-conceptualization is complicated, of course, by the fact that we continue to experience time under the hegemonic mode of Enlightenment calendar and clock time. Abstract Enlightenment time is so rigidly cemented within our culture that it cannot be easily dislodged. Nor do the arguments advanced here suggest that it would be realistic to do so. We cannot simply dismiss this time and aim to put something else in its place. Rather, this book intimates that Enlightenment time, though hegemonic, has never been absolute. It has always been riddled with contradictions, shot through with discrepancies, and porous to other temporalities which exist in its interstices and are constantly becoming apparent in its blind spots (cf Williams 1977: 112–14).

What is at stake, then, is to make more space for these alternative temporalities and to amplify their effects. Just as narrative achron-ism assumes a basic linearity of events which it in fact constantly disturbs, but also more deeply underpins (Currie 2007: 38), so too alternative temporalities will inevitably be perceived against the background of a still-hegemonic Enlightenment time whose environment they actually constitute. None the less, if, as von Weizäcker suggests, the world is always already change, our task then is to join in a process of transformation which we have always been implicated in without knowing (1977: 436). From this point of view, one might want to read Saint Augustine's dilemma, translated again and again over the centuries, not as an expression of a fundamental aporia (Ricoeur 1984–88: III, 241–74), but rather as a persistently reiterated, and none the less unheard assessment of our place within multiple temporalities: 'What, then, is time? I know well enough what it is' – to the extent that I participate in its multiple strands of becoming. But 'if I am asked what it is … I am baffled' (Augustine 1961: 264) – because there is no place outside of those streams of becoming from which, untouched by their dynamic, we could apprehend them. Striving to do so, as we now know all too well, has merely been an active correlative of the catastrophic global consequences terrifyingly evident today. Both halves of Augustine's statement are 'performatives', speech acts with material consequences, and to read his words against the grain is to potentially liberate possibilities of other modes of temporal embodiment hitherto elided.

3

HISTORIES

In Michael Ondaatje's novel *The English Patient* (first published 1992) modernity falters and slides backwards. Eschewing narratives of accelerated technological modernity reinforced by the emergence of rocket and nuclear warfare (Virilio 1986 and 1994), Ondaatje superimposes feudal strife upon mid-twentieth-century global war:

> The last medieval war was fought in Italy in 1943 and 1944. Fortress towns on great promontories which had been battled over since the eighth century had the armies of new kings flung carelessly against them. Around the outcrops of rocks were the traffic of stretchers, butchered vineyards, where, if you dug deep beneath the tank ruts, you found blood-axe and spear.
>
> (Ondaatje 1993: 69)

Ondaatje imagines a European history that is not a narrative of progress but one which turns in circles. Modernity is not as modern as it claims, merely re-enacting pre-modern conflicts and quasi-tribal rivalries. Ondaatje's narrative documents a moment of temporal crisis, given most acute expression at the end of his novel by the dropping of the atomic bomb: at that juncture, modernity reveals its ultimate bankruptcy.

Ondaatje's postmodern fiction diagnoses a malaise not only in modern history but also in modern historiography. For in the midst of this temporal scepticism, the author showcases the slightly disreputable ancient Greek father of history, Herodotus, a purveyor of apocryphal stories. In this Herodotus resembles the eponymous English patient, actually a turncoat Hungarian aristocrat named Almásy, from whom the Allied interrogators can obtain no reliable intelligence. Almásy carries a copy of Herodotus, an unreliable narrative which, however, contains more truth than one might suspect. Almásy's Herodotus is his

> guidebook, ancient and modern, of supposed lies. When he discovered the truth to what had seemed a lie, he brought out his glue pot and pasted in a map or newspaper clipping or used a blank space in the book to sketch men in skirts with faded unknown animals alongside them. The early oasis dwellers had not usually depicted cattle, though Herodotus claimed they had.
>
> (Ondaatje 1993: 246)

Ondaatje's iconoclasm here is double.

First, he confuses the relationship between truth and untruth. Herodotus often functions as the 'other' of factual historiography (Hamilton 2002: 6–11). In contrast to his successor Thucydides, who claimed that his 'factual reporting' was based on events at which 'either I was present myself [or] … I … heard … from eyewitnesses whose reports I have checked with as much thoroughness as possible' (1978: 48), Herodotus epitomizes a form of pre-modern historiography still embedded in myth, legend and hearsay. Yet here it transpires in this passage that Herodotus may not have been so unreliable a source after all.

This transmutation of values – untruth emerging as truth and thus destabilizing what was previously taken for truth – is enabled by Ondaatje's second, more significant iconoclasm, namely an attack on representation in historical writing. Almásy's usage of Herodotus' text treats it as a scrapbook, consolidating and enhancing its materiality as **signifier** rather than its transparency as mediator of a historical **signified**: 'in his commonplace book, his 1890 edition of Herodotus' *Histories*, are other fragments – maps, diary entries, writings in many languages, paragraphs cut out of other books' (Ondaatje 1993: 96). Rather than placing empirically documented events within a linear sequence of causality, Almásy overlays competing versions of the same events, complicating, thickening or obscuring the line of causality. Almásy's scrapbook-like copy of Herodotus mimics its author's strategies: '"This history of mine," Herodotus says, "has from the beginning sought out the supplementary to the main argument." What you find in him are cul-de-sacs within the sweep of history' (ibid: 118–19). The multiple layers of text mimic these lateral shifts and diversions from the main line of historical causation. Almásy's text works by collage, montage, bricolage, taking accretion and opacity rather than transparently delineated causality as its guiding principle.

Linear causality is destabilized by the lateral accumulation of multiple textual versions, glued upon each other and upon the page of the text, thereby disrupting the iconic linearity of reading and questioning the historical fact that reading is supposed to apprehend. The isomorphic temporalities of supposedly linear reading and the historical chain that is read are disrupted. The notion of the historical fact cannot be sustained in any simple sense when each link in the historical chain is overlaid by other texts and other renditions of the same event. Thus the materiality of Almásy's Herodotus, with its wide-reaching implications for the sequential model of temporality underlying historiography, impacts directly upon the very status of the historical fact.

The date 1890, the sole chronological anchor in this mess of textual fragments, is not without significance, because it gestures towards the gradual demise of a nineteenth-century paradigm of scientific historicism that insisted upon the rigorous contextualization of empirical facts in a verifiable chronological sequence. Almásy's Herodotus emblematizes the resurgence of a long tradition of pre-modern forms of historiography displaced by historicism in its dominant nineteenth-century form; in turn, that historicism would lose much of its appeal by the early twentieth century. None the less, the linear chronologies historicism elevated to the status of scientific truth continue to hold sway today in popular consciousness:

the 'history wars' of the 1990s in Australia, for instance, mobilized a vitriolic press campaign harnessing popular belief in historiography. The history wars drew upon the self-evidence of a version of history understood as a sequence of empirically verifiable facts to vilify those who questioned national myths so as to lay bare a history of genocide (Macintyre and Clark 2003; West-Pavlov and Wawrzinek, eds, 2010).

The force of Ondaatje's iconoclasm, then, is less conceptual than performative: it triggers ripples in the transparent surface of the historicist mode of representation still dominant today. Ondaatje's re-visioning of a collage-like history is enabled by the very historicism, and its entanglement in national narratives, that it seeks to disrupt. These hegemonic and contestatory historiographic temporalities exist in an uneasy symbiosis.

This chapter explores the temporal logic underlying nineteenth-century historicism, suggesting that it is very much analogous to the absolute time minted by Newton a century earlier. Rather than regarding that historicism as the teleological culmination of an incremental growth of historical knowledge and methodology, the chapter understands it as the contingent product of a particular configuration of largely imperialist relationships, one which has progressively unravelled during the last half-century. In this chapter, I scrutinize historicism through the lenses of epistemology (Foucault), and phenomenology (Gadamer) so as to demonstrate how the contingent temporal logic of historicity is constructed. The chapter proceeds achronologically, moving backwards from nineteenth-century historicism to its predecessors, early modern and Enlightenment historiographies in their various forms. I lay bare not merely 'the historically conditioned character of the historical discipline' (White 1978: 29) but the temporal 'plot' of the progressivist, evolutionist version of history which, despite a century of waning credibility and mounting attacks, is still largely the one we inhabit. It is because this version of historicist logic, cemented by popular historiography and the educational establishment, is so deeply entrenched, that it bears detailed scrutiny. And for the same reasons it is necessary to present some instances of competing, alternative historiographical temporalities of which historians today have come to take cognizance: counterfactuals (fictive alternative histories), non-linear histories, historical reenactments and climate history.

HISTORY BEFORE HISTORY

What came before nineteenth-century historicism? One line of argument claims that from medieval chronicles and annals onwards there was a steady development that led to the scientifically accurate historical research of the nineteenth century (Butterfield 1955; Fussner 1962). This line of argument would merely project the linear sequences of historical causality back onto earlier epochs, including the development of historiographical method itself within a meta-historical narrative whose apogee would be the historically knowing subject writing its own disciplinary history.

Recently, historians have argued that this narrative of a gradual development of notions of historical methodology and empirical archival accuracy merely imposes retrospectively the teleology which is its own basic principle. Rather, they suggest, the forms of historiography taken by early modern and Enlightenment historical thought did not necessarily or always place them in a direct line of filiation leading to modern historiography (Matchinske 2009: 5–6). For instance, an early modern surge of secular, source-based and context-sensitive *ars historica* (in many ways akin to nineteenth-century scientific historicism) was displaced around 1700 (Grafton 2007); it gave way to what Bacon dismissed as the mere collecting of 'antiquities', manifestations of 'history defaced, or some remnants of history which have casually escaped the shipwreck of time' (Bacon 2001: 77). The history of historical thought is not linear, but appears to advance by 'phase transitions' or abrupt changes of state which may go in several directions, not all of them necessarily pointing forward, telelogically, to our own moment (De Landa 1997).

Many basic elements of modern historiography are far from being the eternal truths we assume them to be, but rather, have a recent history of their own. For example, the concept of an exact system of dating, working forwards and backwards from the birth of Christ (Anno Domini, now known as 'Common Era'), albeit familiar as far back as the sixth century, was properly elaborated only in 1627 by the Jesuit Dionysius Petavius and popularized by Descartes (Wilcox 1987: 8). Similarly, our triad of classical, medieval and modern epochs dates from the 1680s (Osterhammel 2009: 93). Although there were doubtless many predecessors employing methodologies that anticipated later empirical histor-iographies, it would seem that a linear, progressivist narrative cannot account for all the other historiographical models which abounded in the period before empirical historicism. A glance outside Europe reinforces these complications: in China, for instance, whose historiographical tradition is immensely rich, a system of chronological dating was not developed until the 1920s (Kwong 2001).

Given the absence of a teleological narrative, how then did historicism emerge? The European early modern period was characterized by an extremely hierarchical view of cosmic order which placed a high value upon stability and had little place for change (Lovejoy 1957; Tawney 1964: 155, 170). Moments of political transformation, such as the succession to the throne, were causes for apprehension; similarly, periods of social upheaval where subaltern groups demanded social transformation, such as the English Civil War, remained in the collective memory of the establishment as traumatic events decisively inflecting the political settlement of Restoration and eighteenth-century Britain. The passage of social time was thus understood as a process in which tradition furnished the pattern of continuity. Annals and chronicles, for instance, were forms of historical recording composed in an 'epic' mode (White 1973: 7–8) which was in accord with this static notion of historical temporality. They were correspondingly schematic in their notations (Rosenberg and Grafton 2010: 11–12). Chronicles thus displayed an informational paucity underlying the absence of narrative, that is, a story depending inherently upon change and instability to make it worth narrating (Lotman 1977: 237, 233). Early modern histories, while encompassing an exponential increase in the quantity of information to be included, none the less posited a stable background against which historical processes could be sketched. The opening sections of Raleigh's *History of the World* (published unfinished in 1614) began with the Genesis story of Adam and Eve, following a biblical narrative which placed man at the microcosmic (temporal) centre of God's (atemporal, eternal) macrocosm (Racin 1974): 'Man, thus compounded and formed by God, was an abstract model, or brief story of the universal' (Raleigh 1964: II, 58). Eternity, stasis, was the background against which change could be portrayed and, by the same token, constrained.

There were a number of exceptions to this general primacy of stability within early modern thought. One was the cosmic influence of the stars which, far from working in accord with the harmonious revolutions of the spheres, could exert a baleful influence upon events and wreak havoc upon society (Tillyard 1978: 60–68). The image of fortune, either as the mistress of the famous wheel, or the holder of balanced scales of prosperity or cataclysm, mediated a classical narrative of historical change. The notion of fortune's wheel subsumed the unpredictable vicissitudes of human destiny into the constancy of circular motion (Reichert 1985).

The manifest contradictions between an all-encompassing picture of a stable hierarchy extending from human microcosm to the macrocosm of the universe and the disturbances caused by the planets could be resolved only partly by the religious doctrine of the Fall. As Donne wrote,

> Then, as mankinde, so is the worlds whole frame
> Quite out of joint ...
> For, before God had made up all the rest,
> Corruption enter'd, and deprav'd the best ...
> So did the world from the first houre decay.

> (Donne 1964: 213)

Donne's temporality is one of generalized change as decay, sanctioned by a narrative of the fall and the corrupting temporal influence of sin. The temporality of decay or spiritual entropy could be palliated by a narrative of repentance and salvation. Thus Marlowe's Doctor Faustus soliloquizes in a moment of ambivalence, 'O, something soundeth in my ears, | Abjure this magic, turn to God again. Ay, and Faustus will turn to God again' (1985: 279 [1.5.6–8]). Faustus' inner debates offer a vignette of a cyclical 'salvation history' in which temptation, sin and repentance, salvation and damnation, alternate in an endless process of 'turns'. Moving away from a spiritual history with its only partial human agency, Shakespeare's history plays envisaged the search for fame and the production of progeny as two avenues of action contained within the secular *carpe diem* paradigm of human temporal agency (Quinones 1972). Within these broad parameters, the logic of temporality could be conceptualized as a constant agon between time as possibility and time as loss. Raleigh meditated, 'the life of man ... is always either increasing towards ripeness and perfection, or decreasing towards rottenness and dissolution' (Raleigh 1964: II, 61).

What is centrally at stake in these various modes of dealing with temporality, and evinced in their contrasting techniques of managing the passage of time, is the gradually shifting status of contingency, 'the beginning of a climactic change in historical perceptions, one associated with an increasing understanding of change in itself' (Ferguson 1979: ix). An increasing awareness of the materiality of the past, evinced in monuments, inscriptions, urns, the beginnings of archaeology, characterized the antiquarian endeavours of the seventeenth and eighteenth centuries, which constructed a pseudo-classical but also indigenous tradition for an incipient national consciousness. The dialectic of God's universal history as opposed to man's mortality gradually ceded to a dialectic of classical tradition and national tradition, buttressed by a proliferation of texts and artefacts susceptible initially of a primarily museal form of ordering (Parry 1995). In very broad terms, there occurred a gradual shift from a late medieval 'juxtaposition of cosmic-universal and mundane-particular', a simultaneity between past and present, with the connection being made by a God's eye view situated outside of time, to 'an idea of "homogeneous, empty time", in which simultaneity is, as it were, transverse, cross-time, marked not by prefiguring and fulfilment, but by temporal coincidence, and measured by clock and calendar' (Anderson 1991: 23–24). In Shakespeare's dramas, for instance, the former temporality is evinced in the image of 'a preposterous folded cloth in which before and after are coeval', while the latter is prefigured by 'a progressive line that follows the arc of the sun' (Harris 2009: 3–4).

What slowly emerges in the antiquarian work of the incipient Enlightenment, underpinned by an increasingly complex and overwhelming archive, is the concept of 'a sociological organism moving calendrically through empty, homogeneous time', that is, 'a precise analogue of the idea of the nation, which is also conceived as a solid community moving steadily up (or down) time' (Anderson 1991: 26). Antiquarianism's main project is the recovery, based in part upon incipient archaeology and in part upon biblical, mythical or epic narrative, of an invented national tradition (emblematized, for instance, in Camden's *Britannia* [1971] or more radically in the faked Ossian epics [Trevor-Roper 1992]). Historicism is not so much the result of archival perfection, but called forth by the overarching institution of the nation state, which demands a historiography reflecting its own claims for the continuities of a founding tradition.

FROM ORDER TO HISTORY

Historicism, then, emerges as a contingent configuration highly determined, however, by the pressures of national consolidation. The historicist project is coeval with the national-imperial project. Edward Gibbon's massive *Decline and Fall of the Roman Empire* (1776–88) signals the end of antiquarianism, as it does, indirectly, of the *ancien régime* and its respective footholds in Europe and North America, but, but by the same token, heralds the emergence of a new imperial status demanding a new historical vision (Hobsbawm 1992: 7). Historicism, however, also has an internal logic which is worth glancing at prior to reviewing contemporary historiographical alternatives.

It should come as no surprise that late vestiges of the antiquarian impulse and its proclivity to collection may be found in Gibbon's compendium. There one may also glimpse the conditions of possibility for the emergence of historicism. On the final pages of his work, Gibbon takes a look back upon the ambitious project he has undertaken, postulating that every reader's

> attention will be excited by a History of the Decline and Fall of the Roman Empire, the greatest, perhaps, and most awful scene in the history of mankind. The various causes and progressive effects are connected with many of the events most interesting in human annals: the artful policy of the Caesars, who long maintained the name and image of a

free republic; the disorders of military despotism; the rise, establishment and sects of Christianity; the foundation of Constantinople; the division of the monarchy; the invasion and settlements of the barbarians of Germany and Scythia; the institutions of the civil law; the character and religion of Mohammed; the temporal sovereignty of the Popes; the restoration and decay of the Western empires of Charlemagne; the crusades of the Latins in the East; the conquests of the Saracens and the Turks; the ruins of the Greek empire; the state and revolutions of Rome in the middle ages.

(Gibbon 1994: VI, 642)

This summary of the main elements of Gibbon's monumental narrative reads less like a synopsis of a temporal plot than a collection of topoi. For a later reader, looking back through the lenses of nineteenth-century historicism, there is a puzzling sense of excess here, bodied forth by the figure of *copia*, which blurs the clear profile of the temporal chain. Gibbon does speak of causes and effects, but these are somehow obscured by the piling-up of topics, and by the fact that some of them do not seem to be events, susceptible of insertion into a linear sequence. Literally, they are *topoi*, stock common-places which function in their own right rather than as referents of historical events: 'the character and religion of Mohammed; the temporal sovereignty of the Popes'. The modern reader senses less empiricity than rhetoric in this collection, less accurately recorded fact than the play of language itself.

It is significant that we cannot but read such a passage across the mediating screen of 'a revolution in the style of historical writing' which took place in the early nineteenth century, 'a shift from the florid or romantic style of the Enlightenment and Romanticist historians to the plain style of their more "realistic" successors ... seen as a liberation of historical writing from rhetoric in general' (White and Manuel 1978: 4). In supposedly stripping the rhetorical accretions from historical writing, the historians that came after Gibbon, for instance, believed they were recording facts, not collecting artefacts. They claimed to align facts in causal series in a manner more rigorous than, for example, Gibbon, whose 'various causes and progressive effects' resemble a taxonomic order more than a rigorous re-counting, one by one, of events.

That paradigmatic shift is not a purely objective one, but makes possible the very depiction of Gibbon that I am presenting here and you are following. Our own perspective is caught up in that shift and its consequences. To stress the not-quite-yet-historicist character of Gibbon's work is in itself a performative act, in which the reiteration of the logic of historicism depends upon remembering, if only to denigrate it, that which it has superseded and overhauled: namely, a now quaintly archaic notion of taxonomic 'order'.

Classical (i.e. seventeenth- and eighteenth-century) 'order', according to the metahistorical narrative proposed by Michel Foucault in *The Order of Things* (first published in French in 1966), assumed that the profusion of things in the world could be made to yield up a sense by arranging them in tabular systems which would place their constituent parts in relation to each other. The emblematic example of this was the system of botanical and zoological taxonomy constructed by the eighteenth-century Swedish botanist and zoologist Linnaeus, which we have inherited today in the customary classifications of species and subspecies (Foucault 2002).

Classical Order can be most illuminatingly illustrated for our purposes by looking at the visual representation of history. For us, the timeline is one of the most vivid exemplifications of our linear concept of time. It has contributed significantly to the legitimization of professional historians' defence of 'narrative or diachronic, as against an analytical or synchronic, mode of representation' typified, for example, in a 1850 prohibition to French 'historians in universities ... from departing from the chronological order in the presentation of materials' (White and Manuel 1978: 8). When we go back to seventeenth- and eighteenth-century predecessors of today's timelines, say, Christoph Helwig's very popular *Theatrum Historicum* of 1609 (Rosenberg and Grafton 2010: 76–77), we find something that is constructed less as a line than as a table. Its construction is that of a grid pattern, with horizontal cells and vertical columns divided into a chess-board-like space. This is unsurprising, for classical ordering systems assumed a basic, underlying synchronicity of the taxonomic system. This was so even when it was an *historical* system: 'in Classical thought the sequence of chronologies merely scanned the prior and more fundamental space of a table which presented all possibilities in

advance' (Foucault 2002: 237). Such a structure of visual repre-
sentations of temporality would be widespread in Europe until
the late 1700s.

However, the proliferation of elements to be catalogued within
such taxonomies or tables, and the difficulties of knowing where to
place these elements merely on the basis of visual identity (which, as
it transpired, could be deceptive), became so extreme that the systems themselves broke down under the weight of the information
they were designed to accommodate. Not dissimilarly, seventeenth-
and eighteenth-century antiquarianism collected and arranged in
spatial configurations a plethora of artefacts from the past, presenting
them in elaborate engraved plates, as in Edward Gibson's revised
1695 edition of Camden's *Britannia*. Neatly ordered images
belied, however, the perils of the undertaking: the sheer mass of
material the antiquarians collected often exceeded their capacity
to organize it, with the result that many antiquarian works
remained incomplete or unpublished (Parry 1995: 350, 16–17).

Furthermore, the underlying assumptions of synchronicity were
increasingly contradicted by the accumulating scientific evidence
of the changes that the catalogued elements underwent within
their own lifespan. Thus, for biology, what came into view was
not just the visible relationships between entities, but their
common belonging to a temporal system called 'life'. Their own
individual lives, as temporal sequences, were parts constitutive of
the temporal whole (White 1978: 242–44). Research in the history of the sciences corroborates these conclusions: 'Whether we
consider geology, zoology, political philosophy or the study of
ancient civilizations, the nineteenth century was in every case the
Century of History – a period marked by the growth of a new,
dynamic world-picture' (Toulmin and Goodfield 1965: 232). The
underlying structures shifted: 'From the nineteenth century, History
was to deploy, in a temporal series, the analogies that connect
distinct organic structures to one another'; 'from now on, the
contemporaneous and simultaneously observable resemblances in
space will be simply the fixed forms of a succession which proceeds
from analogy to analogy' (Foucault 2002: 237).

This change of historical understanding is most strikingly evident
in the emergence of a new visual format in the historical timeline.

The tabular structure was increasingly superseded, around 1800, by more clearly elongated parallel lines, often extending across spread-sheet fold-out pages (Rosenberg and Grafton 2010: 114–35). The segmented cells of parallel columns employed by the tabular chronologies of the previous century and a half gave way to less clearly segmented bars, whose beginnings and endings often did not coincide with others running parallel to them. It was at the turn of the nineteenth century that the linear, rather than the tabular historical timeline, the visual representation of the passage of time so familiar to us to be unremarkable, became a hegemonic temporal metaphor.

The specific cultural artefact of the timeline exemplifies the rise of history by a visual device frequently used in pedagogical or popularizing contexts. This conveniently concrete example of historical imagination notwithstanding, however, Foucault intends something rather different by his usage of the term History. History 'is not to be understood as the compilation of factual successions or sequences as they may have occurred'. In other words, History is not the *discipline* of history. Rather, Foucault envisages History as something more fundamental, a sort of epistemological foundation which provides the conditions of possibility of specific branches of knowledge (one of which is the discipline of history). According to this conception, in the nineteenth century, History is 'the fundamental mode of being of empiricities, upon the basis of which they are affirmed, posited, arranged, and distributed in the space of knowledge for the use of such disciplines or sciences as may arise' (Foucault 2002: 237). Somewhat akin to the way Saussure's *langue* (as an abstract system of linguistic rules) provides the condition of possibility for real utterances, or *parole*, so too Foucault's nineteenth-century *episteme* of History provides the underlying rules determining how specific branches of knowledge will be organized.

Foucault describes an 'ambiguity that is probably impossible to control' which dictates that 'History becomes so soon divided ... into an empirical science of events and that radical mode of being that prescribes their destiny to all empirical beings, to those particular beings that we are' (ibid: 237). Analogously, History is also 'the mode of being of all that is given to us in experience' and thus 'has become the unavoidable element of our thought'. It is an event, which 'because we are still caught inside of it, is largely beyond our comprehension', the condition of possibility of our thought, but simultaneously (and paradoxically), 'the very being of our modernity', that factor by which we mark ourselves off from earlier ages and other cultures (ibid: 238, 239).

This ambiguity appears very similar to a cognate 'ambiguity' central to Foucault's work. That other 'ambiguity' informs the illusion upon which the human sciences as a whole are posited: namely, 'man' as the subject *and* object of 'his' own knowledge (ibid: 340). This 'empirico-transcendental doublet' is the means by which the human subject, observing the empirical givens about humanity, constitutes itself as a subject in a way never achieved before: a 'paradoxical figure in which the empirical contents of knowledge deliver up, of themselves, the conditions that have made them possible' (ibid: 351). By virtue of this feedback-loop of self-referential knowledge, the human subject comes to see itself as an autonomous rational being which posits its own autonomy 'in the immediate and sovereign transparency of a *cogito*' (ibid: 351; translation modified).[1] The subject forgets thereby the manifold media to which it is beholden for its knowledge – primarily, of course language, but no less importantly, the fabric of natural life from which it comes to see itself as fundamentally different.

The empirical facts of the discipline of history and the underlying episteme of History are caught in a similarly circular relationship. History is the fundamental mode of our being as modern subjects, that which distinguishes us from 'peoples without history' (Wolf 1982). This science of modernity is constituted by putative facts generated by the epistemological grid which also gives rise to 'the analysis of production, the analysis of organically structured beings, and lastly, on the analysis of linguistic groups' (Foucault 2002: 237) – that is, the facts generate the grid which generates the facts.

When, in the twentieth century, this 'doublet' began to be turned inside out, it transpired that History as *episteme* is the condition of possibility of these empirical knowledges of the historical subject, rather than its truth, and the generator of its finitude, rather than of its autonomy: 'the death that anonymously gnaws at the daily existence of the living being is the same as that fundamental death on the basis of which my empirical life is given to me' (ibid: 343).

History as finitude lays bare temporality as the limiting condition of possibility of a contingent self-knowledge. Foucault makes here a masked allusion to Heidegger, his rarely acknowledged mentor (1990: 250) and the equally unacknowledged condition of possibility of the epistemic model of History. Heidegger's notion of temporality as the fabric of our existence, outside of which no knowledge is possible, offers the template for Foucault's notion of the episteme: an invisible underlying grid which underpins the modes of knowledge at a particular historical epoch. Heidegger's idea of temporality provides Foucault with an instrument for rethinking the history of the human sciences, but, by the same token, Foucault turns that notion back upon itself in such a way that it unravels its own fabric. Thus, for Foucault, Heidegger's model of temporal being does not make a claim to absolute truth. On the contrary, its value is merely self-dismantling. It emerges out of the episteme of History to initiate the unmasking of History at the very moment when that paradigm has finally played itself out.

THE TEMPORALITY OF HERMENEUTICS

Gibbon wrote the concluding remarks to his *Decline and Fall of the Roman Empire* on the eve of the French Revolution, that cataclysmic event which catapulted late-Enlightenment Europe into a new and acute sense of historical process. Chateaubriand, in his post-revolutionary reminiscences, wrote: 'If I compare the two terrestrial globes, the one I knew at the beginning of my life and the one I now behold at the end of it, I no longer recognize the one in the other' (qtd in Terdiman 1993: 4n2). Gibbon's own sense of historical contingency nestles on the cusp between the antiquarian's experience of the field of historical knowledge as a collection of ruined artefacts, and an emergent notion of the temporal dynamics of historical process:

> The historian may applaud the variety and importance of his subject; but while he is conscious of his own imperfections, he must often accuse the deficiency of his materials. It was among the ruins of the Capitol that I first conceived the idea of a work which has amused and exercised nearly twenty years of my life, and which, however

inadequate to my own wishes, I finally deliver to the curiosity and candour of the public.

(Gibbon 1994: VI, 642–43)

The device Gibbon employs is the well-known technique of concluding a narrative with the moment of its own inception: paradoxically, at a moment of historical demise, emblematized by the ruins of Rome itself. The history recounted brings the reader up to the point at which the recounting itself begins (Currie 2007: 61–62). An even more perfect avatar of this doubling of recounted and recounting temporalities is Proust's fictional auto-biography *In Search of Lost Time*, in which not merely the beginning of the narration, but its end, converge with the narrated life-story on the very last page. Gibbon's use of the device, though not as temporally tightly woven as that of his successors, is remarkable for the way in which the work compensates, albeit imperfectly, for the ruined state of Rome in its contemporary manifestation; conversely, however, the writer's life, devoured by the task of composing the massive history, is also a displaced synecdoche of the dwindling life of Empire – namely, of the demise of pre-revolutionary, *ancien régime* Europe itself. What Gibbon's portrayal of the time and place of historiographical writing suggests is that the limited, imperfect, contingent moment of history itself is the only place from which history can be understood. Historicism elided its own epistemological foundations. They, however, have once again become manifest at the moment of the twentieth-century demise of historicism, thereby mirroring the moment of its emergence in Gibbon.

The paradoxical nature of historical contingency as the only place to understand history has been most fully explored by the twentieth-century German philosopher of historical hermeneutics Hans-Georg Gadamer. He approaches this complex from two directions: first from the direction of history as 'object', and second from the direction of history as the active process of the reception, or more radically, of the construction of that object by a 'subject'.

The notion of 'play' allows Gadamer, focusing initially on the work of art and particularly on the dramatic work, to conceptualize the manner in which the historical text must be 're-played' again and again in new historical contexts (2004: 156–57). Play is risky: it caries in itself the risk of anachronistic misunderstanding. Yet the time of 'play' (Bateson 1974: 177–93) is one in which the work's 'afterlives' guarantee its 'survival' for subsequent generations of readers or spectators (Benjamin 1999: 72). It is only via the process of play that the risk of misunderstanding can be parried: for 'play' entails a certain amount of 'free play' which contains the flexibility to test and experiment and to change one's attitude in the process of interpretation. Only by being re-activated in a context in which it cannot but be *mis*understood does a historical text have a chance of being understood. Anachronism and the risk of incomprehension is the necessary precondition of comprehension.

In this way, Gadamer reverses the problem of historiography, shifting the temporal perspective from that of the 'object', the past epoch recorded in the historical text, to that of the 'subject' (that of the reader who can only access the past via the historical text). Gadamer begins with Heidegger's notion of the 'pro-ject' ('*Entwurf*') which is necessary to seize the condition of thrownness ('*Geworfenheit*') and convert it into an actively chosen task rather than a passively experienced fate (2004: 268–71). 'Thrownness' (the present situation from which I must read the past, albeit through the distorting lenses of an inevitable, presentist anachronism) is transformed by an act of 'throwing' oneself into the work of interpretation and understanding.

Just as for Heidegger there is no other place to conceptualize the temporality of our being except from within temporal existence, so too for Gadamer there is no way to read historical texts or understand past history except from within the historicity of our own process of understanding (ibid: 267). In other words, there is no position of objective, neutral historical understanding; historical understanding itself is necessarily historically determined. We cannot approach past history or the texts which mediate it except from the necessarily limited and prejudiced historical context which is our own. We thus constantly risk projecting our own prejudices and presuppositions onto the earlier text or historical period, thereby distorting the work of interpretation. The context of the present is both limiting *and* at the same time enabling, for it provides the necessary, if fraught, starting point for an engagement with the past.

The question then becomes, How to both inhabit *and* escape our historically specific moment and its attendant prejudices at the moment of engaging with the past and its textual artefacts? Just as the text's 'afterlives' guarantee its survival, so too they guarantee its being misunderstood *and* its being properly understood. For Gadamer ascribes to the text the power to 'interpellate' the modern reader and shake her or him out of her or his hidebound complacency (ibid: 283; my translation).[2] It is the difference, more precisely the 'temporal distance', between the present and the past, that which makes the past past, which underwrites the possibility of being able to read differently (ibid: 295, 305): 'It is enough to say that we understand in a different way, if we understand at all' (ibid: 296).

The process of engagement with a past text or epoch is understood by Gadamer as a dialogue. The reader's or historian's project poses a question to the text which elicits a response. However, that response itself may function like a question, questioning the questioner and obliging her or him to adjust the very framework from which that question arose (ibid: 351–52, 356–71). In this way, the engagement with the otherness of the past, from the standpoint of the present, ideally induces a new, superior mode of historical comprehension. It is thus a dialectical process (ibid: 341) in which the present and the past interact with each other to produce a new context of understanding, that of the future.

THE NEW HISTORIES

If we cannot but read history from the tendentious, distorting perspective of the present, then nineteenth-century historicism, epitomized in von Ranke's much-quoted injunction to narrate history 'as it was' ('*wie es gewesen*'), becomes an impossible project. What takes its place are forms of historiography which do not disavow their contemporary biases and their immediate political allegiances, but which ostentatiously 'seize hold of a memory as it flashes up at a moment of danger' (Benjamin 1999: 247). When, at the end of the nineteenth century, historicism began to experience a long drawn-out crisis still evident today, critiques came primarily from philosophers such as Nietzsche and writers such as Gide whose 'immoralist' comes to regard an 'abstract, neutral cognizance of the past ... as futile' (2000: 53). In historical research itself, typical reactions came later, with the prominence of Marxist histories in the 1960s and 1970s, such as E. P. Thompson's *The Making of the English Working Class* (1968) or Christopher Hill's *The World Turned Upside Down* (1972). This trend continued with a remarkable pluralization of micro-histories, women's histories, gay and lesbian histories, indigenous histories, disabled histories, and of modes of historical writing, such as oral history or non-archival history.

The school of subaltern history sought to generate a 'history from below' in order to reconstruct the consciousness of Indian peasants of the colonial era. Their absence from archival records, or where they were present, the absence of their own words, rendered them historically invisible or at least inaudible (Guha and Spivak, eds, 1988; Guha, ed., 1997) – with Spivak famously doubting the possibility of restoring a voice to those peasants: 'can the subaltern speak?' (1999: 269, 274, 308). The Australian indigenous author Kim Scott, speaking of his own attempts to reconstruct the story of his family in their ancestral country, observes, 'It's impossible to get a story of such a relationship with country that's from the archival histories' (2010: 68). But his fiction (*Benang*, 1999) and excursions into oral history (*Kayang & Me*, with H. Brown, 2005) have demonstrated alternative ways of recuperating or reconstructing these subaltern pasts.

These new forms of historiography launched 'an interrogation of the relationship between power and knowledge (hence of the archive itself and of history as a form of knowledge)' (Chakrabarty 2002: 8). What they also, if less obviously, undertook was a critique of the temporal logic underlying modern historiography. In some cases, the perspective from which histories were written was questioned, as was the access to discursive power, but the fundamental sequentiality of history and its closure apparently remained largely intact. Thus, for instance, the so-called 'new historicism' in literary studies, by eschewing what it perceived as an outmoded focus upon time, turning instead towards spatiality, unwittingly left intact the very temporal logic it scornfully dismissed (Wood 2009: 5). In other cases, however, there has also been evidence, in the wake of the new histories, of substantial attacks on the sequential causality of modern historiography and its debt to absolute time.

Three recent manifestations of this questioning of the temporal logic of modern historiography are particularly striking.

First, alternative or virtual or 'counterfactual' histories have asked the question, 'What if?', constructing fictive outcomes from given historical events. In this way, counterfactuals question temporal linearity as a mode of historical determinism. They generally do not question irreversible linear narrative in itself (Butter 2009: 69), but rather, the logic underlying that linearity. Because we are so used to history having happened the way it happened, much historiography falls into 'a determinist theory of history' (Ferguson, ed. 1999: 417), assuming that history *had* to happen as it did. This view of history is 'weak' because it '[admits] only one possible outcome' (De Landa 1997: 13). To that extent, it effectively suppresses the contingency and chaos of history, the fact that the most trivial factors may inflect the courses of great events. Alternative or virtual history seeks to lay bare the unpredictability of all life-processes, that contingent productivity of the dynamism of events studied by 'chaos theory' (Gleick 1988: 11–31). Chaos theory does not suggest that causal temporality can be reversed, but rather, that a chain of insignificant events can trigger momentous results. At multiple points of 'catastrophic bifurcation' (Thom 1983), processes can follow multiple routes. The possible chain of cause and effect is impossible to predict; it is only the backwards view of historicism which assumes the inevitability of historical process. Linearity is produced by the backwards view, whereas the forwards view would look more like a splayed out hand whose fingers would each produce subsequent proliferating bifurcations. In his story 'The Garden of Forking Paths', Borges imagined 'a growing, dizzying net of divergent, convergent and parallel times. This network of times which approached one another, forked, broke off, or were unaware of one another for centuries, embraces *all* possibilities of time.' In such a universe of multiple times, 'Time forks perpetually towards innumerable futures' (1976: 53). This is what De Landa (1997) refers to as non-linear history.

Alternative or virtual history deconstructs the linear fiction of inevitability by proposing other courses of history. This has often been the domain of fiction: C. S. Forester (1970: 183–263) imagined the invasion of Britain by Hitler in 1940 eventually being beaten back; Robert Harris (1993) posited a successful invasion with the Third Reich enduring into the 1960s; Ferguson's Second World War began with the invasion of Britain in 1940, witnessed a turning point upon the death of Hitler in the Stauffenberg plot in 1944, but that only came to an end with the Russian invasion of Western Europe in 1950. His narrative is part of a 'counterfactual' history which plausibly remaps European history from Charles I to the imagined break-up of Anglo-American hegemony in 1990 (Ferguson, ed. 1999: 416–40).

In a similar manner, 'ficto-critical' history (Kerr and Nettelbeck, eds, 1998; Muecke 2002) deliberately mobilizes a range of 'calculating infringement of rules' (Pusch 1990: 11–12, 35–36) to radically revise modes of historiography and their temporalities. The Australian cultural historian Katrina Schlunke deliberately sets out to break the rules of colonial historiography. Her technique is to sabotage the necessary 'rarity' of discourse to which historiography owes its coherence (only certain statements can be uttered within a certain genre or context [cf. Foucault 2007: 133–36]), by mobilizing discursive excess. She seeks to overload the historiographical methodology with a plethora of heterogeneous genres which are then piled up against each other. This is most evident in the title of her work: *Bluff Rock: Autobiography of a Massacre* (2005). As she explicitly says, 'How can you have an autobiography of a massacre, an autobiography of an event? ... this is not an autobiography of a self. It is an autobiography of a past, placed, event. It is an impossibility' (ibid: 14). Schlunke's point is that the impossible must be undertaken so as to dismantle historiography's aura of factual authority, thereby opening up novel realms of possibility. Customarily, historiography has worked merely to cement the inevitability of what happened, producing 'a fossilised past, a past that cannot change' (ibid: 35). This historiography 'rests on certain assumptions: there is disjunction between past and present, the past is complete, unchanging and unchangeable, and has an objective existence independent of the present' (Attwood 1996: xx).

The closure of history thus reinforces, in the case of contemporary Australia, the 'inevitable' fact of white European possession, rendering it irreversible. Schlunke's work seeks to open up history, to 'blast a specific era out of the homogenous course of history' in Benjamin's expression (1999: 254). She does this by tampering with the very genre of autobiography, and thus with the temporal regimes which inform it.

Autobiography is usually the temporal narrative of a life, intimately connected with the closure of the autonomous self that has prevailed in European culture since the Enlightenment, and for which Robinson Crusoe's island came to be an emblematic metonym. Schlunke displaces this focus from the self to a natural site, Bluff Rock, with its own agency, especially in the cosmological understanding of the indigenous people. Then it is opened towards the event, something that is past but which continues to resonate in the present by virtue of the effects it had, effects which are perpetuated by a range of other policies, institutions, legislations. 'A rock, an event, a past, cannot write itself ... and yet it does. To claim that such writing is autobiographical shows the ways in which the past is always emerging via someone in particular' (Schlunke 2005: 14). In this way, the past ceases to be read as an inert structure in such a way as to collude with the putative irreversibility of the indigenous peoples' loss of ownership of their country. If the autobiographical element is first marginalized, it is none the less reintroduced in a manner which disturbs traditional historiography. For Schlunke constantly weaves her own narrative in with that of the massacre so as to show how histories are always made by and for a particular group in society, in this case the majority white owners of today's Australia (such as farmers, home-owners and businesses). The putative objectivity of history is destroyed, and so is its closure.

For some, however, contrary to historicism's assumption of causal determinism, the temporal contingency of history may be all too evident; for them, historical reenactments, a second instance of recent questioning of historical temporalities, may offer a way of getting a grasp upon that unnerving contingency. Reenactment is another site where the questioning of the temporal logic of history has become salient. Historical reenactment opens up the closure of the past, making the past in its past-ness present once again, and rendering it available for immediate experience, or indeed consumption. Such re-runs of history are deeply controversial. While they are as old as European culture itself, dating back to passion plays and pageants, they are often taxed with spuriously collapsing temporal differences. Though they claim to mobilize a form of history from below, made vivid again in its prosaic grubbiness, indeed goriness, they may simply depoliticize even further the already sterilized subjects of the school history curriculum (Agnew 2004: 327–28). Reenactments tend

> to hallucinate a past merely as the present in funny dress. ... They patronise the human condition in hindsighted superiority. They remove the responsibility of remedying the present by a distracted, unreflective search for details whose remedying will make no difference.
> (Dening 1992: 4–5)

Yet historical reenactments may mobilize an affective, sympathetic and necessarily performative engagement with the past, with all its associated risks, which is the precondition for all historical understanding (Agnew 2007). Moreover, such reenactments are no more extracted from history any more than the past was, and thus elements of contingency may resurge – as, for instance, when the reenactment gets out of control, or takes untoward turns (Lamb 2009: 1–5).

In many reenactments, the resurgence of contingency is embodied by such manifestations of the agency of nature such as the sea or the outback heat, an agency given renewed force by the reenactors' voluntary relinquishment of modern technology. As in Schlunke's history of a massacre, where the land itself (the site, Bluff Rock) is allowed to speak, these alternative histories articulate multiple temporalities, salient among which is that of the environment itself. In this final shift in the temporal logic of historiographical study, the central conceptual element of Enlightenment time is eroded. Newton's absolute time was predicated upon a separation of time and place. Time became something which was independent of humans and their environment, a sort of abstract container which enveloped events and actors but which was removed from them. This meant that temporality was no longer embedded in specific local sites and their natural processes. This splitting of time from place went hand in hand with the divide between nature and humanity which was crucial to the modern scientific sensibility. Nature became the object of experimentation and knowledge, to be regarded from a distance and manipulated for humanity's usage, rather than a close neighbour to be feared or at the very least respected and cooperated with (Latour 1993; Dux 1989: 23–24). Time was similarly peeled away from natural processes, so as to be implemented as a neutral, unchanging unit of measurement in scientific experimentation. Reenactments are one of the sites of historiographic activity where this neutrality and abstraction is undone.

This Enlightenment separation of time from place and the correlative reification of time is fundamentally questioned by our third instance of recent questionings of historical temporalities: the global carbon-epoch or fossil-fuel-epoch periodization proposed by Chakrabarty (2009) or Smil (1994: 216–18, 223–56). Such periodization is revolutionary to the extent that it undermines the notion of time that we have inherited from the Enlightenment, which has been crucial for scientific modernization. That process of scientific modernization was driven above all by the availability of fossil fuels such as coal and later oil, with their many derivatives, which allowed an extraordinarily rapid and constantly accelerating, indeed exponential rate of technological development. Its consequence, however, has been a global depredation of the environment so radical that the preconditions for long-term human life on the planet have been irreversibly vitiated. Chakrabarty's concept of climate history abolishes the Enlightenment notion of a separation between humanity and nature, insisting instead upon the intimate intertwining of natural history and human history. Climate history stresses the manner in which the temporal regimes of human history, and especially the effects of absolute time as the basis for measuring techniques in scientific progress, have impacted negatively upon the temporal regimes of natural history. The arrow of time is now coeval with the arrow of probably irreversible processes of environmental degradation.

Global climate history reveals what we have known all along but conveniently forgotten since Newton: namely, that temporalities are coextensive with natural processes, the many natural processes of the mineral (above all carbon!), vegetable, animal and human actors, which can only be treated as mere objects of human manipulation at our peril. Chakrabarty's global history is, to employ White's (1973: 29) typologies, a radically Tragic narrative evincing the collapse of a putative human freedom into wilful self-destruction. Its underlying logic is Mechanistic, for it displays a set of rigid laws dictating the consequences of our having disregarded, for three centuries, the intricately interdependent equilibrium between the various actors in the natural world. Its ideological underpinning is Radical, demanding wide-reaching action immediately, for which, however, the time may already have passed: in Derrida's lapidary formulation, it may be 'too late to pose the question of time' (1982: 42).

4

LANGUAGE AND DISCOURSE

'History', as we saw in the previous chapter, is a Janus-faced word, referring as it does to the process of historical causality and to the narrative recounting of that causality. In everyday usage it feels quite unproblematic to us to use the same word for these two phenomena. The reason for this is simple: we have learned to assume that the two usages have the same essential form – namely, that of a sequence of real occurrences and narrated events respectively. The sequence of narrated events refers mimetically, we like to believe, to the sequence of historical events. Narrative sequence transparently conveys historical sequence. In Bertrand Russell's formulation, 'the present contents of my mind have an order, which I believe to be correlated ... with the objective time-order of events to which my recollections refer' (1962: 212).

This was the claim implicitly made by nineteenth-century historicism. Just as eighteenth-century novels had once styled themselves 'histories' in order to distance themselves from earlier 'romances', and thus to underline their claim to veracity, so now historicism sought to rid itself of the vain accoutrements of fiction, sporting instead unadorned factual report (White and Manuel 1978: 4). One of the salient markers of factual veracity in its

nineteenth-century historicist incarnation was its claim to faithfully
replicate chronological order (ibid: 8).

Hayden White contends, however, that factual reporting is as
much a narrative style as the more decorative modes which preceded
it, and proceeds to analyse the narrative structures evinced by
'historicist' historiography. A history, White explains, is 'a verbal
structure in the form of a narrative prose discourse that purports
to be a model, or icon, of past structures and processes in the
interest of explaining what they were by representing them'
(1973: 2). The 'iconicity' (i.e. the mimetic replication of a form)
of historicism reposes in the notion that the micro-sequence of the
sentence and of the macro-sequence of the narrative can faithfully
represent the temporal and causal sequence of historical events.
However, historical stories are anything but mimetic, because
they manifest complex modes of 'emplotment'. That is, their
structure must be formed according to certain patterns which will
inevitably colour the tenor of the story being told (ibid. 1973: 7).
The archetypal story-forms or 'genres' of historiographical writing
(in part derived from Northrop Frye [1957]) are dependent upon
rhetorical strategies taken from language itself – namely, tropes,
or ways of 'turning' putatively neutral language to other ends. One
of these is metaphor, a trope which presupposes the adequacy of
narrative to represent reality, in particular claims to sequential
fidelity. By contrast, another trope, irony, assumes the radical mis-
match of a narrative and reality. The trope of synecdoche posits
the possibility of gaining knowledge of the whole from the study
of a part. Marxist historical theories of ideology and false consciousness would assume a deeply 'ironical' stance in relation to historical actors' own limited knowledge, counterbalanced by the
'synecdochic' knowledge of the historian – that knowledge which
connects a limited, located knowledge to larger historical trends
(White 1973: 31–38).

What historical stories thus lay bare is the contamination of all
faithful sequential narrative by the devices of fictional, and thus
untrue, narration. Such claims mean that fiction, far from being a
secondary, derivative form of temporal recording, moves into the
foreground of the theorization of time. This is why the contemporary French philosopher Paul Ricoeur, at the conclusion of his

magisterial treatise on time and narrative, has narrative figure as *'the guardian of time'*; he claims that access to the experience of time is only available via its narration in language: 'temporality cannot be spoken of in the direct discourse of phenomenology [i.e. as manifested in the direct experience of things], but rather requires the mediation of the indirect discourse of narration' (1984–88: III, 241; translation modified).[1] The relationship between language and time increasingly emerges as one in which the one and the other are isomorphic. Indeed, one could go as far as to claim, with Sartre, that language and narrative can *only* exist in time: '[T]he literary object is a peculiar spinning top which exists only in its movement. To make it come into view a concrete act called reading is necessary, and it lasts only as long as this act can last' (2001: 29; translation modified).[2] In other words, the condition of language being able to map time, as if it were 'outside' time, as no other medium can, is its being 'within' time, which in turn hampers the scope of its knowledge. This is the fundamental aporia that exercises Ricoeur at the close of his three-volume study (1984–88: III, 241–74).

The argument proposed here turns that aporia inside out, suggesting instead that narrative is never 'outside' time, and thus can never genuinely map it. Rather, I posit, it is the very generativity of narrative that makes it a fundamental strand of temporal dynamism itself. The tendency of stories to 'take' time, and to generate more stories which 'make' time (as in *The One Thousand and One Nights*, whose narrator tells stories so as to stave off her death) is what renders them one with time. Fiction is driven by the creativity of language itself. That creativity drives the dynamism of time of which language is one salient strand.

Yet the common-sense notion of the relevance of temporality for narrative is generally restricted to a mimetic conception of narrative according to which 'we tend to think of stories as sequences of events' (Bridgeman 2007: 53). The sequentiality of syntax lends itself quite naturally, we assume, to replicating the sequentiality of events in a self-evident iconic representation (Wenz 1997: 29). A similarly mimetic mapping of temporal sequence might be suggested by Thomas Mann's claim, in *The Magic Mountain* (first published in 1924), that 'time is the medium/element of narration as it is the medium/element of life' (1975: 541; the synonymous translation is mine).[3] However, Mann's apposition of time and narrative is destabilized by his double use of the term medium/element. Clearly, according to this view, time is an environment common to both narrative and life. Yet in what manner might they participate in that common environment? Does their obviously iso-morphic mode of participation tell us more than merely offering the iconic basis for the replication of events in sequential recording? In this chapter I will push these uncertainties further, suggesting that stories do not merely replicate the linear sequentiality of events, nor do they participate in that temporal flow, reporting, as it were, *in media res*. Indeed, as we will see, they more often than not disrupt that sequentiality.

More radically, I will make a claim for narrative which is analogous to my claim about time itself. Time is not an environment in which things happen, but it is the indefatigable happening of things which is time. Like the productivity of time, its constant generativity, narrative is a productive process, a generativity of stories. Narrative is a process of change manifested in the drive to tell stories again and again, always in a slightly different manner. It is the dynamism of narratives, their content and structure, as well as their tendency to be told, which makes up one of the many intertwined strands of the multiple temporalities we call time.

At the beginning of his epic of time, Mann comments that the 'story of Hans Castorp' is noteworthy 'not on his own account, for in him the reader will make acquaintance with a simple-minded though pleasing young man' but rather 'for the sake of the story itself, which seems to us highly worth telling' (1975: xi). The 'tellability' or 'reportability' of stories is that which makes them worth narrating, that element of surprise, suspense, transformation, which will gain the attention of the reader or listener (Labov 1972: 360–67) and create the preconditions for narrating. Lotman suggests that the narrative value of a narrated event is dependent upon the amount of information the event carries: how worth mentioning it is, how improbable its occurrence is. Narrative texts document borders between semantic fields. The narrative-less text 'makes these borders fast' and thus confirms the solid character of schemas of order in the world. In contrast, the narrative-laden text tends to disturb such spatial structures by having their constitutive boundaries crossed by an agent in the text: 'An event in the text is the shifting of a persona across the borders of a semantic field' (Lotman 1977: 237, 233). Bruner speaks more generally of 'canonicity and breach' as the primary criterion of 'tellability' (1991: 11). It is the disruption of a pre-existing order which gives us something to talk about.

An event happens and becomes worth recounting when change is produced, and the tale of that change is itself a form of symbolic change. For every story contains the germ of its own re-telling in a potentially infinite number of versions. Stories generate new stories. According to the criterion of 'tellability' it is not so much the mapping of sequence which characterizes the temporality of narrative as the productive performance of productive transformation. Even the flip side of tellability, the dark 'unspeakable' character of **trauma** or shame (Baroni 2009: 452) may generate repetitive patterns of 'acting out', a morbid, productivity of the same nightmarish experience never able to be banished to past memory (LaCapra 2001: 141–53) (see also Chapter 5).

In this chapter, I will address the various steps in the argument just now rehearsed very briefly. I begin by casting a critical gaze upon narrative beginnings, then address narrative construction and the 'double' temporality of 'story' and 'discourse' (terms deriving from the earlier Russian formalist distinction between narrated *'fabula'* and narrating *'sujet'*). I turn finally to the inherent temporal productivity of language itself as the stuff of which stories are made.

BEGINNINGS

For Hayden White, the minimal form of historical sequence is the genre of 'chronicle'. The chronicle is open-ended, beginning and ending in an apparently quite random manner. By contrast, a historical story sets up a distinctive framework by the imposition of a beginning and an end (1973: 5–7). Beginnings and endings are crucial to narrative because they frame it, shaping the material to be dealt with, and demarcating its 'artistry' from the 'real world' outside and signalling its mode of encoding (Kermode 1967;

Lotman 1977: 215–17; Said 1997). They constitute 'privileged positions' (Rabinowitz 2002: 300–303) establishing the basic parameters of the narrative world and inflecting readerly interpretations of it. Beginnings generate and motivate the ensuing logic of the narrative and endings confirm that logic by fulfilling it in its moment of final closure. Their construction, however, is anything but self-evident and reveals the creativity of language in its temporal dynamism.

In Janette Turner Hospital's novel *Charades*, the eponymous protagonist, a postmodern Scheherazade as her name and that of her interlocutor, Professor Koenig, suggest, tries to tell the story of her family. Koenig is bewildered by the twists and turns of her tale:

> 'Tonight,' Koenig says, 'if you could begin at the beginning perhaps.' The response he gets is uncertain at best:
>
> But where, Charade wonders, is the beginning. And how does she cut her own story free from the middle of the history of so many others? In a sense, she is the epilogue of several lives.
>
> Well then ...
>
> Here's one beginning, she suggests, in the rainforest, where time comes and goes like a bird.
>
> (Hospital 1990: 38)

These quandaries of narration are not new, as Hospital intimates by her intertextual allusions, nor is their problematization within fiction itself.

In *Heart of Darkness* (first published 1899), Joseph Conrad dispenses with the problem of beginning. Introducing the scene on the deck of a yacht where Marlow will tell his tale of a journey to central Africa, the frame narrator refers back to an earlier beginning: 'Between us there was, *as I have already said somewhere*, the bond of the sea' (1990: 135). The frame narrator thus points back to similar comments at the beginning of *Youth* (a long story published a year before [ibid: 93]). Marlow himself employs the same strategy at the opening of his embedded narrative: 'And this also ... has been one of the dark places of the earth' he begins abruptly, obviously continuing aloud a train of thought he has already been pursuing mentally (ibid: 138). Conrad appears not to believe that a story has a clear beginning. Any story refers back to a tale that precedes it. Beginnings, then, are arbitrary, contingent, dictated by mere pragmatism.

Laurence Sterne made the problem of beginnings the subject of an entire novel, *Tristram Shandy* (first published 1759–67). Following the hegemonic form of the novel as a narrative of an individual's life, Sterne's protagonist begins with his own birth (Bennett 1979: 23; Lotman 1977: 214). However, being as thorough a narrator as he is, he realizes that one cannot begin a narrative of life at the beginning (i.e. the birth), but must go back to a moment before the beginning (i.e. the conception), which itself necessitates some considerable explanation about the rituals preceding the conception … and so on. Tristram's beginning gets pushed further and further back into the past, or rather, more and more details shove the recounting of his birth further and further into the future:

> for my own part, I declare that I have been at it these six weeks, making all speed I possibly could, – and am not born: – I have just been able, and that's all, to tell you *when* it happened, but not *how*; – so that you see that the thing is yet far from being accomplished.
>
> (Sterne 1985: 65)

But from the outset, this beginning transpires to be multiple. It immediately splits into its component parts, that of the narrated birth, and that of the birth of narrative. These two components work against each other for the rest of the text, as the burgeoning activity of narration hinders the narrative of the narrator's birth.

STORY AND DISCOURSE

In a very witty manner, Sterne reveals two speaking selves, with their own temporal regimes. One is the self of the tale being told, who has not yet been born; the other is the self telling the tale, already 'at it these six weeks'. They operate respectively on two narrative levels, that of the 'story', the raw material out of which a tale is made, and that of the 'narrative discourse', the activity of putting these materials into a narrative form in the act of telling. These two levels of narrative have their respective chronologies:

that of a sequence of events as they are supposed to have happened in real life ('story-time') and the sequence in which the events are narrated in the process of story-telling ('discourse-time') (Chatman 1978).

Sterne dramatizes the incongruity of these conflicting temporalities by having a tale-telling self announce his own non-existence. The **ellipsis** of the pronoun of the second opening sentence ingeniously highlights the absent selfhood of the 'story' level: ('I declare that I have been at it these six weeks, making all speed I possibly could, – and am not born'). For contrasting effect, Sterne immediately follows this sentence with a reinstatement of the pronoun at the 'discourse'-level: 'and am not born: – I have just been able, and that's all, to tell you *when* it happened, but not *how*; – so that you see that the thing is yet far from being accomplished' (1985: 65). Sterne comically inverts the usual temporalities of individual existence in this sentence by placing them both in the present tense. One has to be born before one can speak. Here, however, it is the process of speaking, as an active utterance, which is holding back the chronology of birth. Paradoxically, it is the generativity of story-telling as a linguistic activity which holds back the business of getting born as a biological activity. The point that Sterne is making is that although biological life is clearly a prerequisite for linguistic life, the latter may have a rebellious dynamic all of its own, with its own tempestuous temporality.

In a final flourish of ambiguity, Tristram triumphantly rounds off, 'so that you see that the thing is far from being accomplished.' But what is 'the thing'? – the tale of his birth, which does not actually occur until well into the third volume of the novel, or the act of narration? Indeed, this process of deferral of accomplishment appears to be self-perpetuating, for the narrator's life constantly provides new textual material ('archives at every stage to be looked into, and rolls, records, documents, and endless genealogies' [ibid: 65]) to feed into the narrative. Thus the temporal march of lived events constantly generates an expanding narrative which pushes away the moment of termination at the same speed as the lived life itself – whence the narrator's promise to continue to write as long as he lives:

I am this month one whole year older than I was this twelve-month; and having got, as you perceive, almost into the middle of my fourth volume – and no farther than my first day's life – 'tis demonstrative that I have three hundred and sixty-four days more life to write just now, than when I first set out; so that instead of advancing, as a common writer, in my work with what I have been doing at it – on the contrary, I am thrown so many volumes back – was every day of my life to be as busy a day as this – And why not? – and the transactions and opinions of it to take up as much description – And for what reason should they be cut short? as at this rate I should just live 364 times faster than I write – It must follow, an' please your worships, that the more I write, the more I shall have to write – and consequently, the more your worships read, the more your worships will have to read.

(ibid: 286)

In contrast to the normal process of autobiographical writing, in which the narrative of the life ('story') progressively gets closer to the real temporal moment in which the writing subject is speaking ('discourse'), the two temporal schemes move further and further apart. The more the author writes, the less hope he has of ever catching up with himself.

What Sterne so comically highlights is the distinction between 'story' and 'discourse', the 'distinction between actions or events themselves and the narrative presentation of those actions' (Culler 1981: 170), one of the most fundamental elements of narrative theory. It was originally theorized by the Russian Formalist critic Viktor Shklovsky. He explained that '[t]he concept of plot (*syuzhet*) ["narrative discourse" in Chatman's terms] is too often confused with a description of the events of a novel, with what I'd tentatively call the story line (*fabula*)' (1990: 170). Shklovsky split the composite 'story-telling' into the 'story' and the process of its 'telling'. He did not stop there, however. Rather than envisaging the 'telling' as a mere mimetic activity in the service of 'the story', he set the 'telling' free from the constraints of representational obeisance, and subordinated the 'story' to it: 'the story line is nothing more than material for plot formation' (ibid: 170), that is, the business of making a story (as 'narrative discourse').

Sterne's love of digression forces a wedge between these two narrative temporal progressions, that of the time-of-the-recounted-life, and that of the time-of-the-recounting. Kenneth Harper comments that the 'fact that this is done consciously, in undisguised defiance of normality, does not point to Sterne's whimsicality; rather, it is an instance of his habit of "laying bare" one of the formal compositional devices *to which all novelists have recourse*' (1954: 94). *Tristram Shandy* is the most typical novel in world literature, as Shklovsky famously claimed (1990: 170), for the simple reason that its principal concern is the making of literature out of the bare bones of a list of events, elaborating a story so that it lasts the length of a book, something all novels do: 'Art in general, and art of fiction in particular, stands or falls with organization' (Erlich 1980: 240). Sterne's novel is a single hyperbolic performance of the multitude of ways a story *makes* and *takes* time. It is only by elaborating, reworking, distorting or refracting a basic sequence of events that a tale emerges. Narratology has until now concentrated upon the product of such working-up, namely, narrative temporality as a construct; what has been overlooked is the process, inherently inimical to any form of closure, of *narrative as temporality*.

Narrative as a process of 'working-up' a putative series of events into a narrative construction, almost always tampers with the temporal order so as to make a story better in the telling than in the experiencing. In *Tristram Shandy* we are confronted with a text which flouts narrative conventions with such ferocity that the customary functioning of such conventions is laid bare in the very moment of being contravened. In the words of Jameson, '*Tristram Shandy* is the most typical novel because it is the most novelistic of all novels, taking as its subject-matter the very process of story-telling itself' (1972: 76).

However, this self-reflexivity may be only the beginning of a more corrosive process, already intimated by Shklovsky, in which the 'discourse' contests the priority of the 'story'. Culler claims that in much postmodern narrative, the arrangement of the events in narrative allows those putatively prior events to become visible as such in the first place (Culler 1981: 175–87); effectively, the 'discourse' produces the 'story'. Even more radically, the 'discourse' may obliterate the 'story' altogether, dislocating it to a point beyond reconstructability: *Tristram Shandy* already comes pretty close to this [*pace* Baird 1936]; in Beckett's fictions, 'discourse' discourses along without any discernible narrative (Richardson 2002: 52–53). It is at such a juncture that narrative *as* temporality begins to come into view as a process whose only product is the productivity of time itself.

Narrative texts undertake a plethora of remarkably complex temporal operations linking 'story' and 'discourse'. Genette (1980) lists three main correlations between 'story'-time and 'narrative'-time, namely, order, duration and frequency. First, order: events occur in a putatively real chronological order, but are then recounted in a more or less different order. Well-known examples of these techniques are 'flashback' (analepsis), or 'fore-shadowing' (prolepsis), or beginning *in media res*. Second, duration: the respective duration of 'story'-time and 'narrative' time may be correlated in many different ways. Bal (1997: 102) delineates five possible durational rhythms: ellipsis, summary, scene, slow-down and pause. Third, frequency: again, variable correlations of 'story'-time singular or multiple occurrences of 'real' events are possible with 'narrative'-time repetition or condensation, possibly by different focalizers, or points of view, often embodied by characters, narrators or narratives voices.

The reason that narrative texts can undertake such complex operations with narrative temporality is that they are multilayered constructs which contain in themselves a number of different temporal strands. Bal (1997: 81–83) identifies at least four temporal linear strands: (1) that of the lines of print, which the reader will consume or construct in a temporal reading process; (2) that of the 'story' which is assumed to be mapped, with more or less acute degrees of 'anachrony', by (3) the linear sequence of the narrative 'discourse'; and (4) the temporality of reading, already referred to, in which the three previous temporalities are woven together as a putatively coherent whole. It is not difficult, however, to imagine clashes and incoherencies between these four linear strands. In their visual arrangement, lines of print are not so much characterized by one-dimensional linearity as two-dimensional spatiality, con-stituted as they are, for instance, between the difference between capital and small letters, and successive lines (a horizontal axis) which descend successively down the page (a vertical axis), page by page (another horizontal axis). And the temporality of reading is merely in theory linear, but may involve frequent interruptions of varying lengths, starting anew to pick up the thread of the plot after a longish hiatus, and skipping to find out what happens at the end before returning to the place where one was (Lotman 1977: 215). Thus the textual experience itself is woven of multiple temporal strands, all the way from the various 'mechanisms by which the temporal ... aspects of this [narrative] world are constructed' (Bridgeman 2007: 63) through to the 'real-life' temporality of reading, not to mention that of writing. Narrative, then, does not so much map, even in a distorting manner, the temporality of the world, as constitute one of its many complex pluritemporal strands.

LITERARY TEMPORALITY AS TIME-PRODUCTIVITY

Gottfried Ephraim Lessing famously categorized the various arts according to their spatial or temporal nature. Literary narrative was, for Lessing, unambiguously linear and temporal (Frank 1963: 3–5). His definition was well-known, being taken up, for instance, by Thomas Mann:

> music and narration are alike, in that they can only present themselves as flowing, as a succession in time, as one thing after another; and both differ from the plastic arts, which are complete in the present, and unrelated to time save as all bodies are, whereas narration – like music – even if it should try to be completely present at any given moment, would need time to do it in.
>
> (Mann 1975: 541)

Oddly enough, however, language, the stuff of which literature is made, has been identified by more recent theoreticians as patently a-temporal. Terdiman, for instance, taking his cue from de Saussure's rejection of diachronic linguistics, imagines 'language ... as a vast structure so intricately and massively architechtonic that it appears characterized not so much by stability as by immobility ... This is the temporality of logic ... Crucially, such systems *take no time*.' He continues, 'Western modernity has increasingly seen the world as a language. But ... [p]aradigms based on language have a low aptitude for modelling time in its productivity' (2008: 136–37). However, we do not have to look very far to find evidence to the contrary in the empirical phenomenon of historical change in language. All-but-obsolete disciplines such as philology focused so obsessively upon language change that de Saussure advocated a methodological clean sweep (1974: 81–83); that gesture of *tabula rasa* notwithstanding, those of us who are a little older will have a very strong sense of the temporal dynamics of language and the manner in which it unceasingly changes and modulates.

More challenging notions of language as an inherently temporal dynamic, however, come from late twentieth-century attempts to rethink linguistic temporality in the wake of structuralism's synchronic ice age. When structuralism had thought in terms of change, it generally assembled a series of cross-sections of the language at a given moment in time. These, however, left intact the notion of a stable systematicity of language, present to itself in some ideal or virtual manner. The notion of **intertextuality** coined by Julia Kristeva in the late 1960s ('any text is constructed as a mosaic of quotations; any text is absorbtion and transformation of another' [Kristeva 1980: 66]) was conceived as a way of introducing a more fluid notion of temporal dynamism into structuralism (Kristeva 2001: 96). Elements of prior texts would resurface in the structure of later texts, transforming the literary system itself, but also responding to transformative influences in the new literary or linguistic context.

Another way of formulating the same concept, not at the level of the text as basic unit, but rather at the more fundamental level of the word, was Derrida's notion of the 'trace' (1976: 66–73). A trace is a present absence, or an absent presence, a sign of something that was present in the past, and is now only present as a shadowy mark of non-presence. A word is always inhabited by 'traces' of other words. Derrida suggests that words constantly lose old meanings and accrue new ones as they reoccur in new contexts. A word used on several successive occasions will have slightly different contextual meanings each time it is used. These different meanings are not clearly distinguishable from each other however. The previous meanings will inhere in the word in a ghostly form as 'traces', jostling with the additional meanings imposed by the new context. In each new context the process will be repeated, with various meanings, often conflicting with each other, occupying the space of the word 'now' as semi-absent or semi-present valencies.

To explain what he means, Derrida sets up an analogy with Husserl's notion of a 'thick' present inhabited by 'retentions' and 'protensions':

> The concepts of present, past and future, everything in the concepts of time and history which implies evidence of them – the metaphysical concept of time in general – cannot adequately describe the structure of the trace. And deconstructing the simplicity of presence does not amount to accounting for the horizons of potential presence, indeed of a 'dialectic' of protension and retention that one would install in the heart of the present instead of surrounding it with it.
>
> (1976: 67)

Derrida takes issue here with Husserl's idea of a present which includes the progressively fading-out 'retensions' of the past and the looming 'protensions' of the near and less-near future. Where Husserl wishes to gather 'retentions' and 'protensions' into 'the heart' of a densely graduated present, Derrida is more interested in the ways in which these traces of past and future may not merely thicken the present moment, but remain exterior to it, 'surround' it, and thereby destabilize it. For Derrida, the past and future give the present a temporal dynamic which makes it not-present to itself. The 'retensions' of the near past may actually alter the present moment upon which they impinge, in turn possibly further modifying the 'protensions' or expectations projected beyond that present. In Derrida's words, the 'dialectic of protension and retension' would 'surround' the present with a context making it not-present-to-itself. Thus the trace shifts the presence of the past and future meanings in the present word away from the present, towards its multiple, conflicting contexts. The present becomes differential, different to itself, with complete meaning always deferred backwards or forwards.

In linguistic terms, the trace describes the manner in which a word or a meaning used in the past will take on different meanings in its future contexts. Meaning is constantly changing over time, and may even do so within the space of a few seconds. When I hear a sentence, I hold in my mind the first words as I move on towards the last words. This may even be a pre-condition for the construction of meaning itself: in a language such as German, which often banishes the most important word, say the verb, to the very end of the sentence, waiting for the end may be a necessary part of making the whole sentence make any sense. The temporal structure of the sentence is one of change and instability. The context which determined my original understanding of the sentence has been displaced by the work done in the sentence itself, and the newly emergent meaning of the sentence will most likely be altered again in unpredictable ways by the impact of future contexts. As Currie says,

> it is only part of a combinative sequence that the word accrues meaning, so that it is marked by the temporal process of the discourse of which it is part. And it is marked by the trace of words which are not part of the discourse at hand.

> (1998: 81)

In writers such as the twentieth-century French, Austrian and German novelists Marcel Proust, Thomas Bernhard or W. G. Sebald, famous for their serpentine sentence structures, the temporal fabric of the prose is the hallmark of literary style.

Conrad in *Heart of Darkness* describes the manner in which perceptions in language change over time. On one occasion he makes a mini-narrative of the way in which signs may undergo a rapid temporal shift of meaning. What Conrad's paddle-steamer captain Marlow initially perceives as 'Sticks, little sticks ... flying about' transpire after a delay to be 'Arrows, by Jove! We were being shot at!' (1990: 199–200). The narrator's focus on negotiating the snag-filled shallows is so total that other signs undergo multiple, staggered interpretations. Likewise, other judgements, such as the African helmsman's and fireman's irresponsibility in abruptly abandoning their duties, are also retrospectively reassessed: they are dead. Watt has famously described this technique as 'delayed decoding' (1981: 270). Conrad's signifiers display a temporal instability within the changing context of other signifiers.

This brief vignette from Conrad's text gives a glimpse of a temporal structure of '*différance*', Derrida's famous neologism (1982: 3–27). 'Differance' is a difference which is also characterized by a 'deferral' of full presence of meaning; 'to defer' in French is '*différer*'; but Derrida replaces the suffix '-ence' by '-ance' to denote a process. Full meaning is never present, but always posited as something that will have happened in the future. Logically, however, this future total meaning is impossible, because the process of deferral of full meaning is potentially infinite. Derrida's picture of an ever-deferred fullness of meaning must by no means be registered as a loss. His hollowing out of full-meaning in 'differance', paradoxically, may transpire to be an unsuspected plenitude, indeed an excess, albeit one that eludes possession. It complements Bakhtin's notion of the novel as the genre of transformation par excellence (1981: 3–40), or suggests the notion of the literary text as the 'completely incomplete' work envisaged by Blanchot as the 'book-to-come' (*pace* Blanchot 1986: 36).[4]

Derrida's slippery sliding of temporalized signifiers can be embraced as a celebration of the infinite productivity of language. Language itself as a system inhabited and sustained by its human users generates meanings with a profusion which cannot be stemmed, so that apparently identical words will gather new and surprising meanings in new contexts. The great neologians of the English language, Shakespeare and Joyce, manifested the manner in which language at its ebullient best can become an immense reservoir of linguistic and conceptual creativity, constantly exceeding its own boundaries to break new semantic and syntactic ground. Language exemplifies one of Manuel De Landa's non-linear processes of material generativity which make up world history (De Landa 1997: 183–255): 'the process of language ... is always marked by the past and the future' (Currie 1998: 81). The time of language itself is a time of constant innovation in which the shared resources of linguistic flexibility and human experimentation drive forward into the future. Indeed they make the future concretely as they together overcome dead metaphors and ossified structures.

Narrative is not merely a way of talking about material processes. It does not consist of idealist signifiers which refer to real signifieds, but is, rather, a material process in itself. Narrative consists of complex chains of aural or visual signifiers which interact with and modify other material signifiers. Words do not merely refer to things, they are things themselves which circulate among and interact dynamically with other things, generating novelty and changing in the process. Since the early modern period we have forgotten the 'thingness' of words (Foucault 2002: 19–50)[5] and the concomitant processuality of language.

As a material process of a very particular sort interacting with other material processes, narration participates in their multiple and interlocking temporalities. Story-telling is a more complex elaboration of this urge to create, not simply a way of filling empty time, wiling away the time, but of 'yarning' (Conrad 1990: 136), weaving threads of narrative which make up one of the many intertwined strands of time which we have identified in this book as the multiple immanent temporalities of existence. Indeed, Conrad thought of the literary text as 'a machine' which 'knits ... us in and it knits us out. It has knitted time space [*sic*], pain, death, corruption, despair' (Conrad 1969: 56–57).

This notion of language itself, then, would offer a profound response to Thomas Mann's question:

> Can one tell – that is to say, narrate – time, time itself, as such, for its own sake? That would surely be an absurd undertaking. A story which read: 'Time passed, it ran on, time flowed onward' and so forth no one in his senses would consider that a narrative. It would be as though one held a single note or chord for a whole hour, and called it music. For narration resembles music in this, that it *fills up* the time.
>
> (Mann 1975: 541)

Mann is right, in one sense. A story which consisted of the words 'Time passed' would certainly not have been considered narrative by many readers in the 1920s. Yet one of his more adventurous contemporaries, Virginia Woolf, could use 'Time Passes' as the title of the central connecting section of her novel *To the Lighthouse* (2000: 135), in an attempt to convey the texture of temporal existence in more immediate ways than Mann himself could do.

According to Mann's (absolute) view of time, time itself cannot be narrated, as it constitutes framework or medium of existence, the invisible container and precondition of all actions, including the narrative portrayal of reality. 'What is then the medium through wh. we regard human beings?' Woolf asked in her rough notes for the section 'Time Passes' (2000: 251 n1). All narrative can do, according to Mann's eminently Newtonian view of time, is to '*fill up*' its emptiness.

Mann none the less yearns for a tighter fit between time and narrative, suggesting that 'time, while the medium of the narrative' is 'also ... its subject', following the impulse of his own 'desire to tell a narrative about time' (Mann 1975: 542). Narratives *about* time have been analyzed most exhaustively by Ricoeur (1984–88). His circular hermeneutics selects the very novels about time (such as *The Magic Mountain*) which will confirm his thesis of time as a theme (Currie 2007: 2–4). In similar vein, Meyerhoff diagnoses a deep-seated temporal malaise in modernity, a crisis coeval with Enlightenment itself, of which narratives of time are a symptom which also claims to be a palliative (1955: 134). In response to such views, Currie has riposted that *all* narrative is about time, proposing that precisely those narratives which do *not* explicitly mention it may be all the more instructive regarding the temporal workings of narrative (2007: 2–4).

Currie abolishes Ricoeur's privilege of a certain sort of narrative *about* time, but one may take this abolition a step further. Where Ricoeur claims the centrality of narrative in our understanding of time, making it '*the guardian of time*' (1984–88: III, 241), I would argue that this privilege is only necessary as a compensatory mechanism. Abolish the gap indexed by the preposition 'about' in 'narratives *about* time' (one introduced, in any case, by Ricoeur's English translator),[6] and there is no lack to be compensated. For, rather than arguing that *all* narratives are about time, as Currie does, one might propose more simply: narratives are time.

Narrative is not merely 'about' time, nor is narrative the crucial medium for conceptualizing time. Both positions, as Ricoeur realizes, merely produce an aporia in which narrative tries to articulate something which it is caught within and thus cannot stand above (ibid: III, 242–43). This, however, is a fallacious problem merely produced by the terms in which it is posed: namely, that of a separation between narrative agency and temporality as a container or 'element'. Narrative is not inside a global, cosmological time that it seeks in vain to encompass by means of its necessarily limited means. Quite simply, narrative is one of the many forms of time itself. When the hapless narrator of Coetzee's *Foe* frets, 'Alas, my stories seem always to have more applications than I intend, so that I must go back and laboriously extract the right application and apologize for the wrong ones and efface them' (1987: 81) she lays bare the dynamic of narrative-as-time. Going back is a *pis-aller* – because stories drive forward relentlessly, always generating new stories, albeit never in straight lines. Narrative produces time itself, in a process of 'non-stop self-regeneration … narrative constantly throws up new stories, it teems; the form – multitudinous', as Rushdie says of his own writing (1991: 16). Narrative should be seen as a strand of that multiple, immanent temporality that we have spoken about from the outset, generating one aspect of the immeasurable and ineluctable productivity which is time in its many specific and inimitable manifestations.

5

GENDER AND SUBJECTIVITY

Simone de Beauvoir famously entitled her mid-twentieth-century feminist manifesto *The Second Sex* (originally published in French 1949) in reference to the temporal sequence in which the Hebrew/ Christian God created man and woman. Gender, it would seem, is a temporalized and thus hierarchical structure from the outset, according to the motto: first come, first served. This genetic, sequential vision of femininity is fundamentally contradicted, however, by de Beauvoir's classic aphorism, 'One is not born a woman, but rather becomes one' (1972: 295; translation modified).[1] Femininity, de Beauvoir contests, is not linked to a putative moment of origin proverbially, marked by the cry, 'It's a girl', which then determines the subsequent status of that human being.

De Beauvoir's polemic was motivated by the suspicion that such a gesture of identification is a moment of fixing which serves to batten down the creativity embodied in gender which, in turn, is coeval with temporality. Gender as the epitome of engenderment or embodied creation, I argue in this chapter, has been contained by being split into two putatively constituent elements — masculinity and femininity. Such splitting assigns different sorts of becoming, that is, existing in a dynamic and constantly changing manner, to different sorts of human beings, thereby limiting the possibilities available to all. This attribution of essential identity thus streamlines, but by the same token dilutes the becoming which is the dynamic of subjective existence. Because we inevitably identify ourselves as human subjects according to our gender, this splitting delimits the constant transformation which is part of our biological and psychic natures, fencing it in within the spurious boundaries of personhood. The splitting and fixing of gender identity, I claim, is central to a larger subterfuge which serves to constrain and curtail the ceaseless processes of engenderment, tantamount to the creativity of temporality itself, not only within subjective selfhood, but also beyond it in the larger world.

GENDERED TIME AND SPACE

From antiquity, time and space have been gendered masculine and feminine respectively. Masculine action occurs within a temporalized framework of historical cause and effect; feminine generativity is reduced to the space (Plato's *chora*; 1952: 124–25) of the fertile womb, and in more recent formulations of the same notion, to the domestic realm (Jardine 1985: 88–89). But does not feminine generativity also produce temporal continuity and renewal? In the mythical tales of the Greek poet Hesiod (c. 750–650 BC), Chronos devours his own children for fear of them usurping his power (2006: 41): the time of chronology appears to be diametrically opposed to, indeed threatened by the time of generativity, which, perhaps precisely for that reason has been relegated to the stasis of space. The linearity of public action vanquishes the 'non-linear' (i.e. unpredictable) generativity of child-bearing. Joyce in *Finnegan's Wake* (first published 1939) playfully rehearses this relegation with his binary 'Father Times and Mother Spacies' (1975: 600), crowding 'species' and 'space' into a punning composite whose uneasy amalgam constantly threatens to burst apart. How that self-evident binary ('Which every lad and lass in the lane knows') might be blurred, both within and without, in its own structure, and in its social context ('in the lane' [ibid: 600]) is the subject of this chapter.

In contrast to these agonistic but seemingly widespread assumptions about masculine time as opposed to feminine time-lessness (e.g. 'The mother of young children has an imperfect sense of time and attends to other human tides' [Thompson 1967: 79]), much recent research has analysed the very real temporal functioning of women's domestic work. Women's 'reproductive' work, usually in the domestic sphere and usually unpaid, continues apace alongside 'productive' labour or professional careers outside the household (Budlender, ed. 2010; Shelton 1992), often, however, without any real transformation or inflection of the latter by the former (Massey 1996). It is time to take another look at such binaries and their temporal structures. This task was undertaken in a notable article by the Bulgarian-French scholar Julia Kristeva, 'Women's Time', originally published in French in 1979, and in English in 1986, but since then somewhat neglected. This chapter revisits that seminal and suggestive piece.

Feminism as an ongoing struggle has its own temporality. First-generation feminists fought principally to gain women political suffrage, or the vote, a struggle which lasted from the early to mid-twentieth century (in countries such as Australia and France respectively). Second-generation feminism sought to secure for women equal access to and status within the public world of salaried employment and careers. Third-generation feminism questioned the symbolic regimes underpinning worldly practices of discrimination, culminating in their rejection of the very category of 'woman'. Kristeva takes issue with the way in which the efforts of second-generation feminists to open up the 'linear' world of professional trajectories, albeit only partially successful, have been rejected by post-1968 third-generation feminists' attention to symbolic and representational economies.

The latter are often averse to accepting the linear temporalities of the competitive male-dominated world of productive work, posited as it is on the temporal projection of competitive individual intentionality rather than communal solidarity. They object to the sinister connections between masculist individualism, national histories based on invented traditions and violent geopolitical aggression, and a Euro-American glorification of 'progress' driven by technological knowledge and instrumental reason. Kristeva summarizes such contestatory stances as ones in which

> linear temporality has been almost totally refused ... These women seek to give a language to the intra-subjective and corporeal experiences left mute by culture in the past. ... By demanding recognition of an irreducible identity without equal in the opposite sex and, as such, exploded, plural, fluid, in a certain way non-identical, this feminism situates itself outside the linear time of identities which communicate through projection and revindication.
>
> (Kristeva 1986: 194)

Kristeva is referring to a range of feminist but also postmodern stances which reject a putatively masculized linear time (for instance Ermath 1992). Many critics share Kristeva's dismay at what they take to be a postmodern rejection of linear time, in particular emancipatory notions of progress and education: 'How friendly is this "postmodern" view of time to the interests of women and other disenfranchised groups? Less than one might think' (Felski 2000: 2). For, would not 'demolishing the idea of linear historical time, and with it the construction of linear historical epochs and periods' amount to 'the abandonment of the concept of modernity' and its 'potentially universal project of enfranchisement and empowerment'? (Radstone 2007: 11). Kristeva joins such voices, insisting that there is no alternative to feminist attempts 'to gain a place in linear time as the time of project and history' (1986: 193), while acknowledging that such linearity may leave intact what she (misquoting and thereby flattening Joyce's creativity) calls 'Father's time, mother's species' (ibid: 190).

Rather, Kristeva argues for a re-introduction of the cyclical, generative, creative time of maternity into the binary deadlock of linear work/project/history vs. non-linear critique. This reinstatement of the time of maternity does not, for her, imply a return to conservative, patriarchal values. It is predicated upon a more complex negotiation, not a mere refusal, of the irreducibility of linear time as the economy of the 'symbolic' order of language as a social fact, to which all human beings are subjected.

THE TIME OF LANGUAGE, TRAUMA
AND THERAPY

Kristeva's equation of linear time with the linear syntax of language intersects with the meditations on the links between temporality and narrative explored in the previous chapter. Linear, sequential language makes communication possible, but only at the costs of regulating and reducing what can be said within the temporal duration of a sentence. The so-called 'rarity' of discourse (Foucault 2007: 133–35) prevents utterances becoming so overloaded with possible meanings that they cease to have any communicative function. The speaking subject is forced to make exclusive (so-called paradigmatic) choices at every (syntagmatic) stage of an utterance in order for the sentence to make sense. A sentence must sacrifice expressive possibilities at every point along its sequential chain if it is to convey a coherent message. The same goes for the subject and its narrative of selfhood: if that narrative is to be coherent, much of the 'truth' of the subject must be expurgated from its tales, by means of what psychoanalysis calls repression. Only in this way will those narratives of selfhood match up with social expectations and regulations. Language as a social medium thus limits the infinite possibilities for the boundlessly experimental semiosis available in the early stages of infancy (Kristeva 1984). Joyce's playful 'Mother Spacies' (1975: 600) resists such linguistic austerity, refusing the choice between 'species' and 'space'. His pun squeezes both words into a single syntactic segment, projecting the 'principle of equivalence from the axis of selection into the axis of combination' (Jakobson 1971: II, 17) and thereby generating a plethora of speculative meanings.

Kristeva's concept of a linear syntax infused with the linearity of sequential temporality emanates principally from her debt to Lacanian psychoanalysis. Lacan reformulates Freudian 'castration' as the necessarily limiting insertion of the subject into the rules and regulations of language, a limitation which is the precondition of participation in society and history. For Kristeva, following Lacan, language instantiates 'a separation from a presumed state of nature' (1986: 198). Words stand in for things; the signifier does not merely refer to the signified, but is necessary because the object referred to is absent (the child's 'ma-ma' is a call for the mother who comes and goes). Language thus enacts a scission between words and things, between desire and fulfilment, which is the fate of the speaking subject. In other words, Heidegger's sense of the way in which death's long shadow stretches back to contaminate every instant of human life ('being-unto-death') is already inscribed in the temporality of the linguistic utterance, predicated as it is upon limitation in order to make sense. The price of taking one's place in society as a speaking subject is to be 'subjected' to the temporal limitations imposed by language. Kristeva accepts this price as being inherent to humanity. It is an acquiescence, however, which is highly problematic and not without formidable opponents, as will become apparent later.

Such a price is perhaps a small one to pay in contrast to a more radical failure of language as the basic fabric of subjectivity. Such a failure is manifest, for instance, in psychosis, but more promi-nently in the experience of trauma. Trauma refers to the effects of experiences that are so awful, shocking or painful, such as torture, rape, genocide, war or terrorist attacks, that they can no longer be encompassed by the representational means customarily employed to make sense of and communicate experience. Bennett notes that

> in the normal course of events experiences are processed through cognitive schemes which enable familiar experiences to be identified, interpreted and assimilated to narrative. Memory is thus constituted as experience transformed into representation. Traumatic or extreme experience, however, resists such processing. Its unfamiliar or extra-ordinary nature renders it unintelligible, causing cognitive systems to baulk; its sensory or affective character renders it inimical to thought – and ultimately to memory itself.
>
> (2000: 81)

Trauma's temporal effects tend to be manifest in phenomena such as 'a tendency to relive the past, to be haunted by ghosts, or even to exist in the present as if one were still fully in the past, with no distance to it' (LaCapra 2001: 142–43). It is in the failure of the temporal distancing instantiated in narrativity, that a specific 'disorder of memory gone awry' is evinced, indexed by a tendency of 'traumatic experiences [to] freefloat in time without an end or place in history' (Rothschild 2000: 36). The traumatic past cannot be consigned to the past, but continues to haunt the subject, as in a recurring nightmare. As the protagonist of Christopher Nolan's 2000 film *Memento* says, 'How am I supposed to heal if I can't feel time?' (qtd in Luckhurst 2008: 206).

A pertinent example of this failure of the temporal function of narrative is Iweala's use of the present continuous form in his harrowing novel about child soldiers in Africa, *Beasts of No Nation* (first published 2005). What theorists have termed the post-modern 'continuous present' (Francese 1997: 156–58) is manifest in a striking stylistic device that gestures towards a partial collapse of narrative memory. The first line of Iweala's novel has the young protagonist, Agu, announce, 'It is starting like this' (2006: 1). The beginning is not in the past ('It started like this'), nor is it in the simple present ('It starts like this'). Rather, from the outset, the protagonist narrates in the continuous present, creating an uninterrupted self-perpetuating span of present time that stretches from the very first page of the novel to the very last. The text does not consist of a succession of discrete present moments, but rather, of a simultaneity of presents which have somehow become interminable. The opening of the novel is permanently extended into an unending, repeating experience. In a sense Iweala's beginning is oxymoronic, for an eternal moment cannot begin if it cannot end. The traumatic experience resists encapsulation (and closure) in narrative, and thus remains as an experience in the (closureless, continuous) present.

The overcoming of trauma, to the extent that it is possible, is thus often posited as a process of re-narrativization of that which resists representation and temporalization. At the conclusion of Jonathan Safran Foer's *Extremely Loud and Incredibly Close* (2006), the young protagonist Oskar confronts instances of trauma across multiple generations: that of his grandfather, who has lost his first love in the fire-bombing of Dresden and has subsequently denied all forms of generativity, including the relationship with his own son; that of his father, who was deserted by the grandfather and never received the hundreds of unsent letters the latter wrote him; and his own trauma, that of his father's death in the terrorist attacks of 9/11, which results in his repeating nightmares: 'The same pictures over and over again. | Planes going into buildings. | Bodies falling. ... | Planes going into buildings. | Bodies falling' (2006: 230). In a moment of resolution, all the letters that Oskar's grandfather never posted to his son are consigned to a grave in Central Park in the place of the father's absent body (2006: 321–22). In a final chiastic image, the full but unopened letters fill the opened but empty coffin. Epistolic narrations until now suspended in their temporal trajectory thus consummate, at least in a symbolic manner, the unresolved trajectory of a narrative of death deprived of closure by the absence of the paternal body. Three intertwined but equally frozen temporalities of trauma and unfinished mourning are thus 'worked through', held together by the clip of narrative. Narrative as a therapeutic response to the unnarratable traumatic event releases the traumatized subject from an eternal present, consigns her or his experiences to the past and opens up the future once again.

Narrative as therapy was in fact the solution proposed by Freud in some cases to trauma (1966: XII, 147–56; XVII: 207–10) but more often to the less dramatic but more frequent condition of neurosis. Many of the emotions that drive a person to seek therapy are temporal in nature: uncanniness, untimeliness, belatedness, delay and failure (Freeman 2007: 163). The archetypical patients on the Freudian couch 'suffer ... from reminiscences' (Freud 1966: II, 7). A repressed past, typically consisting of experiences from early childhood, returns to plague the patient in the form of psychosomatic illness, neuroses, or phobias and anxieties. The goal of psychoanalysis is to lay bare these occluded but active memories and thus free the patient from their grasp.

The unconscious, however, whose translation or decoding is the goal of the therapy, resists simple recuperation as its content has constantly been subject to re-coding in successive present moments according to the principle of *Nachträglichkeit* (Laplanche and Pontalis 1998: 33–36). The repressed contents of the past, as with all memories and all historical narratives, have been retrospectively re-organized countless times before, according to the needs and demands of successive present situations. The distant past is never accessible except via the revisions imposed by later, more proximate pasts, right up to the present moment of therapy. Freud describes the way in which the unconscious is constantly being re-written by using the image of a magic writing pad, in which each successive act of writing disappears when the cellophane is peeled away from the wax surface, only to have a new set of inscriptions superimposed upon it (Freud 1966: XIX: 227–32).

The contents of the unconscious, then, are irretrievably buried in the past. By the same token, however, the past is constantly being pulled back into the present by those self-same re-inscriptions which overlay the past. Freud understood this most concretely in the notion of transference (1966: XII, 199–208, 159–71). Transference refers to the tendency of those situations, relational configurations or interpersonal dynamics from the past that patient and analyst discuss, to suddenly emerge in the present of the therapy, typically 'transferred' by the patient from a family figure onto the therapist her- or himself. Freud's initial impulse was to see transference as a nuisance, as a form of interference disturbing the smooth progress of the analytical cure. It then became obvious, however, that precisely the opposite was the case. Transference was that very past which psychoanalysis wished to retrieve from the oblivion of repression, manifesting itself in the most immediate present of the therapy. The utility of transference as an exemplification of the problematic past that therapy sought to excavate was all the more evident given the fact that some forms of repression could never be undone. Such repressed elements might never be susceptible of revelation by the normal processes of therapeutic analysis, but might, on the other hand offer themselves of their own will in the form of a real-time re-instantiation of past relational configurations. Into such immanent manifestations the therapist could intervene, re-working the past by means of its present repetition.

Psychotherapy in its classic Freudian form is an ongoing process which converts the repressed past and its intrusions into the patient's everyday life, via the ongoing 'presents' of the regular sessions on the couch, into a future in which the patient can live (ideally) freed of symptoms, anxiety or illness. 'The future in psychoanalysis is always bound to be approachable only by a retrospective and retroactive route: the only anticipatory gestures worth making are those that the past – rediscovered, recreated, and re-energized in speech – makes possible' (Bowie 1993: 39). Psychoanalysis sees past, present and future entangled, ideally, in a forward-looking creative process.

CASTRATION AND THE TIME OF LACK

In her article 'Women's Time', Kristeva accepts that taking one's place in the limiting sequential order of language and accepting its temporal limitations is the common lot of humanity. Working through the neuroses associated within the privations of language-in-time-in-society is a fate preferable to the 'frozen' time of trauma or psychosis, especially as it is susceptible of transformation via the rhythmic interventions of psychotherapy, a process to which Kristeva, as a practising psychoanalyst, is heavily committed (Kristeva 1987). Her critique is aimed, rather, at the way in which society places the main burden of 'castration' upon women as supposedly 'castrated beings' (1986: 197). Kristeva does not mean literal castration, but understands this term to refer figuratively to human limitation. Such limitation, for her, is exemplified *par excellence* in the inevitable restrictions upon what can be said in language, by the necessary 'rarity' of discourse referred to earlier (Foucault 2007: 133–35). In terms of popular metalinguistic lore, for instance, a putatively 'feminine' mode of discourse, gossip, is denigrated as trivial and limited, primarily domestic in its scope, and regarded as a waste of time within the larger, more serious world of masculine political or economic agency (Rysman 1977). In a world of discursive and economic scarcity, 'idle talk' by women who supposedly have nothing better to do with their time or tongues must be chastised by reducing it to 'gossip'.

In other words, Kristeva targets the manner in which society unequally distributes its resources at the expense of women simply because they are women. The inevitable costs of living in a temporal-linguistic regime are assigned principally to women, often in the form of a culpabilization which legitimizes discrimination. The monthly cycle of menstruation is construed in many societies as a sign of imperfection, as a recurring reminder of female lack. Almost everywhere, even in progressive European nations, child-bearing and child-rearing, with their unequally distributed temporal investments evident to anyone (female or male) who has raised children, is wielded as a rhetorical pretext and a pragmatic weapon to keep women them out of the progress- (or success-) oriented world of work, fame, prestige and power. Whence Kristeva's recommendation that the cyclical time of maternity be welded onto the linear time of career *and* the poetics of anti-linear gender politics. This strategy, encapsulated in the binary-blurring title of her essay, 'Women's Time', is from one point of view more subversive (in one reading) than Joyce's fence-sitting 'Mother Spacies' (1975: 600); for while Joyce performs a blurring of semantic boundaries, he none the less bows to the shrinking of feminine fecundity to domestic space, enacted in the phrase's work of poetic condensation.

Doubtless Kristeva is right in identifying the fundamentally separative work of the linguistic-social contract (the division between signs and things), and the way it harnesses linearity to the austerity of linguistic expression (extending this to austerity in the realm of unequal opportunities for men and women). To this extent she subscribes fully to the Freudian and Lacanian premise of foundational lack, whether psychic or linguistic. In the Freudian, Lacanian and Kristeva narratives of desire, lack is the foundation of the human subject's experience of temporal existence. Anticipation of the mother and the breast sets the basic temporal calibrations of existence. Whitrow (1988: 5) suggests that the 'first intuition of duration appears as an interval which stands between the child and the fulfilment of its desires'. Green claims that the appearances and disappearances of the object are 'the most powerful agent of the structuring of time'. Thus the alternations of presence and absence impose 'the time of the Other, interpenetrating with the time of the self' thereby inserting the subject into a temporal regime which will henceforth structure the entirety of human existence (Green 2002: 112). Temporal existence is propelled forward by the prospect of a future fulfilment of the felt lack, buttressed by nostalgia for an imagined past before some sort of 'fall'. Such an existence constitutes a narrative of time as lack-waiting-for-fulfilment, in other words, as a 'time of desire'

(Vasse 1969). A temporality of lack is extrapolated as the mainstay of selfhood, with Enlightenment theories of subjectivity stressing that the distance between moments of experience coagulated into a 'self-distance' which in turn founded the self-reflexive nature of consciousness (Siegel 2005: 33, 373, 440). Such narratives of the present-as-lack and consequent self-reflexivity are distilled into a work such as Saul Bellow's 1944 novel *Dangling Man* (1977), which evinces a quasi-diaristic narrativization of what Gurvitch (1964: 13–14, 31–33) called 'retarded time'.

Yet to subsume the temporality of subjectivity into lack, a fundamental conceptual move in much psychoanalytic thought, imprisons subjectivity in a negative structure which largely elides the positive dynamism of subjective existence. It also hollows out a space around the individual which is subsequently internalized as desire, thereby eliding the manifold connections which link human existence to the natural environment.

In our contemporary society, moreover, this tale of lack comes perilously close to a narrative of an 'egos consumans' (Baudrillard 1998: 85) whose existence is driven forwards by an insatiable desire for consumer goods, and whose momentary satisfaction merely amplifies rather than stanches its greed. This mechanism of temporalized lack is more insidiously inscribed in our contemporary culture's temporality of the 'brutal hegemony of the visual's conceptualization of the body – overwhelmingly, in this culture anyway, structured by linear time' (Freccero, qtd in Dinshaw *et al.* 2007: 193). It is the inevitable linear process of aging, with its converse glorification of the youthful body, that condemns the older body to the realm of ugliness. Here, existence is an existence-unto-(aesthetic)-death. It is significant, however, that very different connotations attach to aging male or female bodies. In this way then, the burden of physical temporality and the ravages of time are yet again unequally distributed between men and women, as Kristeva claims, in our society.

TEMPORALITIES OF PLENITUDE

Many psychoanalysts (Osborne 1995: 89; Radstone 2007: 79–80) accept that it is the threat of castration, where for 'castration' may be read insertion into society and limitation by its rules, and by extension the perspective of death as the ultimate limitation of subjectivity, which together define life's temporality in terms of an endstop. Acquiescence to the logic of lack, and acceptance of the temporality of mortality, desire and attendant nostalgia represent, however, a fundamental axiological choice which is by no means accepted by all thinkers. Deleuze and Guattari (1983) claim that this logic of lack displaces a more genuine logic of plenitude, in which all beings are driven not by a lack-motivated desire, but by a positive desire which causes them to connect with other beings. Such connections generate an unending process of further connections, ensuing transformations, new connections, new transformations, and so on. Psychoanalysis, with its rhetoric of eternal lack, convinces subjects that they need help in dealing with the unhappiness that rhetoric produces, thus creating relationships constructed around the therapist's putative knowledge and power and the patient's putative dependence. The narrative of lack as the motor for forward temporal movement and its capacity for setting the agenda for desire elides all the other 'non-linear' temporal routes, unpredictable and unprogrammable, that might otherwise be open to a subject in its existential trajectory. This is the possibility towards which Joyce's 'Mother Spacies' (1975: 600) gestures, with its expansive generativity ('spaces' for 'species') emerging out of the condensed maternal-mythic body.

Kristeva objects to the way our society puts the burden of human limitation upon women, off-loading the universal condition of mortality, for instance, onto those whose regular 'periods' are construed as a sign of inherent decomposition and decay, a 'secret fault' in early modern phrasing (Middleton 1988: 198). Alternative paradigms are proposed by such thinkers as the postwar French philosopher Emmanuel Lévinas (1987: 84–89), who understands the feminine not as a sign of lack, but as an absence signalling the unknown, the future, the potential encounter with an Other whose identity will always elude the grasp of the Self, a reminder of its perennial debt to alterity for its very being. Lévinas chooses femininity as the epitome of alterity because the promise of maternal fecundity, with the unknown possibilities of future generations, seems to emblematize futurity as an unencompassable plenitude. For him, femininity symbolizes the beckoning future which draws the self forward not towards its own dreaded mortality, but to the new lives arising out of an encounter with the Other.

When Lévinas envisions the feminine as the future-as-other, embodying the unpredictable and creative possibilities that lie before us, he goes some way to combatting all the myths from Pandora's box onwards which identify femininity with chaos and disorder. In contrast to those insidious and stereotyping myths, he re-codes femininity as creative futurity. At the same time, however, he merely confirms and reinforces the splitting of engenderment into two halves — that of an active masculine principle and a generative feminine principle. According to this binary division, the putatively natural role of child-bearing underwrites the containment of human generativity to the domestic realm. This manifestation of the unequal burden of temporality instantiates a division of generativity into artificially delimited temporal modes: a brief, punctual ejaculation which initiates procreation but then is largely disconnected from the long-term work of child-rearing; and the longer duration of pregnancy, birth, nurturing and upbringing, all of which take place within the domestic realm. By means of this splitting of procreativity into pre-assigned roles, the inherently unruly potential for the production of unforeseeable futures that is contained within human procreation and generativity, regardless of the gender of the subject embodying that creativity, can be channelled into pre-programmed spatio-temporal trajectories.

Here the work of Judith Butler is salutary in the way it dissolves gender and by the same token renders its temporal structure more fluid. From her classic *Gender Trouble* (1990) onwards Butler has formulated a theory of the performative nature of gender. She argues that gender identities are not stable givens, but are produced by 'repeated acts within a highly rigid regulatory frame that congeal over time to produce the appearance of substance, a natural sort of being' (1990: 33). Butler argues that there is not a biological sex which is reflected in gender discourse, but that discourse and other practices form the gender and even the apparently physiological sex they claim to represent. **Performativity** is the process by which repetition creates an identity which it then retrospectively posits as an origin. Gender is thus a temporal practice in which past sedimentations of performances are perpetuated, newly crafted and even transformed, by subsequent reiterations. Gender is thus always temporal and temporary. Butler's theory offers us a useful way of 'unfreezing' gender practices and reconceptualising them as ongoing practices within time, always open to novel inflections or deflections in the future.

By making all gender 'imitative' or 'derivative', merely bodying forth prior models in performative fashion, which themselves were also derivative, Butler dissolves gender as substance, and declares it merely process. By the same token, fundamental binary differences between masculine/feminine or homosexual/heterosexual identities are also blurred, as the essences upon which they were assumed to repose dissolve into performative iterations. Here, at last, not only the unequal burden of mortality, but also the binary containment of forms of gendered generativity (masculine ejaculation vs. feminine gestation and nurturing) are stripped of their spurious legitimacy. Not only the repressive administration of the burden of mortality (Kristeva's universal 'castration') but also the productive regulation of modes of reproduction, especially the relegation of generativity to the domestic realm of femininity, are opened up. The temporality of all gender, according to the theory of 'performativity', is open-ended and susceptible of infinite transformations whose only limitations are the nevertheless very real coercive measures taken by society to cement traditional gender practices.

MATERNITY

What, then, of Kristeva's attempt to re-insert the cyclical time of maternity in the linear time of the public sphere? Emily Apter objects that 'Kristeva's "creative time" [of maternity] conserves a referential foundation in the act of childbearing', which she contrasts with 'Deleuzian theories of creative time that emphasize the singular, virtual unfurling of being' (2010: 17n1). In part Apter is correct to recognize that by foregrounding maternity, Kristeva implicitly accepts the restrictions of a certain narrative which cancels out possibilities for a multitude of forms of generativity. Apter gestures thereby towards the links between the 'empirical' fact of child-bearing that is identified with a certain set of maternal practices, and the highly normative status of mothering in most societies. This normativity is based upon restrictive teleologies enshrined in a plethora of developmental narratives. Such temporal narratives are varied: they include the traditional 'ages of man'; the stages of maturation assumed by Freudian theory, that range from infantile polymorphous perversity, via the oral, anal and genital stages to mature heterosexuality; or 'straight time' organized in a linear fashion around the 'heteronormative' patterns of family life reposing upon heterosexual reproduction as the goal of marriage (Davies and Funke 2011:1–3). Given the encroachment by such time-hallowed connotations of 'maternity', a broadening of the terms of Kristeva's argument, in line with Deleuze and Guattari's promiscuous, pantheistic generativity (1983) is called for.

But before examining that conceptual widening of perspective, it may be worth lingering over Kristeva's cyclical time of maternity. Without doubt, child-bearing has been privileged by many con-servative discourses in our society and others as part of a massive and powerful apparatus which places the burden of that reproductive work upon the shoulders of women. For precisely this latter reason, it would be ill-advised to dismiss the time of child-bearing as an ideologically inflected but spurious essence. To dematerialize the literal time of work involved in rearing children, comprised successively of the time of gestation and pregnancy, the often drawn-out event of childbirth, the months of sleeplessness and extreme stress, the double trajectories of domestic labour and wage-earning, but also the time of intimacy, proximity and nurturing of emergent embodied selfhoods, would be to fall into the opposite trap. Bearing in mind the very real material process of parenting, and the time involved (for both men and women), it would be more productive to place parenting in the broader field of the ongoing generativity of entities, human and non-human, which constitutes immanent material time.

Therefore, rather than playing off Deleuze's temporalities against Kristeva's as Apter does, it could be more plausibly argued that the generative time of child-bearing and parenting identified as cyclical time by Kristeva, once freed of the restrictive attribution to mascu-linity or femininity, is one salient manifestation of the heterogeneous creative temporalities of being foregrounded in Deleuze's theory. Human procreation would be one facet of a mode of subjectivity unconcerned by a putative foundational lack, involved as it is in constant temporal processes of becoming and unbecoming which participate in the plenitude of the world. By the same token, procreation would be one among many forms of immanent, embodied temporal productivity instantiated in the world's becoming. Human reproduction would be one of the many unpredictable forms of productive coupling which make up the dynamism of multiple temporalities themselves.

BELATEDNESS

Butler's work of 'iterative performativity' implies that all gender is secondary, derivative, imitative; similarly, gender identities which have traditionally been regarded as derivative, secondary or deviant, such as butch lesbians putatively copying a masculine pose, for instance (Jagose 2002), may likewise point to 'the difficult knowledge that all categories of sexual registration are necessarily derivative, secondary and belated' (Jagose quoted in Dinshaw, *et al.* 2007: 179). Butler (2005) has extended these notions as a whole to subjectivity, suggesting that an accumulation of pasts is simultaneously inherited by the subject as an extant, 'sedimented' structure, often constraining, but that may potentially be transformed by those agents who sustain or rework it. Just as gender can be conceptualized not as a primary element of identity, but rather, as a secondary and belated derivation of practices themselves less originary than we assume, so too recent cognitive theory suggests that subjective consciousness itself is secondary.

From this point of view, if phenomenology sought to establish experience as the primary substance of consciousness, it would appear to have been sadly wrong, for consciousness is always a latecomer to the scene of subjectivity. Derrida's quip, 'it is always too late to pose the question of time' (1982: 42), expresses something of the belatedness of reflective consciousness. In a remarkably prescient dramatization of this problem, Conrad in his novel *Lord Jim* (first published 1902) portrays the 'retardedness' of consciousness. The account given by his eponymous character of the fateful jump from the ship that ruins his professional identity as a seaman is riddled with temporal aporia. Jim cannot but offer a 'disjointed narrative' (Conrad 1991: 113), because the temporality of the event itself has become confused: "'I had jumped ... " He checked himself ... "It seems", he added. ... "I knew nothing about it until I looked up", he explained, hastily' (ibid: 111). Conrad's usage of ellipsis and **asyndeton** indicate Jim's difficulty in creating a coherent sequence of events. More radically, however, Jim's use of the past perfect tense, which goes back, beyond an already past moment of narration, to a 'past past', attempts to make sense of a temporal reversal. Jim cannot remember the moment of jumping, nor having made a decision to jump. The act of conscious volition which customarily motivates action is absent. The action precedes knowledge: "'I knew nothing about it until I looked up", [Jim] explained, hastily', his hasty speech betraying a linguistic attempt to catch up on an action which has preceded his consciousness thereof. The entire narrative mimics this, with Marlow, the narrator, tirelessly seeking to recuperate in a compensative narrative the fullness of conscious intentionality Jim appears to have lost to some other more primal agency.

Freudian thought implies that most of our identity is constructed, belatedly, out of the residues left in the wake of the forgetting of forgetting (i.e. repression). Cognitive science corroborates these findings, suggesting that consciousness itself is a mere delayed by-product of the great mass of cognitive activity taking place below the threshold of conscious awareness. Consciousness is not instantaneous: 'Instantaneity is a fiction: even the time of perception takes time' (Terdiman 1993: 9). Consciousness is a mere delayed echo of pre-conscious processes of decision-making.

Building upon the late nineteenth-century work of Wilhelm Wundt, recent cognitive research has discovered that there is a temporal discrepancy between the brain preparing an action (for instance, pulling one's hand away from a hot surface), and the conscious making of a decision to act. It takes around 0.8 of a second, in some cases 1.5 seconds, for the decision to act to be worked-up into a conscious state. Consciousness must be laboriously constructed: 'consciousness takes a fairly long time to build, and any experience of it being instantaneous must be a back-dated illusion' (McCrone 1999: 131). Consciousness only crystallizes with a delay. We are 'late for consciousness' (Damasio 1999: 127).

Several things are worth noting here. First, temporal delay is not an anomaly, but rather is typical of much perception. It is a fairly banal empirical observation that some elements of visual perception exist as an after-effect, for instance the after-image left by a bright light, so that what we are seeing in the present may belong to the past: 'To be aware of an experience means that it has passed' (Norretranders 1998: 128). The presentness of *all* experience is thus an illusion.

Second, far from merely constituting a deficit of conscious perception, however, the 'lateness' of consciousness may be a simple side-effect of underlying cognitive functions. The brain regenerates and re-assesses information several times a second so as to make accurate predictions. The rapidity with which the brain overhauls extant information means that it is constantly running ahead of itself. These ongoing updates mean that neural information has a very short shelf-life; it is constantly being superseded by new information. The lateness of conscious perception may be a direct result of the brain's unseen but vital predictive, futural performance (McCrone 1999: 158); if the brain were to slow down to the speed of consciousness, it would not be in a position to deal with the constantly changing nature of its environment.

Third, this 'post-' character of conscious perception points to a temporal bracket of pre-conscious perception and cognition hitherto neglected by theories of temporality. Thrift accords considerable importance to this 'small space of time which is increasingly able to be sensed, the space which shapes the moment' (2008: 186). This interval of 'bare life', as he calls it following Agamben (1998), because it is life stripped of its thin veneer of merely conscious perception, wins a new salience. This has important repercussions for agency, the central pillar of theories of subjectivity since the Enlightenment. The human subject is constituted of many **actants** which are not immediately assimilable to selfhood: nutrients and oxygen from outside, enzymes, electronic impulses, fight-flight mechanism within, necessitate a reconceptualization of 'self ... itself as an impure, human-nonhuman assemblage' (Bennett 2010: xvii). As Grosz notes, then, 'Subjects ... do not

GENDER AND SUBJECTIVITY **119**

lack agency; on the contrary, they may, perhaps, have too much agency, too many agents and forces within them to be construed as self-identical, free, untrammelled, capable of knowing or controlling themselves' (2005: 6).

Within this perspective, gender, unhampered by the masculine/ feminine binary and its curtailing of modes of procreativity, would in turn merge with subjectivity as an unceasing process of creativity exceeding the myopic provincialism of consciousness. Gender, like subjectivity, would unfold as processes of creativity. Both gender and subjectivity would be released from the narrowly circumscribed compound of being into the dynamism of becoming. This release would place them in a broader context of ongoing transformation. Both gender and subjectivity would thus find their rightful place within a panorama of human and non-human, intra- and extra-human actants whose dizzying multiplicities of agency make up the dynamisms of temporalities themselves.

6

ECONOMICS

'If you've got the money, honey, I've got the time' ran the lyrics of a 1950 pop song written by Lefty Frizell and Jim Beck. The song encapsulated a sentimentalized vision of romance which conveniently obfuscated the real temporal and financial structures of postwar lower- or middle-class gender relations. The song was an immediate hit and underwent later remakes by several artists. Its enduring appeal around the English-speaking world for at least several decades testified to the insidious power of such cultural forms. The innocent coupling of time, money and affect in this instance of popular culture epitomizes the manner in which economics has been fundamental in moulding the modern sense of time.

In this chapter I will argue that capitalism, and its variously evolving forms since the early modern period, the merchant capitalism of the sixteenth and seventeenth centuries, the incipient and fully fledged industrial capitalism of the eighteenth, nineteenth and early twentieth centuries, and finally, the global, post-industrial and finance capitalism of the current era, has from the outset been the primary driving force forging the concepts of time that are hegemonic today. I will argue that economic forces, via the structuring of work and modes of production, have primarily governed notions of time which have been so deeply inculcated that we take them to be coterminous with reality itself. At the same time, however, these temporal structures, albeit roughly gathered together under the general aegis of Newtonian absolute time, have always sheltered regionally specific variations, and a plethora of varying temporal regimes which have continued to subsist alongside increasingly standardized temporal frameworks of modernity.

Newtonian absolute time, which, as we saw earlier, gives us the template for our contemporary common-sense idea of time, is intimately linked with the temporal regimes which emerged in conjunction with incipient merchant and industrial capitalism. The chapter demonstrates how changing patterns of work converged with Protestant notions of time as a resource to be economized, producing an implementation of time as a fetishized and reified **commodity** within the economic framework of capitalist production. The division of labour, commodity turn-around times, built-in obsolescence, and the central importance of logistics in the global economy from the nineteenth century onwards have been important temporal components in the logic of capitalist expansion. Time itself appears less as a pre-existing factor towards which industrial processes increasingly oriented themselves, than as one of the products generated by those processes, an ideological practice which in turn represses other temporalities.

The chapter then proceeds to examine the ways in which more recent transformations in post-industrial capitalism have produced a shift towards an economy of consumer-time, and most recently, of flow-time linked to the service industries, the market for digital technologies, and the global speculation on 'futures' at the turn of the century. If absolute time is produced by capitalism in its industrial phase, it would appear that in recent decades, with the rise of global finance capitalism as the dominant mode of profit-generation, other temporal regimes have arisen alongside and in complicity with absolute time; these variegated temporal regimes have co-opted the very terrain upon which alternative temporalities might have had the potential to re-emerge in the century since the advent of relativity.

What, then, of the immanent regimes of temporality which I have been proposing as an always present but elided alternative to absolute and universal time? If, as many commentators intimate, industrial capitalism and its more recent global variants have been the driving force behind the rapid depletion of the earth's resources and its accelerated plunge into unsustainability, then alternative temporal regimes are an integral part of a response to this fatal dynamic. An ethics and an aesthetics of immanent temporalities would acknowledge the primacy of the agency and existence of all entities as the forward-moving dynamic of time itself. Such an ethics and an aesthetics would radically displace humanity as the central actor in the natural global economy, inculcating a new respect for other beings and things as co-actants, thereby contributing to an alternative ecology and 'oekonomy' (in the etymological sense of management of resources) of the global system.

INDUSTRIAL TIME AND ABSOLUTE TIME

The notion of absolute time was formulated by Isaac Newton in England at the dawn of the Industrial Revolution (see Chapter 2). Its characteristics appear to have been embodied in a number of social or political phenomena in different parts of Europe, work-houses, schools, armies (Foucault 1991: 149–6), at varying historical junctures in the eighteenth and nineteenth centuries, but always in connection with capitalism in its respective forms. Absolute time, regular, external and independent of place, may have been formulated in the rarefied context of a Cambridge college, but its substance emerged out of the factories of England. Absolute time was from the outset intimately linked to the emergent capitalist system. Both absolute time and capitalist production detached temporal and productive structures from the traditional matrix of nature, locality and social networks. Indeed, it is possible that the capitalist system provided the primary contours of absolute time, with the theoretical notion legitimizing *a postiori* what the industrial revolution forged as one of its most potent productive processes.

A number of aspects of industrial time closely resemble absolute time, suggesting that practice and concept emerged in conjunction with one another. First, industrial time was effectively separated from the task itself and became an abstract standard of measurement imposed upon varying pre-existing temporal patterns, not unlike the framing time of the Enlightenment's container-like temporality within which events are held to occur. Prior to this, time had little existence outside of the rhythms of day and night, inflected by the seasons, which were in turn intimately bound to the exigencies of a specific local context. In rural, pre-industrial France, for instance,

> [s]easonal and liturgical rhythms governed people's sense of time ... Past and present were not two but one: a continuum of time lived, not a series of units measured by the clock ... Proximity in time was relative, almost unimportant. Traditional time had no fixed units of measure, there was not even a break between leisure and work.
>
> (Weber 1979: 482)

In the course of Enlightenment modernization, time was separated from locality and removed to an abstract, framing position encompassing all places, though this abstract absolute time was only universal in principal before the spread of coordinated, universal time in the late nineteenth century (as shown in Chapter 1). In concrete processes of work and production, this abstraction and removal of time from the immediate local context took the form of its extraction from the task of manufacturing and from the commodity itself. The gradual transition from place-based task-orientation towards timed labour is evident, for instance, in the 1641 account books of the Yorkshire farmer Henry Best, which refer to 'the Cunnigarth, with its bottomes, [as] 4 large dayworkes for a good mower' (quoted in Thompson 1967: 61). Time was less and less the 'immanent' texture embedded inextricably in the task itself, but increasingly became an abstract, external measure utilized to record how long it took to complete that duty, and thence to calculate its cost for the manufacturer.

When Marx speaks of the way in which work-time becomes an inherent part of the value of the commodity, his own formulation performs this shift from the concrete and the local, to an abstract and delocalized universal framework. In Marx's conception, the **exchange-value** of a commodity is measured by the quantity of labour objectified in it, that is, by being removed from the connection to the worker, and this quantity can in turn be measured in terms of work-time. The more effort and work-time that goes into a product, the greater its value (1976: 129–31). Marx describes a first stage of abstraction when he explains that 'As exchange values, all commodities are merely definite quantities of *congealed labour-time*' (ibid: 130). This 'congealed', lifeless labour-time, however, will be subject to a further degree of abstraction, rendering uniform different types of work: 'Commodities which contain equal quantities of labour, or which can be produced in the same time, have therefore the same value' (ibid: 130). In other words, the now frozen labour-time disappears into the potentially mobile and decontextualized commodity; the commodity itself loses its specificity, sharing with all other commodities produced in the same time the same time-related value. Labour-time has now diminished to the status of an abstract and thus universal measure of conversion of values. It has become a cognate of absolute time. With the increasing volatility of exchange values, however, the abstract, objective, externally imposed time of production begins to veer towards a more radically fluctuating temporality indexed by mercurial forces of inflation/devaluation and obsolescence. At this point, absolute time undergoes a fluid transformation to which we will return later.

A second aspect of industrial time which closely resembles absolute time is its tendency to atomize a temporality that was previously fluidly modulating, into discrete units. This segmentation was a direct consequence, as Marx demonstrated, of the practical imperatives of production deadlines and profit margins:

> An increased quantity of the article has perhaps to be delivered up within a given time. The work is therefore divided up. Instead of each man being allowed to perform all the various operations in succession, these operations are changed into disconnected, isolated ones, carried on side by side; each is assigned to a different craftsman, and the whole of them are performed simultaneously by the co-operators. This accidental division is repeated, develops advantages of its own and gradually ossifies into a systematic division of labour.
>
> (1976: 456)

The production line embodies this process of atomization. The commodity itself, as one of a series of identical products being assembled and then delivered, moves along a temporal trajectory, that of its gradual construction from a number of basic elements. The workers at each stage of the process repeat, over and over again, one element of this construction process, where once they would have been involved in its many phases. Thus time as the dynamic process of production is converted into mathematical values and measured by the imposition of a deadline. By the same token, lived time is atomized into parts in the same way as time itself as a flow is atomized into the calibrations of time-as-measure. The internalization of time segmentation and the discipline it inculcated, down to the temporal patterns imposed by the machines themselves, has been documented by Thompson (1967: 82).[1] A whole array of temporal strategies, from the development of shift-timetables, bells and horns to mark the passage of time, via long-service rewards such as pocket-watches, through to the rhythm of the machines themselves, created a deeply ingrained consciousness of industrial time, and a sense of discipline which became part of the worker's subjectivity.

A further refinement of this cutting-up of the temporal sequence of production was to analyse the individual segments of the process-segment to which the worker was assigned, then to time both the optimal segment completion time and the sub-segments, and finally to have the worker compete against the clock. In this way, the production tempo could be constantly accelerated. This analysis and synthesis of the temporal components of the production process was formalized early in the twentieth century by Taylorism, a forerunner of contemporary managerial science which measured and then shortened production times (Kern 1983: 115–16). Such formalization, however, merely documented practices that were long established in the workplace and were deeply ingrained in workers' *habitus*.

The philosophical idea of the divisibility of time was a correlative, perhaps even a residue or a spin-off of the division of labour. The concept of temporal divisibility facilitated the increasingly hegemonic, but at root coercive logic of industrial time. When Hume, in his 1738 *Treatise of Human Nature*, postulated the divisibility of time, the factory had already contributed to the intuitive rightness of his conception:

> It is a property inseparable from time, and which in a manner con-
> stitutes its essence, that each of its parts succeeds another, and that
> none of them, however contiguous, can ever be coexistent ... every
> moment must be distinct from, and posterior or antecedent to
> another. It is certain then, that time, as it exists, must be composed
> of indivisible moments.
>
> (Hume 1961: I, 38)

Thus, when Oliver Heywood's *Youth's Monitor* of 1689 intones
time 'is too precious a commodity to be undervalued ... This
is the golden chain on which hangs a massy eternity' (quoted in
Thompson 1967: 61), time itself has become a commodity, a series
of measurable, valuable units linked along a linear chain, with the
once-preponderant eternity now becoming a secondary, dependent
factor. The earlier relationship between time and eternity, central
to time-discipline in its monastic avatars (Foucault 1991: 149–50),
had been fundamentally reshaped.

Heywood's conceit mixes references to eternity with the language
of commodity and money because it expresses a transitional phase in
these developments. The time-eternity dualism slowly modulates,
via the mediation of the time-unit as commodity, towards a novel
dualism: that of an objective time-framework vs. the commodified
time-units and events which inhabit it. Strikingly, Heywood's
metaphorical materials are antiquated: time itself is a 'golden
chain' and eternity a 'massy' pendant. These markers of value are
still cast in the medium of bullion. They precede more fluid
forms of wealth, and by extension, more fluid forms of commodity-
time which will increasingly supersede absolute, divisible time.
Although merchant and industrial capitalism went hand in hand
with the increasingly complete command of absolute time over
every aspect of life and of thought, the gradual replacement of
absolute time by other temporalities of economics has not seen a
weakening of its everyday conceptual hegemony.

TIME IS MONEY

From the outset, then, absolute time went hand in hand with economic processes. Absolute time followed on the heels of commodified

industrial time, but as a conceptual system, fed back into the maintenance and perpetuation of industrial time. Quinones explains that '[w]e segment time, we schedule time, and when it is thus segmented and scheduled, we regard it as an indispensable, precious commodity' (1972: ix). In practical terms, this meant, historically, that not only were daily rhythms standardized against an objective, external clock time, which was then translated into bells, whistles, sirens and so on. Additionally, both the workers' time, in the form of wage-labour worth a certain amount per hour, and the employer's time, involved in his purchase of hours of labour, became increasingly commodified:

> Those who are employed experience a distinction between their employer's time and their 'own' time. And the employer must 'use' the time of his labour, and see that it is not wasted: not the task but the value of time when reduced to labour is dominant. Time is now currency: it is not passed but spent.
>
> (Thompson 1967: 61)

Such attitudes became common currency. For example, Wordsworth in *The Prelude* of 1805 arraigned 'Stewards of our labour, watchful men | And skilful in the usury of time' (1990: 444). These topoi were also omnipresent in nineteenth-century fictions such as Dickens' *Hard Times* (first published 1854):

> 'You see, my friend,' Mr Bounderby put in, 'we are the kind of people who know the value of time, and you are the kind of people who don't know the value of time.'
>
> 'I have not,' retorted Mr Childers, after surveying him from head to foot, 'the honour of knowing you – but if you mean that you can make more money of your time than I can of mine, I should judge from your appearance that you are about right.'
>
> (1985: 72)

Bounderby's binary of time-value knowledge vs. ignorance is re-minted by Childers as a spectrum of degrees of exploitation and profitability, but both use and thus perpetuate, in their capacity as discursive actors in Dickens' text, the common currency of time as money.

By the end of the nineteenth century, other forms of time commodification began to manifest themselves. In the process of the standardization and coordination of time (see Chapter 1), chronometrical time became a valuable form of information that could be sold from one local timekeeping network to another. The technological devices (clocks, telegraph instruments), the infrastructure (telegraph lines), and the services (installation and maintenance) necessary for the coordination of varying local times were also a source of gigantic profits for the companies concerned (Galison 2003: 107–12). Thus new forms of incipient universal time, embodied in information, technologies and services, came to be marketed as a bundle of commodities.

But what is a commodity? A commodity is a product which has been reified, that is, torn out of its original context, shorn of its erstwhile immediate **use-value**, and now floats free on the ebb and flow of market forces. Not only is it free to circulate in space, but also it lost its moorings to the past. In reality, any product is a temporal complex, consisting of

> both past material that has been reworked as well as present, reworkable potential that presumes a future. Materiality thus articulates temporal difference. ... in collating the traces of past, present and future, [materiality] also pluralizes and hence problematizes the time of the object.
>
> (Harris 2009: 7–8)

This temporal complexity is repressed in the reified, or fossilized object. Its reification consists, precisely, in the forgetting of its process of production. As Adorno once quipped to Benjamin: 'every reification is a forgetting' (quoted in Jay 1984: 229). The reified commodity has undergone a process of 'genesis amnesia' (Bourdieu 1977: 23, 79). As Terdiman (1993: 12) comments, 'The experience of commodification and the process of reification cut entities off from their own history.'

An example of such temporal reification, at every scale from the micro to the macro, is Montecasino, a mode-retro shopping centre and casino complex on the northern outskirts of Johannesburg in South Africa. Montecasino is an immensely detailed replica of a

Tuscan village, complete with an authentic Fiat 500 parked on a street corner and washing strung out on lines above the narrow streets. Montecasino houses restaurants, fashion stores, a cinema and, as its name suggests, a casino. Its architecture draws upon a repertoire of elements from a romanticized European agrarian past (appropriately, the original Montecasino was totally destroyed in the Second World War), one conveniently removed from the conflicts and complexities of post-apartheid South Africa. Montecasino also painstakingly elides its own more immediate historical past, the dismantling of state-legislated racial segregation, reconstituting a neo-apartheid almost-Whites-only zone via security systems and the power of the credit card. To that extent the entire complex underwrites the elided visibility of the underwaged Black subproletarian or other Third-World labour which provides the services or has produced many of the commodities purveyed there. Like the entire complex, the commodities it channels onto the market are multiply reified, cut off from the past of their production.

Mbembe (2008: 62) characterizes Montecasino as 'post-apartheid commercial architecture constitute[ing] a mode of erasure all the more dramatic because it is accomplished with painstaking care against the duties to memory ritualized by the Truth and Reconciliation Commission.' Mbembe acknowledges that the architectural vernacular of Montecasino evinces

> new genres of writing time. But this new inscription of time is paradoxical. For it to be possible at all, the built form has to be constructed as an empty placeholder for meanings that have been eroded by time rather than remembered by it. That is why they are largely the manifestation of the failure of the racial city to assimilate the passage of time. While bearing witness to a demand that the past be forgotten, this architecture asks the spectator to forget that it is itself a sign of forgetting. But in so doing it reiterates the pathological structure and hysteria inherited from the racial city.
>
> (Mbembe 2008: 62)

Recent historical time as a process of heavily conflicted transformation and of uneven democratization is sidestepped by the construction of a protected space in which everything (setting, products, and consumption itself) is reduced to a temporal mode which forgets the very forgetting of the intertwined temporalities of production which constitute it. These extend through to the temporalities of the place itself, South Africa as it redefines itself as a neo-liberal, post-apartheid semi-democracy characterized by a 'shifting terrain of desegregation and resegregation' (Nuttall 2009: 155), apparently intent on replicating, in many domains, the old exclusions (Marais 2011).[2] Montecasino's fortress structure is a spatial assembly which facilitates temporal amnesia, that is, reification on a grand scale.

Montecasino suggests, however, that not only commodities themselves become atemporal. The same process infects time itself. Lukács reflects upon the way in which, under the auspices of commodity capitalism, subjects increasingly lose a sense of history, with their momentary experiences becoming caught in a series of hermetically sealed presents: 'Time sheds its qualitative, variable, flowing nature; it freezes into an exactly delimited, quantifiable continuum filled with quantifiable "things" … in short, it becomes space' (1970: 90). What ensues is the reification of the moment which has been so lamented by theorists of the supposedly postmodern present (see Chapter 7). Multiple temporalities are streamed into a putatively singular absolute time; in its abstraction, absolute time can then be segmented into infinitely divisible units, and these temporal units in turn contain infinitely divisible commodified products isomorphically modelled on their respective temporal sites. That is, the reified, discrete commodities enjoyed by consumers in the capitalist economy have the same fragmented form as the temporality of their enjoyment, without any connection to a past or a future except in the ever-renewed lust after the newest model on the market.

THE FLUID TIME OF CREDIT AND FINANCE CAPITAL

Up until now, we have described time, segmented, abstracted and commodified, as if it were stable, just as absolute time regards time flowing evenly and indifferently to events it envelops. However, labour time, once it is abstracted and set free in the form of commodities, undergoes some startling transformations.

As soon as commodities go onto the market their value, as we well know, can fluctuate dramatically according to a range of interlocking factors: supply and demand, competition with other commodities of the same sort, obsolescence, whether built-in or not, etc. The value of work-time, itself a commodity to be bought on the labour-market, becomes similarly abstract and fluid, having undergone a transformation from a real activity via a use-value to, in the end, a mere exchange-value. The value of work has become, stage by stage, abstract, then delocalized rather than immanent, and thus universalized; and finally, it has become liquid and fluctuating.

In real terms, this translates into constantly reduced 'turnover' times. 'Turnover time' is the total time necessary for the production of the commodity, its launching onto the market and distribution, and finally, the return of the profits to cover the original outlay invested by the capitalist owner of the production plant and process (Harvey 2006: 61–63). This acceleration of 'turnover' times is mirrored in the 'half-life' of the commodity, which becomes obsolescent in a shorter and shorter period of time (Harvey 1989: 156). Fashions change with ever-increasing rapidity, so that the shelf-life of products contracts faster and faster, thus accelerating the 'take-up' on the successor or replacement product.

Ideally, 'turnover' time and 'half-lives', both necessarily connected to the materiality of the commodity, can be eliminated altogether if production short-circuits the material object entirely. The instant production of virtual values via the global exchange of or speculation on electronic assets and currencies (since the gradual erosion of the 1944 Bretton Woods Agreement, which fixed exchange rates in a rigid global framework, in the course of the 1980s), has reduced 'turnover' between production and profit to a matter of seconds. The profits to be made on this form of global electronic trading are infinitely greater than those to be made on the production of 'real' commodities (Harvey 2010: 21). This is one form of the volatility of time under global late-capitalism. Ultimately, it seems to generate a quite new sense of temporal rhythm:

> The narrowing and the urgency of the [finance capital] time frame need to be underscored here and the way in which a novel and more

universal microtemporality accompanies and as it were condenses the rhythms of quarterly 'profit taking' (and is itself intensified in periods of crisis and uncertainty). The futures of the stock market – whether in the literal and traditional sense of investments in crops and other seasonal goods not yet in existence or in the more figurative sense of derivatives and speculations on the company reports and the exchange listings – these 'futures' come to be deeply intertwined with the way we live our own individual and collective futures generally, in a period in which careers are no longer stable and layoffs a seemingly inevitable hazard of professional and managerial as well as proletarian levels of society.

(Jameson 2003b: 704).

The latter aspect of the volatilization of work-times has become ever more widespread and more and more brutal in its human consequences. Many different work-times go into this total 'turnover time': production time, transport time, advertising time, selling time, and so on. All of these are related to the time of the working day, the tasks to be performed in that day, and the salaries to be paid, all of which are constantly being squeezed to maximize profit: more has to be done in less time for less pay.

As a global trend, wages in general, with the exception of elite constructions such as the corporate managerial bonus, have been stagnating or dropping since the 1980s. The low-wage service sector has expanded exponentially, with a concomitant shrinkage of blue- and white-collar employment. The mobility of production sites, with production increasingly being shifted to South-East Asia and Eastern Europe in recent decades, tapping into an immense pool of sub-proletariat, often female labour, has accelerated this trend. Across the globe there has been an increasing polarization towards the extremes of unemployment and overemployment (e.g. unpaid overtime) (Zoll, ed., 1988). Furthermore, the spread of precarious or sporadic employment has meant that employees, particularly in the non-West, can go from one extreme to the other at the drop of a hat (Mbembe 2001: 54–57). Temporary or part-time labour, serial unpaid internships (Perlin 2011), and redundancy without notice, have increasingly become the norm even in Europe and North America. The threat of outsourcing to cheaper production sites, with loss of jobs as a result, as been one of the most effective means of intimidating and disciplining labour. The temporal patterns not only of the commodity, but also of labour itself, have become increasingly mercurial, and their fluctuations increasingly rapid.

DEBT, CREDIT, RISK AND THE FUTURE

Production-distribution-profit-return times are one aspect of the constantly accelerating, and increasingly fluid time of capitalism. But there are other ways in which 'moments', in Marx's terminology, are crucial 'elements of profit' (1976: I, 352). From time immemorial, the natural environment, 'eternally renewed and eternally unpredictable', obliged humans, like all other beings, to organize production along temporal lines. From the medieval period on, a range of technological innovations, such as improved transportation, more sophisticated commodities with more complex production processes and, increasingly complex exchange mechanisms, added new factors demanding a more stringent and accurate measurement of time (Le Goff 1980: 34–35). What loomed increasingly large on the financial horizon was the measurement of risk and the assessment of future time. Thus Shakespeare's merchant Salanio '[peers] in maps for ports and piers and roads' to make out 'every object that might make me fear | Misfortune to my ventures' (*The Merchant of Venice* 1.1.19–21). Commercial undertakings usually demanded an outlay not available to the merchant, so money had to be lent in advance, on the assumption of a later profit, with interest paid to cover the risk of the lender-creditor's possible loss; the borrower-debtor in turn had to weigh up the risks of the undertaking against the costs in interest. Most commercial undertakings thus possessed a temporal element, but for those merchants trading overseas within the emergent imperial-colonial economic system, transport time extended that temporal dimension to a major element to be factored into investments and potential returns.

Production and consumption have always moved forward by the mechanism of credit. Credit simply means making available in the present funds which are predicated upon profits imagined or expected in the future, thus injecting a future element of the cycle in its present state and thereby accelerating it towards that future stage. This futurity appears to lie at the heart of capitalism itself, which is always reaching into the future to generate more profit which in turn will pay off the debts incurred in today's investments: 'Money values backed by tomorrow's as yet unproduced goods and services, to be exchanged against those already produced today: this is credit or bank money, an anticipation of future value without which the creation of present value stalls' (Kunkel 2011: 14).

In the emergent Atlantic trade triangle, for instance, consisting of the transport of slaves from Africa to the Americas, raw materials from the Americas to Europe, and commodities from Europe to Africa (and the Americas), the round circuit of an initial investment and the return in profit could take many months. This temporal delay, plus the risk of loss on the way and the concomitant growth of an insurance industry, generated a credit system in which time was a crucial factor. The promissory notes which underwrote the investments themselves became the objects of exchange during the hiatus awaiting their being honoured. They became a new form of currency, a fullness of value entirely posited upon an elided future, a 'performative' whose future realization in profit or loss was pulled back into the present (Baucom 2005). A financial market of 'speculation' on 'futures', to take the terminology of contemporary finance capital, thus arose at the nexus of the industrial revolution and imperial-colonial financial investment.

The investor needs tomorrow's money so that he can invest it today; he also needs tomorrow itself so that he can invest the returns on today's investments, in order to generate profits the day after tomorrow. As Marx noted in the *Grundrisse*, 'The surplus value created at one point [or at one time] requires the creation of surplus values at another point [or at another future time]' (1993: 407). Capitalism depends on the future, and that future is its weak spot not only because investments may not bring a return, but also because there may not be an opportunity to re-invest those returns. Capitalism thus depends upon a continuing expansion, both in space and time, of the sites where surplus capital can be disposed of profitably by investing in new markets. Capitalism is posited on the accumulation of more capital, but paradoxically, it also depends upon reinvestment for the cycle of continued accumulation to function. Capital which cannot be reinvested, or can only be reinvested at a loss, does not produce new profits, resulting in the machine slowing to a halt. This is financial crisis. When Balzac, in *Old Goriot* (1834), employs the topos of fortune's wheel to explain excessive aristocratic spending, subsequent debt and ruin (1955: 70), he is using an archaic notion to elucidate a residual quasi-feudal mode of conspicuous consumption. In fact, even as he wrote, the wheel had already become that of the giant machine of industrial capitalism; the machine's periodic failure resulted from the loss of future avenues for investment and provoked recurrent 'crises of over-accumulation' up to and beyond the Great Depression of the 1930s.

In recent decades the global economy has expanded in two ways. First, a crisis of over-accumulation in the real productive sector in the 1980s led to a shift towards virtual finance (Harvey 2010: 216–17). Aided by the rapid development of electronic communications, not only did the financial markets dispense with the real production and exchange of commodities, but also they increasingly moved into the realm of speculation on electronic currencies, assets and investments. Second, and concurrently, since the 1980s the global economy also based its profits upon an increasing gap between wages and profits, fuelling surplus profit. However, this gap has also meant that future consumer expenditure has had to be maintained via an expanding credit system, familiar to most of us in the form of credit cards and home loans: 'The gap between what labour was earning and what it could spend was covered by the rise of the credit card industry and increasing indebtedness' (Harvey 2010: 17). Taken together, these two elements led to an extraordinary fluidity of financial markets (Knorr Cetina 2004). The markets reached further and further into the domain of the virtual and the imaginary, posited upon the availability of future capital. The imaginary *time* of credit came to dominate the global economy, right down to the lives of individual shoppers or home buyers. At the same time, however, consumers' real buying power continued to shrink: 'by the late 1990s ... [f]inancial institutions, awash with credit, began to debt-finance people who had no steady income' (Harvey 2010: 17). In other words, more and more buying power in the present, from the level of individual households to that of international banking systems, was drawn from a hypothetical future; at the same time, real opportunities for investment and consumption contracted.

The world economy rode a wave of capital which, once it was perceived to be merely 'futuristic', possibly never to be realized, evaporated like a morning mist. In 2008, much of this debt, acquired against the promise of fictitious capital from the future and in double denial of contracting income and investment opportunities in the present, was suddenly revealed to be unredeemable. This double revelation provoked a worldwide crisis as both investors and institutions had the financial ground pulled from under their feet. Huge amounts of taxpayers' money were siphoned back into private banks that were declared 'too big to fail' as governments rushed to fill the monetary void the imaginary future had made in the greedy present. Taxpayers' money is of course taken from *their* futures: imaginary speculative futures have robbed taxpayers and their children of real future educational provision, real future health-care services, real future pensions.

In the 'flow economies' (Knorr Cetina 2004) of contemporary global financial capitalism, it would appear that the absolute time evolving out of industrial time has become a more ephemeral, relative time, loosed from the temporal restraints of material production altogether. The sundering of time and place was the foundation of Enlightenment absolute time and of the commodity's release from its production-place and its production-time-value. Post-industrial time has become entirely fluid and relative, but it has not brought back together the long-dichotomized time and space factors. Rather, the time of global financial capital is one of instantaneous exchange regardless of time and place as 'electronic brokering systems' carry out financial trading deals between banking systems around the world.

We tend still to think intuitively in terms of absolute time, but much of our everyday experience is increasingly contoured, in fact, by a temporal regime utterly contemptuous of both human and non-human (or natural) temporal rhythms. That temporal regime is the autonomous, but ultimately self-vitiating regime of global speculative finance which is the hallmark of the late-modern epoch.

7

POSTMODERN TEMPORALITIES

If late-capitalist electronic financial speculation appears to have cut value entirely loose from space and reduced 'turnover' times to negligible split-seconds, postmodern culture, by contrast, frequently seems to have brought time and space back together. Postmodern time imagines 'pleats' or 'wrinkles' in time (Hospital 1990: 161; L'Engle 1962) – for example, conjuring up 'islands of the day before' (Eco 1995) where temporal sequence appears to double up or loop back upon itself. Postmodern time is a temporal logic in which the suppressed aporias of absolute or universal time begin to re-emerge, often manifesting themselves in spatial form.

For David Harvey, it is the incremental process of 'space-time compression' which has produced these aporias. He argues that 'the history of capitalism has been characterized by a speed-up in the pace of life ... so overcoming spatial barriers that the world seems to collapse inwards upon us'; these processes 'so revolutionize the objective qualities of space and time that we are forced to alter, sometimes in quite radical ways, how we represent the world to ourselves' (1989: 240). According to Paul Virilio (1991: 15), post-modern time is the disembodied and constantly accelerating time of technology, 'pure computer time ... [that] helps to construct a permanent present, an unbounded, timeless intensity'. Ursula Heise (1997: 42–43) suggests that the yawning chasm between, for instance, the micro-time of an atomic clock's nanosecond accuracy and the macro-time of the history of the cosmos generates temporal discrepancies too great to be encompassed by subjective understanding. Whence Elam's claim that 'postmodernism is the recognition of the specifically *temporal* irony within narrative' (1993: 217) by virtue of which no single temporal perspective ultimately underwrites the logic of a given narrative.

These theorists attempt to articulate a range of conceptual paradoxes by virtue of which the evenly flowing linear and universal time of modernity reveals its internal contradictions and begins to fragment into a plethora of incoherent mini-temporalities. In Jean-François Lyotard's (1984: xxiii) account, postmodernism is characterized by the failure of modernity's grand narratives of reason and progress, whose bankruptcy became all too evident in the course of the twentieth century's Holocaust, Gulag Archipelago, Hiroshima, Vietnam, to mention only a few of its notable catastrophes. In place of these discredited grand narratives, more modest micro-narratives emerged, but lacked any overarching explanatory power. Accordingly, the twinned grand narratives of absolute Newtonian time and coordinated universal time fragmented into the multiple micro-'social times' of Gurvitch's (1964) temporal sociology. Even more radically, as Ermath (1992: 11) suggests, 'postmodern sequences make accessible new temporal capacities that subvert the privilege of historical time and bind temporality in language', in a post-Saussurean revamping of the Kantian categorical *a priori* which posited time as a fundamental category of thought that provides the subject with a framework for articulating and understanding existence.

But these postmodern tales about time themselves throw up another set of paradoxes. How much has really changed since the advent of the postmodern 'condition'? A century has elapsed since the Einsteinian revolution which declared that time and space mutually inflect each other, thus destabilizing the very parameters of Newtonian absolute time. Notwithstanding widespread awareness of this 'difficult and contentious topic', as Harvey points out 'we do not usually let that interfere with the common-sense of time around which we organize our daily routines' (1989: 201). We take cognizance of various culturally inflected time-schemes, but '[i]n spite of (or perhaps precisely because of) this diversity of conceptions [of time] and the social conflicts that flow therefrom, there is still a tendency to regard the differences as those of perception or interpretation of what should fundamentally be understood as a single, objective yardstick of time's ineluctable arrow of motion' (ibid: 203). In similar manner, Ashcroft has asked, 'To what extent does a paradigm actually affect the behaviour of subjects? Have people really abandoned the Newtonian world-view?' (2001a: 104). Newton's absolute time, it seems, is remarkably tenacious. So much for the legacy of Einstein, and so much, then, for postmodern time.

The unbroken hegemony of Newtonian time a century after Einstein may be confirmation of Marx's law of the relationship between base and superstructure. According to White,

> whenever there is any transformation in the Base (comprised of the means of production and the modes of relationship between them), there will be a transformation in the components of the Superstructure (social and cultural institutions), but that the reverse relationship does not obtain (e.g. changes in consciousness do *not* effect changes in the Base).
>
> (1973: 11)

In other words, ways of understanding the world do not change ways of organizing the world, whereas transformations in the organization of society may very well change ways of understanding its dynamics. According to this idea, relativity was a radical but ultimately irrelevant paradigm shift which left absolute time largely intact because its impact was restricted to the realm of ideas and concepts.

A different picture emerges, however, if we ask the same question about the ways in which new notions of time emerge out of modes of production and the relationships between them. In that case, as enumerated in the previous chapter on economics, we see a panorama of increasingly accelerating production processes (faster turnover times, shorter product shelf-lives, increasing production of services and digital commodities, etc.) accompanied by increasingly ephemeral forms of capital accumulation and reinvestment. If, according to the old adage, 'time is money', then the century since the proclamation of relativity would indeed have witnessed a remarkable increase in the flexibility of temporal regimes as a result of the liberalization of monetary regimes, and of the concomitant shift away from the production of goods towards the production of speculative financial values.

A paradoxical situation arises as a consequence of this. On the one hand, temporal 'relativity' is 'disavowed' in something akin to the psychoanalytical meaning of the term, that is, simultaneously acknowledged as a fact but ignored in practice. On the other, a remarkable fluidity of time as it is organized under late capitalism has become prominent among our repertoires of temporal experiences, usually as a highly ambivalent phenomenon. To take one banal example: seven-days-a-week, morning-to-midnight shop opening-times may flexibilize my working day, making it possible to restock my fridge after staying late in the office – but what of the working conditions of the underwaged staff who are behind the counter until midnight? The apparent discrepancy between the persistence of absolute time in many areas of everyday life, and a truly astonishing increase in the flexibility of temporal regimes as consumer values invade the most intimate niches of the same everyday life, is the subject of the main sections of this chapter on postmodern temporalities.

In this chapter I argue that much of what is touted as postmodern time, in particular the loss of temporality in the face of a superficial spazialization of experience, is less momentous than the more subtle intrusion of late-capitalist symbolic economies into the temporal fabric of everyday life. These economies are symbolic, in the sense that what is increasingly exchanged are images, increasingly often digitally produced and consumed, and purely virtual values rather than tangible goods. With the ubiquity of the internet, mobile phones, Skype, and so on, such operations have become a familiar part of the intimate fabric of everyday life. I then go on to argue that such developments, however, are not genuinely postmodern to the extent that they merely evince the intensification of trends present in modernity from the outset. This in turn begs the question of the temporal narrative that postmodernism claims as its own, making it likely that the very notion of the 'post' in postmodernism in fact perpetuates the temporal logic upon which modernity itself is predicated.

What was signalled by some theorists of relativity and quantum theory (for instance, Müller 1972: 266–315) but was largely overlooked by postmodern theory until the advent of 'post-humanist' thought, however, is a more radical temporal plurality which I investigate in the final section of this chapter. Spacetime as it emerged in the theory of relativity abolished what had been the main precept of absolute Newtonian time (and, in parallel, that of fully emancipated Euclidean space): namely, the rigorous severance of time and place. Spacetime proclaimed the rehabilitation of intertwined temporality and spatiality. What we may now call post-relativity temporality consists of the various sites, both human and non-human, at a multiplicity of scales, from the very small, to the very great, and the dynamic changes and the transformations which inhabit them. These immanent, entity- and material-inhabiting temporalities and their respective time-trajectories are bound together to make up a complex interwoven time with a plethora of different tempos.

An example of such intertwined human and non-human trajectories with differing tempos might be the superimposed portrait-landscape photographs created by the Australian Indigenous artist Leah King-Smith. Her photos overlay in palimpsest form colonial photos of long-since deceased Indigenous people from Victoria upon photographs of the landscape, sometimes in panorama, sometimes showing details of the trunk and bark of a eucalyptus tree (King-Smith 1994). In this way, they blend the temporality of the landscape with that of individual human lives. The photos evoke the 'ghostly' haunting of the postcolonial present by the victims of colonial genocide; they also suggest, however, that Indigenous temporalities, defying the erstwhile colonial rhetoric of 'the dying race', continue to be coextensive with the vibrant life of the landscape itself, despite the ecological depredation it has undergone in several centuries of European settlement. The photos dramatize the complex imbrications of human and nonhuman temporalities over several centuries, using the genre of the double-exposed reproduction of earlier photographs to denote the endings and new beginnings that characterize the temporality of material substances themselves. The photos could easily be characterized as postmodern, but the real symbolic and material work they do is more radical, enacting the intersection of time and space heralded by twentieth-century relativity; this 'spacetime' is all too often forgotten in everyday thought but is rejuvenated by the contemporary Indigenous ethos of 'country' as the bedrock of all life (see Chapter 8). It is to such post-Enlightenment temporalities, and not to their postmodern alibis, that we should be paying attention.

POSTMODERN TIMES

As the Berlin Wall fell, Francis Fukuyama (1992) announced the 'end of history', a claim made to look somewhat rash by several decades of subsequent post-socialist turbulence. At the same moment, Fredric Jameson (1992:16) more cautiously advanced the idea of a 'waning of the great high modernist thematics of time and temporality, the elegiac mysteries of *durée* and memory'. 'I think it is at least empirically arguable', he continued, 'that our daily life, our psychic experience, our cultural language, are today dominated by categories of space rather than by categories of time.' More recently, he has continued to rehearse this argument, diagnosing an

> 'end of temporality' ... faced by postmodernity in general and ... characterized as a dramatic and alarming shrinkage of existential time and the reduction to a present that hardly qualifies as such any longer, given the virtual effacement of that past and future that can alone define a present in the first place.
>
> (Jameson 2003b: 708)

Such tones are echoed frequently in postmodern theory: the present age is losing 'its capacity to retain its own past, has begun to live in a perpetual present and in a perpetual change that obliterates traditions of the kind which all earlier social formations have had in one way or another to preserve' (Jameson 1992: 179); the stasis of the database and the computer game produce 'a permanent present, an unbounded, timeless intensity' (Virilio 1991: 15); according to Nowotny we live in an 'extended present' (1989: 47–76, esp. 51–54). Such trends are epitomized in Barack Obama's 2008 election slogan 'The time is now!' The tautological temporality of this slogan suggestively evokes 'opportunity' but refuses to specify any form of progressive content. It epitomizes a political scene where 'the present is all there is' (Harvey 1989: 240) because the future has failed as a receptacle for collective wish fulfilment or hope (Desroche 1979). This sense that 'the future cannot begin' (Luhmann 1976) has been consolidated by the definitive failure of socialist utopias and of panoramas of endless consumer prosperity at the beginning of the twenty-first century.

What takes their place are mildly dystopian future prospects. Granted, the great nuclear holocaust or Third World War feared at the mid-twentieth century never occurred, merely generating, however, a schizoid divide 'into a false future in which we all live and a true future which by virtue of being true does not have us in it' (Hayles 1990: 279–80). Yet global warming is accelerating inexorably; a number of critical ecological thresholds within the 'planetary boundaries' model have been overstepped (Foster, Clark and York 2010); major nuclear accidents appear to be pre-programmed to recur at periodic intervals (Three Mile Island in 1979, Tschernobyl in 1989 and Fukushima in 2011 to name only those the media have publicized); the global economy seems to be bogged down in serial crises indicating a long-term recession (Lanchester 2011); and a major world food-shortage is already looming on the horizon (Ambler-Edwards *et al.* 2009). If there is a future, it is a grim panorama of serial emergencies: '[T]he trouble with normal is it only gets worse', as Bruce Cockburn (1983) was already singing a few decades back.

But despite the eternal present which we supposedly inhabit, the past has not been entirely lost. Huyssen (1995: 5) perceptively notes that, paradoxically, the 'undisputed waning of history and historical consciousness, the lament about political, social and cultural amnesia, and the various discourses, celebratory or apocalyptic, about *posthistoire* have been accompanied in the past decade and a half by a memory boom of unprecedented proportions.' Even Jameson acknowledges 'an omnipresent, omnivorous, and well-nigh libidinal historicism' which manifests itself, however, in varieties of historical 'pastiche', in a 'random cannibalization of all the styles of the past' that goes hand in hand with 'consumers' appetite for a world transformed into sheer images of itself and for pseudo-events and spectacles' (1992: 17–18). Symptomatic of this is the imminently postmodern rage for 'citation' evinced, for example, in 'mode retro' phenomena such as classic car remakes of the Mini Minor, the Volkswagen Beatle and the Fiat Cinquecento, in the revisiting of past sartorial trends, or in the playful recreation of past architectural styles: for instance, Montecasino near Johannesburg, analyzed in Chapter 6. Currie (2007: 11) calls these strategies 'accelerated recontextualization', as they involve a process in which past styles, designs and fashions are reactivated again and again in anachronistic contexts at ever-reduced intervals.

This paradoxical relationship between past, present and future reaches its postmodern apogee in what Derrida (1998) has named 'archive fever'. The ubiquitous availability of digital recording technology in the form of digital cameras in ever-smaller dimensions means that every moment can be recorded and archived as if it was already past. Increasingly this means that we experience our present through the lens of a digital camera, already imagining it in the moment of immediate presence as if, in the future, we would read it as past. This leads to a curious hollowing-out of present experience, as it is constantly being projected into a future-preterite structure (i.e. 'this moment will have been'). This paradoxical temporal structure in turn disturbs relationships of representation, as a present event is recorded *in order* to archive it; the intended archivization determines the selection of the moments deemed worthy of archivization; thus the future-past actually governs, in the very moment of its happening, what constitutes the present. According to Currie,

> Archivisation is the experience of the so-called news media because the cause-and-effect sequence of an event and its recording as news is reversed in a highly developed media capitalist society: an event is recorded not because it happens, but happens because it is recorded.
> (2007: 11)

This reversal is endemic in narrative in general, in which the 'narrative discourse' often serves the 'story-line' or chronological order of the facts far less than one might expect; often, rather, it is the 'narrative discourse' which allows the chronological events in their putative sequential order to come into view in the first place (Culler 1981: 175–87). None the less, the 'archive fever' with which we are all more or less infected in our everyday lives indexes a more massive and fundamental shift of consciousness than that associated with the age-old tricks of story-telling.

TIME IN REVERSE

'The past is unpredictable', says Kishlansky (2011: 20), retooling an old Russian proverb. Appropriately, the past archive of oral lore is itself translated and recast here for contemporary purposes. The aphorism imagines a complex and temporally extended interplay between past, present and future. In a manner not dissimilar to 'accelerated recontextualization' or 'archive fever', the proverb thrusts the past forwards into an infinite number of futures, which, retrospectively, will re-mould that self-same past again and again in different forms: 'time is an "open whole" where the past can always produce new potentials for new futures, which in turn open up new pasts' (Colebrook 2009: 14). A number of postmodern writers or thinkers have re-imagined the very temporality of the past so as to reverse the causal relationship between past and present. Borges envisaged a mode of intertextuality according to which 'every writer *creates* his own precursors' (Borges 1976: 236), just as Benjamin claimed that translations consecrate their originals, which, without them would not gain the status of classics (Benjamin 1999: 71–72). The protagonist of Jean Rhys' fictional *Jane Eyre*-remake, *Wild Sargasso Sea* (first published 1966), is propelled inexorably forwards towards the death by fire that her fictional predecessor in Brontë's novel, Bertha, has prepared for her: '[I]t was as if the fire had spread across the room ... it reminded me of something I must do. I will remember I thought. I will remember quite soon' (Rhys 1968: 153). Rhys's protagonist lives a fictional trajectory that is determined from the outset by the plot of the earlier text, yet gives that earlier character a new lease of life and a qualitatively different nature.

These examples instantiate one of the fundamental topoi of postmodern temporality: namely, the interrogation of reversible linear time. Nineteenth-century thermodynamics and the notion of entropy, the tendency of all bodies to lose heat and more broadly to disintegrate incrementally until reaching the simplest possible state, consecrated the notion of *irreversible* time. Irreversible linear time was one of the few stable elements in the physics of temporality not to have been shattered by the attack mounted by quantum theory on Newtonian absolute time. Interestingly though, it does appeal to literary artists for whom the juggling of temporal order is one of the major resources of their craft. An episode in Kurt Vonnegurt's *Slaughterhouse-Five* (first published 1966) has the protagonist coming 'unstuck in time' when he watches American war footage, with a bombing raid on German cities related in reverse gear (1968: 73–75). One of the narratorial voices of Calvino's *If on a Winter's Night A Traveller* (first published 1979) expresses a desire to have time run backwards (1982: 18). More poignantly, Foer's youthful narrator in *Extremely Loud & Incredibly Close* likes to play with a flip book allowing him to make the people falling from the twin towers on 9/11 float back upwards. The book's final pages feature such a flip-book segment that the reader her- or himself can activate (2005: 327–55). These experiments with reverse linear temporality appear to be elaborate but ultimately superficial exemplifications of postmodernism's ludic questioning of temporal order.

A more complex answer to the issue of unpredictable pasts may be found in Martin Amis' *Time's Arrow* (1991). Amis offers a biography recounted as much as possible in reverse. His narrative re-winds the story of Odilo Unverdorben, a Nazi war criminal who changes his name and makes a new life in the USA after having been a concentration-camp doctor in Auschwitz. The reversed narrative order implies the gradual revelation of the horror of Auschwitz, which the reader knows about but which the frame-narrator, intimately connected with Odilo but only cognizant of the reverse story he relates, does not suspect. Appreciation of the constantly surprising effects of the reverse narration depends upon knowing the 'real' order of the story being run backwards: if we are not familiar with the history of the Holocaust, we cannot appreciate the irony of an SS-doctor in Auschwitz 'helping' the Jews by rescuing them from the gas chambers (1991: 16) or by 'deconcentrating' them: 'the Jews were being ... channelled back into society' (ibid: 149). The reader's implicit knowledge of a 'real' chronology that is itself necessary for the reverse chronology to make sense is matched in the text by a 'doubly linear story that simultaneously moves backwards and forwards in time' (Richardson 2002: 49). The frame-narrator-voice of the text must narrate forwards, just as the reader must fundamentally read forwards. This textual split is a clear example of the narrative concomitant of the irreversibility of time: the narrated story (Odilo Unverdorben's life as a series of ghastly events) can be narrated backwards, but the narration of those events, even in their reversed order, must progress forwards, as must also its reception in the process of reading. In narratological terms, the 'story-line' can be juggled, even reversed, as can the order in which the text is read, but 'narrative discourse' cannot, just as reading itself must proceed forwards in time. In Ricoeur's formulation, though the narrated chronology may flow in several directions, it still has to be configured into a narrative (quoted in Currie 2007: 95–96).

This necessity of the irreversibility of narrative discourse may appear to offer a bedrock of temporal certainty untainted by postmodern scepticism. In fact, it generates a more profound critique of Enlightenment temporality. The all-pervasive subject of Amis' novel is of course temporal difference, evinced in the simple narrative device of reverse time. At the foundation of Enlightenment modernity's self-understanding is its difference from earlier eras. Modernity is modern because it is supposedly, in some fundamental way, different to pre-modernity. This simple difference is then constantly replicated at the level of epochal difference, for example the nineteenth and twentieth centuries, or pre-war and postwar (de Certeau 1988: 3–4). Such differences paper over historical continuities and allow successive generations to forget that epochal difference is a mere performative gesture, albeit one with powerful and enduring effects. The epochal binary is not merely replicated along a sliding timeline; it is more significantly transmitted down to the infinite divisibility of time as discrete, atomized instants. However, this temporal difference as it has been understood since the Enlightenment, essentially the difference between before and after, is also factitious.

It is no coincidence that Amis chose the Holocaust as the central narrative seme for his novel. Many critics took him to task for an alleged disrespect for the victims of the Holocaust in his treatment of that event (Self and Amis 1993). But the Holocaust was one of the main factors to shatter the dominant sense of Western European culture's sense of its own superiority and self-legitimacy (LaCapra 2001: 175–76). Whence, for instance, Adorno's famous quip that poetry after Auschwitz is barbarism (2003: 30). Adorno's 'after', with its concomitant reduction of poetic 'high' culture to 'barbarism', upsets the Enlightenment logic of temporal priority which equates 'before' with barbarism and 'after' with modernity. The temporal disturbance that this double gesture translates thus corroborates Amis' choice of the Holocaust as the site for his questioning of Enlightenment's temporal self-identity.

The succession of a distinct 'before' and 'after' is the principal victim of Amis' postmodern narrative experiment, not by virtue of simply reversing it, but by juxtaposing two countervailing examples of that distinction, thereby confusing the very moral terms attached to it. For example, in his American life, under an assumed name, the erstwhile camp doctor does damage to his patients, sending them away from the hospital with awful injuries, whereas in Auschwitz he heals them, extracting poison from their veins and repairing the wounds caused by ghastly experiments. This grotesque reversal highlights the perversion of the Hippocratic oath embodied in spurious concentration camp medicine. The doctor's oath reposes upon an ethical imperative, *primum non nocere* (first of all, cause no harm). This 'first of all' is a temporal injunction with its attendant moral sequentiality, namely the duty to transform sickness into health. This moral sequence is complicated, but not fundamentally shaken, by the (proto-postmodern) assertion of the impossibility of returning the body to its originary state of health (Canguilhem 1978: 137). It is this moral relationship of 'before' and 'after' that Amis scrutinizes. The example of the Holocaust reveals how shaky this 'before' and 'after' really is as a supposedly stable moral, civilizational distinction.

Temporality, as I will point out in more detail in the final section of this chapter, is not a matter of succession, for succession is based on the atomization of time and the concomitant self-identity of the instant. Rather, the moment is different *within* itself. This difference does not consist of being infinitely divisible into ever smaller but always discrete sub-instants, for that would merely translate to ever smaller scales of proportion the self-identity of these instants. On the contrary, the difference within the moment is infinitely more complex, and consists of existing as and within a complex of overlapping and intersecting temporal strands. It is this heterogeneity of every moment which eschews any atomization and demands the instant be defined by the ambient temporal fabric it is part of, and not by its difference from other instants, which truly makes up temporality. The interaction of many temporal strands is the productivity inevitably emerging out of self-difference. Any moment includes within and around itself interwoven differences, and this is what generates the dynamic productivity of the material world which is time's real 'arrow'.

TOWARDS A CRITIQUE OF POSTMODERNIST TIME

Amis' performative enactment of intertwined temporalities deliberately complicates the binary before/after. To this extent, Amis' *Time's Arrow* offers an indirect commentary upon all usages of chronological series employed to underpin a term involving the prefix 'post'. Amis' novel may thus disturb the very temporal logic underlying the postmodernism it is often taken to exemplify.

As the term 'postmodernism' itself suggests, there could be no postmodernism without the modernism it claims to supersede but simultaneously perpetuates by maintaining its label as a root term. This leads Frow (1997: 13–63) to conclude that postmodernism is largely a discursive effect, produced by the logic of modernism itself. Modernism imposes a repeatedly new moment of the new, a logic which is self-contradictory, since the new cannot remain eternally new. Modernism can only be new, paradoxically, if at some point it exhausts itself. Whence the necessity of something which comes *after* modernism. Frow claims, therefore, that postmodernism is largely the result of a discursive operation which, paradoxically, proclaims the end of modernism and the advent of something which comes after it by appropriating the same epochal binary (before/after, modernism/postmodernism) as employed by modernism itself (pre-modern/modern). Postmodernism thus constitutes a repetition of modernism which is also a suppression of the evidence of that repetition. What might these aporia mean in terms of the temporal logic of postmodernism?

One of postmodern theory's main claims about temporal disarray has concerned the increasing evidence of incommensurable time-scales juxtaposed upon one another but no longer susceptible of any form of reconciliation. These temporal rifts appear to be a particularly postmodern manifestation. Heise finds a bitter-sweet example of such a disparity of timescales in Woody Allen's 1977 film *Annie Hall*. A nine-year-old boy suffers from a very Woody-Allen-ish melancholy and is sent to consult a psychologist. When asked the reason for his depression the bookish lad replies, 'the universe is expanding'. The gaping incommensurality between pre-teens blues, and the incomprehensible cosmic timescale of centrifugal effects of a fifteen-to-twenty-billion year-old big-bang, is indicative of such temporal rifts (Heise 1997: 42–43). Such chasms show that

> [o]ur image of the world now routinely includes a time scale that lies so far above human experience and all but mathematical manipulation that our time sense quite literally 'falls apart' into different temporal scales which have a simultaneous reality and yet cannot be contemplated simultaneously.
>
> (ibid: 42)

In this definition of postmodern temporalities, it is the absence of any all-encompassing paradigm to hold these scales together in a single framework which generates unresolvable dilemmas of stymied knowledge.

However, the gigantic disparities identified by Heise between a child's time and that of the universe, between nano- and cosmic-time, are merely avatars of the Modernist chasm between public and private time (Stevenson 1992: 83–124). Heise (ibid: 49–53) suggests that the precarious capacity of modernism to reconcile public and private time in narrative has been eroded by postmodern scepticism. The gap Heise finds exemplified in the Woody Allen anecdote is supposed to epitomize the temporal break which also informs the 'post' of postmodernism. Yet the very example she provides exemplifies just such a narrative articulation and negotiation of that putative temporal schism, suggesting fewer differences between modernism and postmodernism than similarities. Postmodern time increasingly looks, from this perspective, like modernist time in an accelerated, intensified form. Postmodern temporality evinces an 'exacerbation of modernity' (Frow 1997: 3), not its aftermath.

By stressing the difference *between* these apparently incommensurable timescales, Heise merely replicates the differential structure upon which Enlightenment time is based. The unbridgeable gulf between before and after re-emerges as an unbridgeable gap between synchronous but incommensurable timespans. But the chasm between nano- and cosmic-time is entirely spurious. That chasm can only appear so great in Heise's account because her version of a temporal rift suppresses the many intermediate temporal strata whose intersections and overlaps provide the real mediating strands connecting them. Heise neglects the differences *within* the connective tissue of a given temporal bundle, differences which prove to be constitutive of that complex. In the example Heise gives from Woody Allen's *Annie Hall*, some of these temporal interlays might be, *inter alia*: diaspora Jewish tradition, the vicissitudes of the psychoanalytic concept of neurosis and its narrativization in therapy and in art, the temporal life of New York City, the development of Woody Allen's own *oeuvre* (in which the film represented a significant turning point), and of course the narrative temporality of the filmic genre itself, all of which combine to create an infinitely differentiated temporal complex. The manner in which differences within *and* outside structures tend to blur the very notion of inside and outside, generating the dynamic productivity studied by chaos theory (Hofstadter 1980) has not impacted on most postmodernist theories. Greater attention to the interconnecting links between temporal regimes, or the manner in which epochal transformations are in fact highly complex composites of many forms of continuity and rupture, with multiple temporal strands intertwining, evolving, modulating into other forms, would allow a more accurate picture of temporality.

The notion of a radical but spurious caesura between modernist and postmodernist time is corroborated by Bruno Latour's even more corrosive dismantling of modernity and its putative postmodernist avatar (1993). Latour interprets modernity itself as a rhetorical gesture designating a before/after caesura. Modernity believes itself to inaugurate a new regime in which humans and nature, words and things, superstition and knowledge, once confused with each other, are now radically pared off from each other. Latour regards this division as a mere sleight of hand because, he claims, in fact 'hybrid' composites of humanity and nature continue to exist and have always done so. However, untrammelled by society's awareness of their existence, they could proliferate unmonitored in the service of technological progress, resulting in the swarms of human-technological mixes which we know today, from *in-vitro* fertilization to all the technical devices which effectively function as prosthetic extensions of our everyday activities and indeed even of our thought processes.

Latour sees in postmodernism the ultimate manifestation of a putative scission between the human and the non-human worlds which, having been the lynchpin of thinking about science and technology, is now transported into the domain of signification and meaning. According to postmodernist thought, meaning circulates among sign systems, totally separated from the world to which it is incapable of referring descriptively or connotatively (Latour 1993: 61–65, 73–74). Postmodern signifying play merely consummates the imaginary scission between 'words' and 'things' heralded by Foucault as the dawn of modernity (2002: 19–50). For words, as modernist culture knew when it celebrated the materiality of the signifier, as for example, in Dada's collaged poems, or in Freud's dream language, which uses words as if they are objects (Freud 1966: IV, 303), have never ceased to cohabit with things and display their thingness. Postmodernism, once again, appears as the perpetuation and intensification of a modernity which, however, in reality never took place. Postmodernism fulfils the same alibi function as modernity, masking an ever greater proliferation of human-natural hybrids, building upon the legacy of the rhetorical smoke-screen of a modern divorce between the human and the natural which is fictive rather than factual.

Postmodernism, then, on the one hand denies the continuities of capitalism's ultra-modernity with which, none the less, it is intimately entwined; on the other hand, this postmodernism exacerbates, under the aegis of the floating signifier, the same human/non-human divide which has allowed the undisciplined proliferation of cross-border hybrids and the alienation of humans from the places to which they owe their being. The human/non-human dichotomy facilitated the accelerated production of modernity by virtue of human/non-human hybrid constructions immune to any sort of ethical scrutiny. Postmodernism elevates this chasm to the status of an epistemological principle, thus consecrating an alibi which has merely generated the uncontrolled proliferation of often-toxic hybrids. Postmodernism thus offers little to palliate this catastrophic situation.

The abstraction of absolute time facilitated the atomization of segmented time units in order to put them back together in optimized production processes. Integral to the temporal segmentation is also the separation of the event not only from its temporal neighbours but also from its environmental fabric, not only from the 'site' in which it occurs, but also from the materiality of the very elements that make it up. This separation in turn allows the ruthless exploitation of the environment and all the material entities which constitute it. Postmodernism functions as one more alibi under whose threshold hybrid connected networks have proliferated in ways which have effectively ravaged the environment; the neglect of a more responsible participation in the natural world, and a recognition of immanent time as the dynamic interaction of beings, has had apocalyptic consequences for the global community of all beings.

BEYOND POSTMODERN TIME: TOWARDS ATTENTIVENESS TO PLURAL TEMPORALITIES

What are the alternatives? Latour urges us to become attentive to the interconnections between the human and the natural world, interconnections that the temporal caesura of modernity claimed to put behind itself. This does not mean, however, going back to some mythical pre-modern epoch. More pragmatically, it implies becoming attentive in the present moment (Nancy 2007; Waldenfels 2004) to the interconnections between the various temporal strands which make up existence, and whose dynamic becoming is time itself. This may sound excessively abstract. Two examples should help to bring out the full concrete immediacy of immanent intertwined temporalities.

John Cage's classic 1952 experimental musical composition, entitled simply 4'33", illustrates an emergent consciousness of alternative temporalities. At the inaugural performance, the pianist David Tudor sat down at the piano and did nothing except close the lid and then open it again, for 4 minutes and 33 seconds. The audience was presented with a 'framed' period of silence, four minutes and thirty three seconds long, punctuated by the closings and re-openings of the lid. Other than the wind in the trees outside the hall and the drumming of the rain on the roof, nothing was heard by the puzzled audience. Or was it? 'What they thought was silence,' Cage later said, 'because they didn't know how to listen, was full of accidental sounds' (Gann 2010: 4). By evacuating musical notes from a musical composition, Cage asked his audience to pay attention to the natural material processes of which temporal duration is concretely made up. By virtue of its title, 4'33", the piece advertises itself *as* duration, refusing to elide its own temporal materiality. It proclaims itself *as* time, rather than facilitating the common assumption that music merely occurs *in* time (as in Thomas Mann's formulation quoted earlier [1975: 541, see p. 97 above]). Cage foregrounds adjacent, overlapping temporal processes, of which music is now proclaimed to be one strand. Braidotti comments,

> In music, time can be heard. It is a pure form of time through the mediation of rhythm. ... How to make us hear the inaudible, the imperceptible, that roar which lies on the other side of silence, is what is at stake in this process.
>
> (2002: 154–55)

Time is not some sort of yardstick for measuring those transformative processes, it is the dynamism and rhythm of these processes themselves as they occur. Their self-productivity, their becoming (or un-becoming) from one moment to another are all that there is to time. Their complex overlappings and interactions make up the plural temporalities that all along have been proposed in this book as the constantly present alternative to a singular and abstract 'time'.

To get a sense of what precisely those overlappings and interactions might actually look like, I turn to a second example which may provide an allegory for a conception of the temporal interactions between multiple human and non-human actants: contemporary 'free-soloist' rock climbing. Free-soloist climbers dispense with the customary equipment of the 'assisted' ascent, such as ropes, carabiners, wedges, chocks or metal pins. Free-soloists thus rely entirely upon the interaction of their own balance/weight with the contours and texture of the cliff face:

> The free-soloists must flow up the mountain, flow or 'tack' against the downward gradient of gravity – but also must become hypersensitive tamers and channelers of the gravitational sink, masters at storing it in their muscles or making it flow through certain parts of the pelvis, thighs, palms, and this only at certain times; they must know how to accelerate the flow into a quick transfer that could make the difference between triumph and disaster, to mix and remix dynamic and static elements in endless variation.
>
> (Kwinter 2003: 29)

We customarily think of gravity as a derivative of inertia, hindering freedom, keeping things in their place. Kwinter's lyrical description unexpectedly imagines gravity as a positive flow of energy which traverses the climber's body and is diverted along the body's own paths and routes, setting up a body-gravity dynamic: 'Thus the body ... must be broken apart into a veritable multiplicity of quasi-autonomous flows – conditions on the mountainface vary critically from centimetre to centimetre' (ibid: 30). That bodily dynamic in turn facilitates the dynamic interaction of the climber and the rock face.

Similarly, common sense thinks of both climber and rock face as opposed givens, according to a scheme in which 'material objects are characterized by inertia and by temporal self-containment (i.e. by being) that the organic world enlivens (through becoming)' (Grosz 1999: 23). Here, rather, we must reimagine climber and rockface as reciprocally interconnected processes of becoming, as incarnations of immanent time in its inherent self-productivity.

What emerges out of this reconceptualization is an interaction of varying timescales:

> it is the mountainface itself whose flow is most complex, the most intractable and problematic of all. The mineral shelf represents a flow whose timescale is nearly unfathomable from the scale of duration represented by the electrolytic and metabolic processes of muscles and nerves ... nanometric in relation to the millennia that measure geological flows.
>
> (Kwinter 2003: 31)

In this conception of immanent plural temporalities, every entity becomes dynamic, flowing at a greater or lesser speed. Any situation is the sum total of the interactions between these multiple temporal flows.

If all temporal entities are dynamic, we can no longer assign agency to human or, to a lesser extent, to animal subjects, and withhold it from mineral or other non-organic entities. All these entities must be recognized as actants in their own right, acting at their own speeds. As Anne Michaels has a character say in her novel *Fugitive Memories*, '[I]t's no metaphor to hear the radiocarbon chronometer, the Geiger counter amplifying the faint breathing of the rock, fifty thousand years old' (1998: 53). It is all too easy to dismiss the 'it's no metaphor' precisely because the phrase occurs in a fiction: but we must learn to un-learn our over-hasty dismissal of nature's agency (Bastian 2009). We need to reverse the epistemological-developmental chronology according to which, in the words of Jean Rhys' protagonist in *Wild Sargasso Sea* (1966), '[L]*ong ago, when I was still babyish* [I was] sure that everything was alive, not only the rivers or the rain, but chairs, looking-glasses, cups, saucers, everything' (1968: 32; emphasis added). These literary examples themselves must be thought of as reiterated temporal speech acts, sites at which words-as-things and discourse-as-flow reactivate their participation in the dynamism of immanent time. Such speech acts have the potential power to trigger new connections and temporal dynamics around us as responsive readers.

Subsisting, then, within the interstices of an ostensibly overarching, calibrated, abstract clock-time which continues to regulate our lives and regiment the processes of contemporary economic existence, *and* the putatively incommensurable and irreconcilable nano- and macro-times of postmodern temporalities, are infinitely more complex temporalities: a plurality of interacting temporal flows immanent to the world of organic and non-organic things themselves.

In place, thus, of the human/non-human divide there emerge complex interactions between a plurality of actants, some of them organic, some non-organic (Bennett 2010). This conception of a multiplicity of human, animal, plant or mineral actors 'blurs the organic and inorganic ... by emphasising an order of ceaseless connection and reconnection ... [and] networks which are circulations, rather than entities or essences' (May and Thrift 2001: 27). The various actants inter-act in mutually independent processes which make up a bundle of plural temporalities beyond which there is no 'real' time.

Postmodern temporality is a chimera; far more real are the pre- and post-Enlightenment temporalities, newly discovered, which have always made up the world's temporal dynamism. We need to recognize anew these temporalities across the human/non-human border, and to re-find our own humble but exhilarating place within this complex but democratic order of immanent flows of becoming.

8

POSTCOLONIAL TEMPORALITIES

In his postcolonial epic *Midnight's Children* (first published 1981), Salman Rushdie has India ushered into independence (for independence, read: modernity) by the 'ticktock' of Mountbatten's countdown to political emancipation. This metonymic 'ticktock' is structured, in contrast to the normative identity-based copula between vehicle and tenor that we find in metaphor, by looser relations of causality, contiguity or association. The metaphorical English-made clock of imperial-industrial modernity, with its 'relentless accuracy', is sidelined and replaced by a more fluid metonym that functions as an index of the multiplicity of temporal schemes at work in the novel. 'Time, in my experience,' says the narrator, 'has been as variable and inconstant as Bombay's electric power supply' (Rushdie 1995: 106). In general, in Rushdie's narratives, 'Time cannot be homogenized like milk' (1984: 13), thereby making his fictions giant laboratories of 'alternative' modernities (Gaonkar, ed., 2001). Rushdie's temporal experimentation is emblematic of much postcolonial fiction, indeed of postcolonial thought in general, in the confrontation it stages with forms of temporality identified as specifically European and imperialist, and the ways it proposes alternatives that may elude this imperial time.

Temporality, in the guise of models of history, has received considerable attention in postcolonial studies. Edward Said has commented that, 'So far as Orientalism in particular and European knowledge of other societies in general have been concerned, historicism meant one human history uniting humanity. It either culminated in or was observed from the vantage point of Europe.' Western history was 'a homogenising and incorporating world historical scheme that incorporated non-synchronous elements to it' (Said 1985: 22). Robert Young has undertaken a sustained critique of this singular, teleological history with its universal pretentions (1990). History in the colonial context is supremely important, because 'History, and its associated teleology, have been the means by which European concepts of time have been naturalized for post-colonial societies' (Ashcroft 2001b: 82). The temporalities identified as those inculcated, for instance, by colonial education, were those of the forward vector of progress and incremental acquisition of civilization, which provided a legitimizing alibi for the more direct forms of exploitation carried out in the colonies by the imperial powers. Paradoxically, however, by identifying European conceptions of history as universal and singular, and then posing contestatory forms against that singularity, much postcolonial analysis of temporality has tended to replicate the very structure it critiques, 'collapsing different histories, temporalities and racial formations into the same universalizing category' (Hall 1996: 243).

This chapter begins by reviewing the ways the 'post' in 'post-colonialism', which, like the 'post-' in 'postmodern', one of its cognates (Appiah 1992: 221–54) has been intensively debated by scholars. Issues of temporal sequence are central in these debates. The chapter then goes on to critique the Orientalist binary pre-modern/modern which often survives intact in postcolonial studies, despite the discipline's questioning of chronological sequence. As an alternative to such sequential binaries it proposes, in accord with recent work on postcolonial ecocriticism but going beyond mere consideration of the 'racism/speciesism nexus' (Huggan and Tiffin 2010: 137), a renewed attention to temporalities which eschew a human/non-human schism. It exemplifies these temporal projects by readings of contemporary Caribbean and Indigenous Australian narratives.

THE POLITICS OF *POSTCOLONIALISM*

The narrow canon of works of English Literature studied in universities around the world was gradually displaced in the 1960s by a broader palette of texts belonging to what was briefly known as 'Commonwealth literature'. When the residual imperial connotations of that term became untenable, writing in English coming from outside Britain came to be known as 'post-colonial literature', subsequently acquiring the methodologies of cultural studies to become 'post-colonial studies'. The 'post' in post-colonial studies was rapidly subjected to scrutiny, as it implied an excessively simplistic periodization of colonialism and its demise. In many Latin American countries or in 'dominions' such as Australia, New Zealand and Canada, independence from the metropolis (Spain or Britain) was gained as early as the nineteenth century; yet in a number of these technically post-colonial nations, oppression of indigenous peoples continued, and indeed in a number of cases, was exacerbated after independence (Young 2001: 79). Furthermore, in many erstwhile colonies that gained independence in the decades after the Second World War, neo-colonial structures meant that postcolonialism was political but not economic. *Post*-colonialism is clearly a misnomer in a world in which colonialism lives on in neo-colonialism, and imperialism continues under another flag. Stuart Hall notes that 'In this scenario, "the colonial" is not dead, since it lives on in its "after-effects"' (1996: 248). As recently as 2008, for instance, the Australian government declared a state of emergency in the Northern Territory, brought in the army, and reintroduced measures which for many Indigenous people signalled a return to modes of repressive colonial governance (West-Pavlov 2011).

The temporal status of the 'post' in 'post-colonialism' is clearly problematic. Critiquing Ashcroft, Griffiths and Tiffin's seminal *The Empire Writes Back* (1989) for its pedagogically motivated attempt to gather up a multiplicity of postcolonial phenomena into one single definition, Hodge and Mishra claim that postcolonialism is far too complex to allow such a brief: '[W]e are really talking about not one "post-colonialism" but many postcolonialisms.' They distinguish between two sorts of postcolonialism, 'viewed as ideological orientations rather than as a historical stage': first, the 'more readily recognizable [variant], is ... oppositional postcolonialism, which is found in its most overt form in post-independent colonies at the historical phase of "post-colonialism" (with a hyphen)'. The second variant, 'equally a product of processes that constituted colonialism but with a different inflection, is a "complicit post-colonialism" ... an always present "underside" within colonialization itself' (Hodge and Mishra 1993: 284). The hyphen, in their usage, has a temporal valency. Its presence ('post-colonialism') thus signals some sort of rupture in a strictly historical sense. The absence of the hyphen ('postcolonialism'), by contrast, points at the ways in which postcolonialism both precedes independence, *and* remains entangled with colonialism in its various historical forms, especially after the historical demise of colonialism. As exemplifications of these temporal anomalies, Hodge and Mishra mention Australian colonial writers, such as Charles Harpur, Marcus Clarke or Christopher Brennan, who were members of a colony striving towards autonomy, but also engaged in highly ambiguous relationships with the indigenous culture, or V. S. Naipaul, a writer with a strong ideological commitment to the erstwhile colonial undertaking in a postcolonial age.

Hodge and Mishra's own 'fused' term 'post(-)colonialism' (1993: 288) represents a typographical attempt to acknowledge the difficulty of keeping these two varieties apart, and is perhaps also an acknowledgement of the danger of binarism lurking even in their apposite critique. Many theorists of postcolonialism have sought to complicate the temporalities of colonialism, post-colonialism and neo-colonialism in similar manner. Hall detects something like Hodge and Mishra's non-hyphenated 'post-colonial' in all these epochs, from two points of view. On the one hand, the 'post' in 'postcolonialism' charts a significant caesura, in which colonization as a major, extended, and world-historical event becomes the bearer of a global process of violent transformation. As Hall puts it,

> It is the retrospective re-phrasing of Modernity within the framework of 'globalisation' in all its various ruptural forms and movements (from the Portuguese entry to the Indian Ocean and the conquest of

the New World to the internationalisation of financial markets
and information flows) which is the really distinctive element in a
'post-colonial' periodisation.

(Hall 1996: 250)

On the other hand, the 'post' in 'postcolonial' reflects a contestatory
vision triggered by colonization itself, from the very outset: a
disrupted, decentred way of seeing, 'a critical epistemic shift
within the colonizing process' (1996: 252). If, as Hall suggests,
'"Colonialism" refers to a specific historical moment (a complex
and differentiated one ...) ... it was also a way of staging or
narrating a history' (1996: 253), so that *post*colonialism signified a
mode of resistant thinking emerging at the moment of colonization
itself and disrupting its own self-legitimizing narratives. In Gaylard's
formulation, 'postcolonialism is not just a time period, but an
idea' (2005: 314). Thus, in similar vein, if Shohat understands
the 'post' in 'postcolonial' as fallaciously signalling 'closure of a certain historical event or an age', she also glosses the prefix as enabling
a 'going beyond ... commenting upon a certain intellectual movement' (1992: 101, 108) which inhabited colonialism, eroding it
from within, from its founding moments.

HISTORY WITHOUT TIME

If the colonial epoch, in such formulations, has been already interpreted as containing anachronic 'postcolonial' impulses which
worked to bring about the historical end of colonial rule, the nature
of the forces activated by such impulses remains a subject of debate.
Often, despite the dismantling of the binary sequence colonialism/
postcolonialism, another binary creeps in through the back door
of postcolonial studies to explain such forces: modernity versus
pre- or countermodernity. Foucault, responding to interrogations
by his Japanese translator, attempts to break up the unicity of a
single Eurocentric history: 'European space is not space in its
entirety ... there is not a single history ... there are several histories,
several durations ... two durations, two evolutions, two lines of
history' (1994: III, 581; my translation).[1] The single history is
supplanted by a duality hardly less schematic. Ganguly comments

on 'the ways in which ... the postcolonial has been taken to represent an "other" time whose logic and historical expression have been incommensurable with the normative temporalities of clock and calendar associated with western modernity' (2004: 162). For Homi Bhabha, for instance, postcoloniality contains a 'contra-modernity' that introduces 'other, incommensurable cultural temporalities into the invention of tradition' (1994: 2). Rushdie's evocation of 'closed systems, under intense pressure, [where] time can be persuaded to run backward, so that effects precede their causes' (1984: 22) points towards this putatively retrograde counter-modernity. Effectively, postcolonial theory has often worked with an 'exclusionary' model of time which 'neglected the study of the "distant" past, positing instead the anteriority against which modern regimes of power have supposedly arisen' (Cohen 2003: 19). Postcolonial theory questions modes of colonial knowledge which legitimized geopolitical domination, but even at the moment of denouncing such frameworks for exploitation, it has often still held on to a binary notion of modernity and premodernity imposed by the Orientalist perspectives instrumental in colonization; or it has simply made pre-modernity a positive attribute without questioning the Orientalist binary at work as part of its definition.

How did that binary arise? The universalizing nature of European history was not simply given, but rather *produced* by the contact with other cultures assumed to be primitive in proportion to their distance from Europe, as one commentator observed in 1800: 'The ... traveller, sailing to the ends of the earth, is in fact tra-velling in time; he is exploring the past; every step he makes is the passage of an age' (Degérando 1969: 63). At a larger scale of analysis, history emerged out of the specific chronology of imperial expansion's growing purchase on the colonized world. As Dipesh Chakrabarty has observed,

Historicism is what made modernity or capitalism ... global *over time*, by originating it in one place and then spreading outside it. ... Historicism thus posited historical time as the measure of cultural distance ... that was assumed to exist between the West and the non-West.

(2000: 7)

The trajectory of individual or cultural movement away from Europe was projected onto a linear sequence which ran counter to the direction of travel.

That linear sequence, however, was rarely graduated. Backwards travel meant travel out of a single global history into a temporal void. Non-European societies, according to Fabian (1983: 35), have been subject to an 'all-pervading denial of coevalness' and thereby deemed to exist, via 'a cosmological myth of frightening magnitude and persistency', in a radically other timeframe. Thus Africa, for instance, for the early nineteenth-century German philosopher Hegel, 'forms no historical part of the World; it exhibits no movement or development' (1956: 91; translation modified).[2] Likewise, the Martinique writer and theorist Edouard Glissant describes 'the Caribbean notion of time [as] fixed and stabilized in the void of an imposed nonhistory' (1989: 65; translation modified).[3] Non-European society waits, immobile and timeless, to be drawn into the slipstream of a European trajectory of progress that is dynamic and forward-looking. Thus Marx could write in 1853: 'Indian society has no history at all, at least no known history. What we call its history is but the history of its successive intruders who founded their empires on the passive basis of that unresisting and unchanging society' (1969: 132–33). Invasion is merely the obverse side of assimilation: both bring time to the primitive world, or bring the primitive world into time. The rapport between time and timelessness can oscillate, albeit within strictly circumscribed limits. V. S. Naipaul writes vindictively of a thinly disguised Congo after it has thrown off the yoke of colonialism, 'You were in a place where the future had come and gone' (2002: 30). Briefly, it would seem, the colony had hooked itself onto the chariot of progress, albeit in a clearly subsidiary relationship, only to now fall by the wayside back into a temporal void. Once out of time, always out of time.

The logic of Europe's temporal self-conception dictates that non-Europe must be a temporal abyss. Mbembe suggests that modernity is a largely self-referential term which Europe uses to define itself, arising out of its own engagements with tradition and authority since the Enlightenment. It is thus an essentially tautological term (Modernity = the West = Modernity = ...) (2001: 9–11). To this extent it does not engage with its others, but simply negates them, working 'to deny African societies any historical depth and to define them as radically *other*, all that the West is not' (2001: 11). Mbembe claims, then, that modernity's principal function, when applied to other cultures, is to castigate them for their non-modernity *in order* to constitute itself as modernity. It is for this reason that the binary modernity/pre-modernity, even when its negative term is recast as a positive force, may continue to poison the emancipatory projects it informs.

Thus Chakrabarty, discussing peasant religious beliefs as a factor in subaltern agitation in Indian pre-independence history, comments that historical analysis can ascribe agency to the belief in gods, but not to the gods themselves who are supposed to have participated in the making of history in peasant narratives. The historian cannot invoke the supernatural in explaining the event. There is no resolution between these various experiences of historicity, only an 'irreducible plurality in our own experiences of historicity' (2000: 104, 108). Mishra and Hodge (2005) perpetuate just such evocations of the pre-modern in suggesting that such elements (ancestral spirits, mythical beings) may be the key to a rejuvenation of the discipline of postcolonial studies. They argue that '[o]nly by contemplating itself in the past tense', by which they mean attending to the temporalities discredited and marginalized by the modern,

> may postcolonialism still continue into the future. The past it needs to accommodate includes a serious engagement with those premodern (and countermodern) tendencies that colonial instrumentalism systematically excised under the sign of the rational 'man' ... those life-worlds of spirits, myths, religions, indeed of poetry, that cannot be explained in totally modern terms, but which are nevertheless (as sites of contradmodernity) so essential for a proper postcolonial reconstruction.
>
> (2005: 391–92)

In the Australian context, this binary has been identified as an Antipodean variation of a *differend*, a dispute based on incommensurable founding claims which thus cannot be resolved but must be negotiated (Gelder and Jacobs 1998: 18–20). The binary of modernity and pre- or counter-modernity continues to hamper postcolonial studies, even when it poses as an emancipatory strategy opening the discipline up to other regimes of belief and epistemology.

In what follows I suggest that in order to dissolve this binary, it is necessary to abandon the sequence it relies upon altogether, whose underlying structure is that of segmented absolute time. In its place, it would be helpful to take up a notion of overlapping, non-segmented temporal planes which credit many actants with agency. In this way, such putatively pre-modern elements such as nature religions, mythological beings, or ancestral spirits might be understood differently, along with many other human, non-human, organic and non-organic, material and immaterial actants whose being would be that of the continuous becoming of the world.

PLURAL TEMPORALITIES

The postcolonial critique of the singular linear temporality of colonialism has been superseded in recent years by a broad critical consensus that colonial and postcolonial histories in fact consist of a plurality of heterogeneous temporalities. Postcolonial temporality is 'a plurality of times existing together' (Chakrabarty 2000: 109); it is emphatically 'not a series but an *interlocking* of presents, pasts and futures that retain their depths of other presents, pasts and futures, each age bearing, altering and maintaining the previous ones' (Mbembe 2001: 16). For the Irish context Lloyd has proposed a complex dialectic of modernity and its predecessors in which

> Formations that are recalcitrant to capitalist logic, and therefore targeted for destruction are in the first place not backward remainders of outmoded traditions, but already themselves adaptations of older formations in response to previous confrontation with earlier forms of modernization. What that implies is ... that modernity does not replace tradition, but that modern forms and institutions emerge in differential relation to their non-modern and recalcitrant counterparts.
>
> (Lloyd 2008: 4)

In a not dissimilar manner, Edouard Glissant, whose texts I will focus on here, uses the Caribbean, with its history of transplantation and mixing of very diverse populations, as a test case for just such an interlocking of plural temporalities. Such multiple temporalities are dramatized in Glissant's novel *Mahogany* (1987), which fictionalizes the layered co-existence of multiple Caribbean time-planes: 'we have acquired the habit of jumping from one time to another: our times link up with each other' says the narrator Matthieu Béluse (Glissant 1987: 158).[4]

However, it is not enough merely to multiply and overlay the sequences of historical events. More decisively, the sequences themselves must be retrieved from their reified isolation from their environment. Walter Benjamin, in his seventeenth thesis on the philosophy of history, observes of historicism that '[i]ts method is additive; it musters a mass of data to fill homogeneous, empty time.' (Benjamin 1999: 254; translation modified).[5] This version of linear, sequential (additive) time is homogeneous because it is empty, and empty because its context and environment have been cleared away, leaving an arena to be filled by events alone. The linear shape of temporality is thus the result of a streamlining and pruning process which abstracts its trajectory from the tangled thickets of being in which events are immersed. Linear time is connected, at the very most, to other events, in relationships of simultaneity (Foucault 2007: 8), but not to their environs. Faithful to this logic, Coetzee's violent Vortrekker figure in *Dusklands* (first published 1978) boasts that 'the master-myth of history [has] outdated the fiction of the symbiosis of earth and heaven' (2004: 26). Glossing such attitudes, Glissant notes that 'History and Literature agree ... to separate man from the world, to subject nature to culture', but in place of this violent decontextualization and isolation of things and events, he proposes a newly evident 'product of the link between nature and culture' (1989: 73, 92). His fictions flesh out such a programme.

The narrator of Glissant's *Mahogany* tries to reconstruct a Caribbean history, first of all, by the respectable method of a 'collection of dates', which is nothing more than a 'series of erasures in the mess of time'. This form of historiography is merely complicit in the ontological rarefaction (whence 'erasures') upon which 'homogeneous' time depends. Rapidly, however, he discovers other 'relationships and equivalences', namely, connections through multiple layers of past, present and future: 'I wouldn't be the last negro runaway slave in this history/story, even though there were no longer any fugitives on the hills ... I was pure Contamination' (1987: 28).[6] This oxymoronic 'pure Contamination' articulates the essence of Glissant's sense of multiple temporalities. The confused lines of historical destiny repose upon a hybrid mixture of human and natural interactions. This is why the main characters of Glissant's recon-structed history, the *marrons* or runaway slaves, are so important. In their persons, the alienation of plantation labour gives way to a symbiosis with the natural environment that offers them refuge. This is also why, in Glissant's novel, trees are characters on a par with human beings, emblematizing a nature-culture relationship which even the narrator only gradually comes to understand: 'I didn't make the connection between the ebony trees and the mahogany ... I didn't enter the unity of the place' (ibid: 20).[7] Little by little, the complexity of these Caribbean temporalities, silenced by Euro-historicism, emerges. It is located at ground-level, at the point where the visibility of trees, and their hidden root systems, converge symbiotically:

> But in truth, what hovered at the level of the grass silvered by the wind or between the rotting trunks framing the moss under the ebony trees was the withdrawn, silenced clamour ... buried in the earth itself to the point of spreading the giant ants, subterranean dwellers, to the four corners of the land ...
>
> (ibid: 19)[8]

The tree is both a visible sign in the landscape, but also rooted in the earth in ways that are not immediately evident. The tree emble-matizes a non-sequential plurality of temporalities (a 'clamour') inti-mately linked to its environment. The opening lines of *Mahogany* are programmatic: 'A tree is a whole country, and if we ask what this country may be, immediately we plunge down to the dark rootedness of time that we are labouring to clear of brushwood' (ibid: 13).[9] Why? the reader asks. 'The reason is that [a tree] reads/spells out/deciphers the forest, whose depths it multiplies everywhere' (ibid: 13).[10] The tree, by virtue of its root and branch systems, is one with the forest. That 'forest of the runaway slave' was the 'first obstacle the slave opposed to the transparency of the planter. There is no clear path, no straight line, in this density.' The forest thus becomes emblematic of a contestatory nature-culture spacetime-complex subsisting in the interstices of European historiography and its singular, rarified, reified linearities (Glissant 1989: 83, 85). Glissant's evocation of these multiple temporalities of Caribbean history makes its trajectories inextricable from nature. Their dynamism is intimately linked to the impetuous growth of tropical life itself. Temporalities are indistinguishable here from life-processes, both human and natural, better defined as a 'pure Contamination' of the human-natural world.

Postcolonial temporalities, as exemplified in the work of Glissant, thus lay bare apparent tangles of plural, non-sequential historical processes which cannot be abstracted from the regenerative processes of nature itself. If we are not to fall back into the polarized, binary structures of European dichotomies, however, we must pursue this 'pure Contamination' back to Europe. The 'pure Contamination' that Glissant foregrounds in his novels and criticism eschews just such spatio-temporal dichotomies and thus imposes the task of conceptualizing European modernities as equally hybrid and entangled.

European modernity itself is neither singular nor free from ambivalence. European modernity itself depends upon an internal temporal 'other' often provided, for instance, by constructions of the medieval period (Johnston 2008). Horkheimer and Adorno's (2002) notion of the brutal shadow-side (or dialectic) of Enlightenment, together with Latour's (1993) dismissive claim that Europeans 'have never been modern', imply that European modernity itself is riven with contradictions, more heterogeneous than it is customarily prepared to admit.

From there, it is only a step to opening up modernity's own contradictory temporalities to the other temporalities with which it has always co-existed in a hybridized interweaving. These entanglements have been heavily conflicted, with other temporal regimes being re-worked to suit the purposes of European modernities; the latter, however, have been transformed in the process, so that the sum total of temporalities we now inhabit is inescapably hybrid and plural in character. Contemporary modernities are far from being 'singular', and nor are they in any simple way 'of the same age' (*pace* Jameson 2003a, Fabian 1983: 159). None the less, there are good reasons for accepting 'the mutual embeddedness of European and "non-Western" history' (Ganguly 2004: 169) even as we might wish to reject the insidiously recurring binarism manifest even here. Their material histories have become inextricably intertwined with each other through the workings of imperialism, colonization and globalization. Likewise, conceptualizations of history, in which it is no longer possible to prise apart the theories of European thinkers (for instance Hegel, see Young 1990) and non-European critics, or vice-versa, as in an African concept such as 'ubuntu', which states that humans only gain their humanity in relation to other humans, have been reciprocally influential. We thus live in a postcolonial world in which countless temporalities make up plural, hybrid 'modernities' and whose analysis ultimately resists the implementation of such categories as 'pre-modern', 'Enlightenment', 'post-colonial'. What might such multiple, entangled histories mean when interpreted as the intertwined temporal dynamics of multiple planes of becoming?

ENTANGLED MULTIPLANAR TEMPORALITIES

In contemporary Australia, such a reciprocal contamination of 'Euromodernities' and traditional temporalities has taken place in a now inextricable process of usually conflictual entanglement. In its 1992 Mabo decision, the Australian High Court ruled that, contrary to previous *terra nullius* understandings, traditional Indigenous ownership of territory could persist unbroken from before the arrival of white settlers in 1788 and the massive displacement, dispossession and indeed genocide which ensued. Subsequent legislation made it possible for Indigenous groups to lodge claims for the reassertion of traditional land ownership where an unbroken connection and a continuity of traditional practices could be proven (Butt, Eagleson and Lane 2001).

Paradoxically, the land rights legislation demanded as proof of ownership the very sorts of continuity which had been virtually obliterated in the long two-hundred year war of attrition against Indigenous culture and the confiscation of Indigenous territory upon which it was based. The very necessity to reassert ownership was predicated upon the loss of ownership, whose proof then became the precondition for return. Equally paradoxical was the demand for proof of 'authentic traditional' continuities from a hegemonic white society which had, until a decade before, actively pursued various policies contributing to the destruction of such continuities of 'authentic' traditional culture (Povinelli 2005), most prominently through sustained and widespread child removal practices that broke up families, disrupted communal solidarity and interrupted the transmission of traditional lore (Haebich 2000; Holt 2001; HREOC 1997; Mellor and Haebich, eds, 2002).

These double-bind demands frequently placed Indigenous people in an impossible position, one frequently encountered by those once-colonized peoples seeking to reconstruct traditional culture. Hegemonic European culture demanded, in a post-traditional epoch, as fossilized historical artefact or as legal evidence, the very authenticity whose demise it had actively brought about. Such demands for a frozen authenticity ignore, by contrast, the more dynamic and resilient temporalities of Indigenous cultural survival, and constant negotiation with and adaptation to invasive modernities (Muecke 2004). Eze's description of the dilemma of the African writer articulating a relationship to past oral tradition is emblematic in this respect:

> On one level, the tradition one presumably writes about, or out of, is experienced by the writer as alive – a source of inspiration and creativity. But on another level, the writer also knows that the tradition in question has been 'damaged' and transformed in an irreversible manner. In fact, the act of writing is itself a mark of the time of deconstruction, transformation and renewal.
>
> (Eze 2008: 26)

These entangled questions about the status of overlapping temporalities, ancient, modern, nostalgic, recuperative, eroded, or resilient, are characteristic of postcolonial societies. They are typical of the temporal phenomenon Mbembe has described as 'the postcolony', which 'encloses multiple *durées* made up of discontinuities, reversals, inertias, and swings that overlay one another, interpenetrate one another, and envelope one another: an *entanglement*' (2001: 14).

Correspondingly, under the conditions of postcolonial reconciliation and reparation, Indigenous people in Australia often operate within heterogeneous and contradictory temporal frameworks. In order to clarify what this might mean, let us examine two examples from Indigenous Australia. One group lodging a land claim found themselves fighting for Catholic mission lands they had occupied since the 1950s, rather than the 'genuinely' traditional lands from which they had migrated in response to the missionaries' offer of employment and education. Thus the appeal to traditional ownership, based on a long period of connection and ritual and myth, and involving notions of timeless traditional ownership, had to be adapted or appropriated for a more recent, and thus putatively 'inauthentic' past, with its own clearly dated history of connection (Duelke 2008: 110–14). What emerged was a newly forged connection to land and place, not faked or fraudulent, but drawing upon various 'polychronic' temporal regimes, the 'timeless' traditional past versus the recent timed past, and the rhetorical resources, involving appeal to the repertoire of customary law and collective ritual in ancient and contemporary versions, associated with those regimes (ibid: 116).

Over and above such heterogeneous temporal regimes, however, the 1992 Mabo decision brought into contemporary Australian modernity an understanding of the land, characterized by the denotation of 'country' and rendered generic by the absence of the article, which unsettles even further such hybrid temporalities (see Rose 1996: 6–15). Indigenous lore reposes upon two fundamental concepts which transform extant notions of temporality. The first is that the ancestral past is embodied in the country itself. Features of the landscape or creatures of nature *are* the Dreaming ancestors, so that the 'past does not so much precede the present, as lie contained within it' (Rickard 1996: 4). The second is that the landscape is endowed with a powerful agency which makes human beings mere residues or 'manifestations of place' (Scott 2009). Greer has gone as far as suggesting that 'aboriginality ... is ... a characteristic of the continent itself' (2003: 72). Together, these two precepts

make the landscape an embodiment of ongoing, immanent temporalities constituted by nature itself as a community of actants,
including human beings as subordinate custodians in those processes (Rose 1996: 6–15; Swain 1993). Thus in Kim Scott's
Benang (1999), a narrative which traces both the twentieth-century
destruction of Indigenous society and late twentieth-century
attempts to recuperate Indigenous culture and identity, it is place
which plays a central role:

> Here.
> Here.
> Here.

(Scott 1999: 189)

These deictic markers create their own sequence, one which is
chronological within the textual discourse as activated by the
reader, but stubbornly eschews any temporality which is not that
of the land itself, or of its custodial response, the twinned Indigenous
customs of travelling along a dreamtime track and recounting successively the stories associated with its respective sacred sites. Such
markers contradict the customary ego-based notion of language's
capacity to point to place. Rather, they understand these deictic
speech acts as responding to and drawing upon an agency which
enables them. That agency is dynamic and ongoing: the fabric of the
multiple entwined temporalities of the land which underpin and bear
along the productivity of language itself (cf. West-Pavlov 2010).

At a late stage in Scott's story, when the protagonist has made
contact with family members and is visiting traditional country
on the coast with them, his attention is drawn to a bird hovering
above the rocks and the sea. 'I felt something particular about the
place, reminding me of something, somewhere, some other occasion. ... "That bird wants us," I said ... "That bird is trying to
tell us something."' The protagonist tells his elderly relatives
about this, and they reply: '"Those birds. That was the spirit of
the land talking to you. Birds, animals, anything can do it. This
is what we Aboriginal people see"' (1999: 453–55). Place, natural
actants, and a past which is present in 'country', are manifest in such
experiences. Textually re-enacted as what Bakhtin (1981: 84–85)

termed a '**chronotope**', a complex of concept and image whose dimensions are both spatial and temporal at once, they empower other actants, and thus trigger a mode of environmentally immanent 'remembering forward' (König, Evans and Falk 2011) which provides genuine alternative temporalities for our own late-colonial, late-modern, late-capitalist age.

CONCLUSION

In this volume, I argue that absolute time emerged in the Enlightenment as a radically disruptive understanding of temporality that abstracted it from the spatial sites and the material processes of being and production that it had previously inhabited. Enlightenment time replicated this abstraction within itself, segmenting time into atomized units susceptible of measurement and quantification. This, in turn, provided the template for a plethora of modern conceptions and material practices: for the reified, commodified object; for the monadic bourgeois individual hollowed out by the desire and greedily searching for satisfaction in the acquisition of consumer goods; for the periodization of history, the banishing of the past, and the denial of coevalness to people deemed to live in 'pre-history'; and for the instrumentalization and depletion of actants, whether animal, vegetable or mineral, of nature. Above all, the extraction and abstraction of time has been implicated in and driven by the forces of merchant, industrial and finally speculative finance capital. Absolute time is thereby implemented as a measure of productivity, reflecting the reification of the commodities it contributes to producing.

Against this still hegemonic model of absolute time, I argue for an alternative model of multiple temporalities which are immanent to the very processes of material being itself in all its manifestations. Whether human, animal, vegetable or mineral, all being is 'a continuous stream of occurrence' (Whitehead 1920: 172), an 'uncaused causality that ceaselessly generates new forms' (Bennett 2010: 117). Its dynamism constitutes the very momentum of time itself. These temporalities are specific to the processes whose energy they are identical with, and to the particular sites they inhabit. These temporalities are not abstracted from place, but provide the infinitely heterogeneous manifestations of what modern physics calls 'spacetime'. In a previous book I sought to open up a forum for the agency of 'place' (West-Pavlov 2010); the present book complements that concept by describing the immanent temporality which constitutes that agency; together these two concepts make up a multifaceted model of 'spacetime'. A notion of multiple, heterogeneous, immanent temporalities embedded in what is henceforth recognizable as a dynamic, generative 'spacetime' is of inestimable significance because it casts into question the entire structure of our modernity with its destructive tendencies.

In the service of capitalism, the separation of time and space has been heavily involved in two closely interrelated processes of subjugation: that of colonized peoples and their territories, and that of exploited natural resources and their biotopes. These distinct processes have become visible as two faces of the same phenomenon since the advent of globalization. Awareness of the global, gendered 'international division of labour' (Spivak 1999: 274), the global climate problem, global economic crises (Harvey 2006), and global food shortages (Ambler-Edwards *et al.* 2009) have contributed to our consciousness of an interconnected complex of problems, of potentially cataclysmic proportions. If the Enlightenment project, with its central 'racism/speciesism nexus' (Huggan and Tiffin 2010: 137) depended upon a fundamental time/space schism, recent scientific and philosophical theory brings these two terms back together.

Fabian has analysed the alternate mobilization of both space and time in the colonial relationship when he writes that:

[I]t is not difficult to transpose from physics to politics one of the most ancient rules which states that it is impossible for two bodies to occupy the same space at the same time. When in the course of colonial expansion a western body politic came to occupy, literally, the space of an autochthonous body, several alternatives were conceived to deal with the violation of that rule. The simplest one, if we think of North America and Australia, was of course to move or remove the other body. Another one is to pretend that space is being divided and allocated to separate bodies. South Africa's rulers cling to that solution. Most often the preferred solution has been simply to manipulate the other variable — Time. With the help of various devices of sequencing and distancing one assigns to conquered populations a *different* Time.

(Fabian 1983: 28–29)

Curiously, however, this 'denial of coevalness' (ibid: 35) implements space (geographical distance from the West) to assert an absolute temporal difference. Colonial exploitation wielded a perverse version of 'spacetime' which produced a spurious non-connection between colonizers and colonized. It created in the process hybrid connections between Western and non-Western spaces and technologies which produced the colonial and neo-colonial relationship and the various power relations they imply, as well as the commodities flowing out of that power differential (e.g. cash crops, cheap clothing), and the environmental changes which have ensued. If twentieth-century physics coined the term 'spacetime' to overcome the Enlightenment scission of time and space, it was in fact merely laying bare time-space-hybrids which had never ceased to proliferate since the advent of absolute time.

However, physics, although it produced the first refutation of that separation by providing the concept of 'spacetime', has none the less failed to engender, in popular consciousness, a counterpoise to the hegemony of absolute time and space. Similarly, Liberal humanism posited the singularity of the human in opposition to the natural world of things: analogously, abstract absolute time extracted temporality from the things to which time had previously been immanent. This dual separation was the precondition for a code of ethical conduct predicated on the refusal to treat people like things. This ethical code, however, has manifestly failed to realize its promise; on the contrary, it has produced an exclusionary definition of the human (generally, white, European, Christian, male) which has underpinned most of the discriminatory and exploitative practices of recent centuries (Bennett 2010: 11–12). Both the sciences and liberal humanism, then, have failed to provide a counterbalance to the exploitation of humans and of the global environment. A new collaboration between the sciences and the humanities, foregrounding novel forms of attentiveness to 'spacetime', is required. Such collaboration would be capable of suggesting an ethics of the interconnectedness of the human and the non-human. By furthering a recognition of their common material dynamism, agency and creativity, this sort of collaboration would contribute to a different morality on the basis of shared but heterogeneous temporalities.

One impulse within this book, then, is descriptive, seeking to map the emergence and transformation of concepts of time over past centuries, in particular since the Enlightenment. Another impulse is critical, motivated by the conviction that absolute time is partial and biased, and that its obfuscated imbrications with capitalism in its various guises need to be laid bare. Clearly, however, the critical brief of the humanities does not suffice to induce real societal change. A third impulse in this book, then, is utopian, gesturing at possible models and alternative conceptions of temporalities which would possess the potential to significantly inflect the way humans interact with their environments. This utopian project would begin, precisely, by revising the very binary of humans versus the environment:

> In lieu of an environment that surrounds human culture, or even a cosmos that cleaves into three ecologies, picture an ontological field without any clear demarcation between human, animal, vegetable or mineral. All forces or flows (materialities) can become lively, affective, and signaling.
>
> (Bennett 2010: 116–17)

A fundamental recognition of such flows as the very substance of time would be anything but idealist. Even ideas are material actants, and open up engagement with other actants in ways which can transform real practices.

Rather than issuing critiques of power which all too often merely work to provide an alibi activity for erstwhile radicals (Bachelard 1966: 14–17; Grosz 2005: 2–3; Paulson 2001), such utopian intellectual work would seek to provide imaginations of feasible alternatives to extant models with concretely conceivable results. Jane Bennett asks,

> How would political responses to public problems change if we were to take seriously the vitalism of (nonhuman) bodies? ... How, for example, would patterns of consumption change if we faced not litter, rubbish, trash, or 'the recycling', but an accumulating pile of lively and potentially dangerous matter? What difference would it make to the course of energy policy were electricity to be figured not simply as a resource, commodity, or instrumentality but also and more radically as an 'actant'?
>
> (2010: viii)

Such a brief, explicitly pragmatic and political in its scope, would seek ways of recognizing anew the agency of immanent temporalities so as to curtail the myopic and destructive annexation of agency by humanity at the expense of its own planetary conditions of possibility. Such a brief would propose a new role for literary-philosophical enquiry as a subset of the 'experimental humanities' (Muecke 2012) working within existing knowledge networks via all the genres of exploratory thought (philosophy, art, fiction, poetry, mixed-genre writing, film, documentary, performance, etc.).[1] Producing performative models of a multiplicity of immanent 'space-times' would contribute to restoring ethical relationships not only between human actors but also with the many natural actants of the animal, vegetable and mineral environment. Such instantiations of the 'experimental humanities' would understand themselves not as meditations 'about' time, but as exemplifications of the creative agency of immanent temporalities themselves. The very temporality of the 'experimental humanities' would resonate with the non-linear, unpredictable dynamism of the universe itself in its becoming. Thus, as Liz Grosz (2004: 261) suggests, 'The task is not so much to plan for the future, organize our resources towards it, to envisage it before it comes about, for this reduces the future to the present. It is to make the future, to invent it.' Or even better, to be invented by it.

These experimental humanities would resonate with the polymath sciences of the early modern age, one of whose central figures, Sir Francis Bacon, posited that 'innovations ... are the births of time', taking his attribution of agency a step further to proclaim that 'time is the greatest innovator' (1999: 63). This book seeks to emulate such an eclectic purview in its attempt to provide a brief overview of theories of temporality across a range of disciplines from philosophy via historiography, narratology, gender studies, psychology, cognitive theory, through to economics, and postmodern and postcolonial theory. In the time of its writing, as it has come to be inhabited by multiple concepts and language constructs with their own agency, it has embodied something of the unceasing generativity of the immanent temporalities it describes. I believe that in its reception for you as readers, the book's conceptual and linguistic actants will continue to exert their unpredictable agency, thus generating in 'non-linear' fashion, unforeseeable, indeed turbulent waves of innovation and creativity around it as it follows its own trajectories through 'spacetime'.

Glossary

absolute time also known as Newtonian time, this was a concept of time which enabled modern scientific procedure by providing a standard of time measurement which was extracted from local particularities. It was deemed by Newton to flow evenly and without regard to external influences.

actant a term which ascribes agency to any entity, whether human or non-human, whether animal, vegetable, mineral, or even conceptual. It seeks to dismantle the wall between creatures and things, between sentient and non-sentient beings, broadening the palette of active power to work upon other beings and thus make change happen.

asyndeton a rhetorical strategy which consists of separating from one another certain syntactic elements which would normally be placed next to one another.

atomic time abbreviated to TAI, a time measurement based upon the radiation cycles of Caesium 133.

chronotope a term coined by the Russian literary scholar Mikhail Bakhtin to describe a conceptual literary image which combines the dimensions of spatiality and temporality.

commodity an object produced within the capitalist industrial economy for sale on the market.

cosmological time Ricoeur's term for an encompassing time framework which envelopes and exceeds all human experience of time and thus eludes explanation or comprehension within human understanding, and in particular narrative.

delta time abbreviated to ΔT, a time measurement based upon the difference between UT (universal time) 1 and atomic time (TAI), is employed by astronomers to calculate planetary positions.

differend a concept coined by the French philosopher Jean-François Lyotard to describe a controversy or debate in which no consensus or closure can be reached because the underlying assumptions of the warring partners are fundamentally incommensurable.

ellipsis a rhetorical strategy which consists of omitting certain words.

episteme a term invented by the French philosopher Michel Foucault to describe the tacit categories of knowledge underlying and making possible, at a given historical epoch, a whole range of forms of knowledge, scientific disciplines and the statements that could be made within them.

escapement a mechanism which allowed the primary driving force of a clock (a spring or a weight) to be released in doses. This stop-go mechanism could then be harnessed to calibrate the passage of time in a measured rhythm and attached to a time indicator such as an hour- or minute-hand.

GPS Global Positioning System using a network of satellites to allow users of a GPS device to exactly determine the position of a point on the earth's surface.

Greenwich Mean Time the reference time for universal time, set at Greenwich Observatory in London, at the so-called Prime Meridian, i.e. the longitudinal ground-zero from which all geographic measurements are derived.

intertextuality a term coined by Julia Kristeva to describe the way in which any text, deliberately or not, is constructed of citations from, allusions to, and echoes or fragments of earlier texts, which may or may not be visible to the writer and to readers.

latitude the east–west grid of measurements of positions on the earth's surface determined by distances (in 'hours' and 'minutes' and 'seconds') from the equator. Together with longitude allows the precise identification of any point on the earth's surface.

longitude the north–south grid of measurements of positions on the earth's surface determined by distances (in 'hours' and 'minutes' and 'seconds') from the Prime Meridian passing through Greenwich, London. Together with latitude, it allows the precise identification of any point on the earth's surface.

metaphor/metonymy two closely linked tropes which replace one literal term by a more poetic equivalent. Metaphor connects 'vehicle' and 'tenor' by a relationship of identity or substitution; metonymy links them by a looser relationship of contiguity, causality or association.

Nachträglichkeit German word meaning 'retroactiveness'; it refers to the manner in which unconscious memories are re-worked, after the event, into another form which takes their place, so that the original memory becomes inaccessible.

performativity A concept, elaborated on the basis of Austin's and Searle's linguistic 'speech act' theories, of the ways in which reiterated enactments of certain linguistic attributions gives them the appearance of substantive reality. What language then purports to describe as an objectively existing reality, such as masculine or feminine gender, can thus be deconstructed as the coagulation of a set of attributes repeatedly evoked by acts of language that take effect in material ways (so-called 'performatives'), but are conversely susceptible of transformation by subsequent, differing acts of language.

reification Marx's term for the ways in which entities become 'things', isolated from their context and stripped of their connections to a prior history of production.

relativity Einstein's Theories of Relativity showed that time could not exist independently of space, but that they influenced each other reciprocally. Time could only be measured from a specific local context. Einstein's special theory of relativity (1905) dealt with the relative movements of bodies and the manner in which this impacted upon time, while the general theory of relativity (1916) expanded the earlier theory to include the influence of gravitational fields upon the measurement of time.

signifier/signified a distinction made by the linguist de Saussure to tease out the material sign (the word, whether written or spoken) from the concept it denotes.

spacetime a term coined by modern physics to take into account the inextricable interrelatedness of the concepts of space and time. Together they make up a 'space–time continuum' used for instance to explain time-dilation or curved space.

story/discourse a distinction originally conceptualized by Shklovsky, and elaborated by Chatman, Genette and others, between the 'what' and the 'how' of story-telling. 'Story' refers to the chronological sequence of events as they might have occurred in reality; 'discourse' refers to the order in which they are recounted in narrative (and also to the frequency and duration of their occurrence within the narrative).

trauma refers to the effect of experiences so horrific that they resist capture in representational or narrative form. Because they cannot be encompassed within narrative, that is, cast in the closure and pastness of a story, these experiences often persist in modes of repetition or recurrence, such as nightmares.

universal time The global articulation of times to Greenwich Mean Time, abbreviated to 'UT', with internal discrepancies, such as UT0 (the ideal standard), UT1 (which takes into account variations in the rotation of the earth so as to produce an astronomical and navigational norm), UT2 (UT1 corrected to take account of seasonal oscillations) and UTC (Universal Coordinated Time, or Global Mean Time).

use-value/exchange-value Marx's distinction explaining how the pragmatic utility of an object is transformed into its economic value on the market.

Notes

INTRODUCTION

1 On a number of occasions where an English translation fails to convey the subtlety of the original as it pertains to issues of temporality, I modify the translation, giving the original in the endnotes so as to facilitate comparison. Compare Mann's German: 'Was ist die Zeit? Ein Geheimnis – wesenlos und allmächtig' (1991: 472).

2 Compare Ricoeur's French: 'notre hypothèse de travail revient ainsi à *tenir le récit pour le gardien du temps*, dans la mesure où il ne serait de temps que raconté' (1983–85: III, 349). The extant English translation ('our working hypothesis thus amounts to taking narrative as a guardian of time, insofar as there can be no thought about time without narrated time' [1984–88: III, 241]) removes Ricoeur's italics, changes the article determining 'guardian' from a privileged 'the' to a vaguer 'a', and expands and thus weakens Ricoeur's tightly elliptical final clause by adding an 'about' to 'time'.

2 PHILOSOPHIES OF TIME

1 Marx's German: 'Es ist nicht mehr der Arbeiter, der die Produktionsmittel anwendet, sondern es sind die Produktionsmittel, die den Arbeiter anwenden. Statt von ihm als stofflicher Element seiner produktiven Tätigkeit verzehrt zu werden, verzehren sie ihn als Ferment ihres eigenen Lebensprozesses, und der Lebensprozeß des Kapitals besteht nur in seiner Bewegung als sich selbst verwertender Wert' (1975: I, 329).

2 Some exceptions, such as Rumania, Russia and Turkey, remained right up into the early twentieth century (Osterhammel 2009: 92).

3 A much more comprehensive list of the plurality of calendars in use around the globe up until the present time can be found in Osterhammel 2009: 89–93.

4 Heidegger's German: 'das, von wo aus Dasein überhaupt so etwas wie Sein unausdrücklich versteht und auslegt'; '*Horizont des Seinsverständnisses*' (1953: 17).

5 Heidegger's German: 'Die Übernahme der Geworfenheit ist aber nur so möglich, dass das zukünftige Dasein sein eigenstes "wie es schon war", das heißt sein "Gewesen", *sein* kann. Nur sofern Dasein überhaupt *ist* als bin-gewesen, kann es zukünftig auf sich selbst so zukommen, dass es *zurück*-kommt' (1953: 325–26).

6 Fraser's (1978) insistence upon a hierarchy of scales of time represents an attempt to resist the ineluctable complexity of the world as processual dynamics.

7 Bergson's French: 'Or, la vie est une évolution. Nous concentrons une période de cette évolution en une vue stable que nous appelons une forme, et, quand le

changement est devenu assez considérable pour vaincre l'heureuse inertie de notre perception, nous disons que le corps a changé de forme. Mais, en réalité, le corps change de forme à tout instant. Ou plutôt il n'y a pas de forme, puisque la forme est de l'immobile et que la réalité est mouvement. Ce qui est réel, c'est le changement continuel de forme: *la forme n'est qu'un instantané pris sur une transition*. Donc, ici encore, notre perception s'arrange pour solidifier en images discontinues la continuité fluide du réel' (1932: 327).

3 HISTORIES

1 Foucault's French: 'un redoublement empirico-transcendental ... cette étrange figure où les contenus empiriques de la connaissance délivrent, mais à partir de soi, les conditions qui les ont rendus possibles ... la transparence immédiate et souveraine d'un cogito' (1966: 333).
2 Gadamer's expression is 'angesprochen' (1965: 266), translated by Weinsheimer and Marshall as 'addressed' (Gadamer 2004: 283); I have deliberately adopted Althusser's (1972: 175, 181) notion of 'interpellation'.

4 LANGUAGE AND DISCOURSE

1 Ricoeur's French: '*tenir le récit pour le gardien du temps*'; 'la temporalité ne se laisse pas dans le discours direct d'une phénoménologie, mais requiert la médiation du discours indirect de la narration' (1983–85: III, 349). See my comments in note 2 to the Introduction.
2 Sartre's French: 'l'objet littéraire est une étrange toupie, qui n'existe qu'en mouvement. Pour le faire surgir, il faut un acte concret qui s'appelle la lecture, et elle ne dure qu'autant que cette lecture peut durer' (Sartre 1970: 52).
3 Mann's German: 'Die Zeit ist das Element der Erzählung, wie sie das Element des Lebens ist' (1991: 738).
4 I have deliberately given a more playful translation of Blanchot's phrase: 'L'œuvre de Proust est un œuvre achevée-inachevée' (1986: 36). The title of his book, *Le livre à venir*, 'the book to come', contains a homophonic pun on *Le livre-avenir*, 'the book as futurity'.
5 The title of the English translation, *The Order of Things*, chosen because Ernst Gellner had already published a book entitled *Words and Things*, loses the central importance of the original French title, *Les Mots et les choses* (Foucault 1966).
6 Once again, see my comments in note 1 to the Introduction.

5 GENDER AND SUBJECTIVITY

1 De Beauvoir's French: 'On ne naît pas femme: on le devient' (De Beauvoir 1976: II, 13).

6 ECONOMICS

1 Thompson's now classic account of time structuring and time discipline has been subject to a number of trenchant critiques. See, for instance, Glennie and Thrift 1996, May and Thrift 2001.

2 For alternative modes of memory in South Africa, see Part II, 'Sites of Memory and Identity' in Murray, Shepherd and Hall, eds 2007: 83–180.

8 POSTCOLONIAL TEMPORALITIES

1 Foucault's French: 'l'espace européen n'est pas l'espace dans son entier ... on vit dans une série d'espaces polymorphes. ... il n'y a pas qu'une seule histoire ... il y en a plusieurs, plusieurs temps, plusieurs durées ... deux vitesses, deux évolutions, deux lignes d'histoire' (1994 : III, 581).

2 Hegel's German: 'Afrika ... ist kein geschichtlicher Weltteil, er hat keine Bewegung oder Entwicklung aufzuweisen' (1961: 163).

3 Glissant's French: 'le temps antillais ... stabilisé dans le néant d'une non-histoire imposée' (1981: 133).

4 Glissant's *Mahogany* has not been translated into English. All translations here are my own. Glissant's French: 'nous avons pris l'habitude de sauter d'un temps à un autre: nos temps se relaient' (1987: 158).

5 Benjamin's German: 'Ihr Verfahren ist additiv: sie bietet die Masse der Fakten auf, um die homogene und leere Zeit auszufüllen' (Benjamin 1991: I.2, 722).

6 Glissant's French: 'Je me voyais ainsi ramené à mon recueil de dates, à ma série de ratures dans l'embrouillé du temps, à mes projets de mise en relations, d'équivalences; pour finir, à cette épure de personnage dont j'avais voulu m'évader. Je ne serais pas le dernier nègre marron de cette histoire, tout de même qu'il n'en restait pièce sur les mornes. Tout autant que cet auteur, j'étais le pur Contaminé' (1987: 28).

7 Glissant's French: 'je n'établissais pas le rapport des ébéniers au mahogani ... que je n'entrais pas dans l'unicité du lieu' (1987: 20).

8 Glissant's French: 'Mais à la vérité, ce qui flottait au ras de l'herbe argentée par le vent ou entre les souches pourrissantes qui cadraient la mousse sous les ébéniers, c'était la clameur tue, rentrée ... à fond dans la terre elle-même, jusqu'à éparpiller aux quatre coins du pays les fourmis-folles, habitants des profondeurs' (1987: 19).

9 Glissant's French: 'Un arbre est tout un pays, et si nous demandons quel est ce pays, aussitôt nous plongeons à l'obscur indéracinable du temps, que nous peinons à débroussailler' (1987: 13).

10 Glissant's French: 'C'est qu'il épelle la forêt, dont il multiplie partout la profondeur' (1987: 13).

CONCLUSION

1 I wish to thank Stephen Muecke for telling me about his projects in the field of the 'experimental humanities', and for providing me with a pre-publication copy of his work in this area (Muecke 2012).

Bibliography

Adorno, Theodor W. (2003) *Kulturkritik und Gesellschaft I: Prismen; Ohne Leitbild.* Frankfurt am Main: Surhkamp.

Agamben, Giorgio (1998) *Homo Sacer: Sovereign Power and Bare Life.* Trans. Daniel Heller-Roazen. Stanford, CA: Stanford University Press.

Agnew, Vanessa (2004) 'Introduction: What Is Reenactment?' *Criticism* 46.3 (Summer): 327–39.

——(2007) 'History's Affective Turn: Historical Reenactment and its Work in the Present.' *Rethinking History* 11:3 (September): 299–312.

Althusser, Louis (1972) *Lenin and Philosophy and Other Essays.* Trans. Ben Brewster. New York: Monthly Review Press.

——(1997) *Reading Capital.* Trans. Ben Brewster. London: Verso.

Ambler-Edwards, Susan, Kate Bailey, Alexandra Kiff, Tim Lang, Robert Lee, Terry Marsden, David Simons, Hardin Tibbs (2009) *Food Futures: Rethinking UK Strategy: A Chatham House Report.* London: Royal Institute of International Affairs. URL: www.chathamhouse.org.uk/files/13248_r0109foodfutures.pdf Accessed 18 October 2010.

Amis, Martin (1992) *Time's Arrow.* Harmondsworth: Penguin.

Anderson, Benedict (1991) *Imagined Communities: Reflections on the Origin and Spread of Nationalism.* London: Verso.

Appiah, Kwame Anthony (1992) *In My Father's House: Africa in the Philosophy of Culture.* London: Methuen.

Apter, Emily (2010) 'Women's Time in Theory.' *Differences* 21.1: 1–18.

Aristotle (1952) *The Physics.* Trans. Philip Wicksteed and F. M. Cornford. London: Heinemann/Cambridge, MA: Harvard University Press. 2 volumes.

Ashcroft, Bill, Gareth Griffiths and Helen Tiffin (1989) *The Empire Writes Back: Theory and Practice in Post-Colonial Literatures.* London: Routledge.

Ashcroft, Bill (2001a) *On Post-Colonial Futures: Transformations of Colonial Culture.* London: Continuum.

——(2001b) *Postcolonial Transformation.* London: Routledge.

Attwood, Bain (1996) 'Introduction: The Past as Future: Aborigines, Australia and the (dis)course of History', in Attwood, ed. *In the Age of Mabo: History, Aborigines and Australia.* St Leonards, NSW: Allen & Unwin: vii–xxxviii.

Augustine, Saint (1961) *Confessions.* Trans. R. S. Pine-Coffin. Harmondsworth: Penguin.

——(1972) *City of God.* Trans. Henry Bettenson. Harmondsworth: Penguin.

Bachelard, Gaston (1966) *La Philosophie du non: Essai d'une philosophie du nouvel esprit scientifique.* Paris: Presses universitaires de France.

Bacon, Sir Francis (1999) *Essays.* ed. Michael J. Hawkins. London: J. M. Dent.

——(2001) *The Advancement of Learning*. Ed. Stephen Jay Gould. New York: Modern Library.

Baird, Theodore (1936) 'The Time Scheme of *Tristram Shandy* and a Source.' *PMLA* 51: 803–20.

Bakhtin, Mikhail (1981) *The Dialogic Imagination: Four Essays*. Ed. Michael Holquist. Trans. Vadim Liapunov and Kenneth Brostrom. Austin, TX: University of Texas Press.

Bal, Mieke (1997) *Narratology: Introduction to the Study of Narrative*. 2nd edn. Toronto: University of Toronto Press.

Balzac, Honoré de (1955) *Old Goriot*. Trans. Marion Ayton Crawford. Harmondsworth: Penguin.

Baroni, Raphaël (2009) 'Tellability', in Peter Hühn, John Pier, Wolf Schmid and Jörg Schönert, eds *Handbok of Narratology*. Berlin: de Gruyter: 447–54.

Barth, John (1969) *Lost in the Funhouse: Fiction for Print, Tape, Live Voice*. New York: Bantam.

Barthes, Roland (1977) *Image – Music – Text*. Trans. Stephen Heath. New York: Hill & Wang.

Bastian, Michelle (2009) 'Inventing Nature: Re-Writing Time and Agency in a More-than-human World.' *Australian Humanities Review* 47 (November): 99–116.

Bateson, Gregory (1974) *Steps to an Ecology of Mind*. New York: Ballantine Books.

Baucom, Ian (2005) *Specters of the Atlantic: Finance Capital, and the Philosophy of History*. Durham, NC: Duke University Press.

Baudrillard, Jean (1998) *The Consumer Society: Myths and Structures*. Trans. Chris Turner. London: Sage.

Beauvoir, Simone de (1972) *The Second Sex*. Trans. H. M. Parshley. Harmondsworth: Penguin.

——(1976) *Le deuxième sexe*. Paris: Gallimard/Folio. 2 volumes.

Bellow, Saul (1977) *Dangling Man*. Harmondsworth: Penguin.

Benjamin, Walter (1991) *Gesammelte Schriften*. Ed. Rolf Tiedmann et.al. Frankfurt am Main: Suhrkamp. 7 volumes.

——(1999) *Illuminations*. Ed. Hannah Arendt. Trans. Harry Zohn. London: Pimlico.

——(2002) *The Arcades Project*. Trans. Howard Eiland and Kevin McLaughlin. Cambridge, MA: Belknap Press/Harvard University Press.

Bennett, Jane (2010) *Vibrant Matter: A Political Ecology of Things*. Durham, NC: Duke University Press.

Bennett, Jill (2000) 'The Aesthetics of Sense-Memory: Theorising Trauma through the Visual Arts', in Franz Kaltenbeck and Peter Weibel, eds *Trauma und Erinnerung / Trauma and Memory: Cross-Cultural Perspectives*. Vienna: Passagen: 81–95.

Bennett, Tony (1979) *Formalism and Marxism*. London: Methuen.

Berger, Peter L. and Thomas Luckmann (1971) *The Social Construction of Reality: A Treatise in the Sociology of Knowledge*. Harmondsworth: Penguin.

Bergson, Henri (1911) *Creative Evolution*. Trans. Arthur Mitchell. New York: Henry Holt.

——(1932) *L'Évolution créatrice*. 38th edn. Paris: Alcan.

Bhabha, Homi K. (1994) *The Location of Culture*. London: Routledge.

Biarne, J. (1984) 'Le temps du moine d'après les premières règles monastiques d'occident (IVe–VIe siècles)', in *Le Temps du Chrétien de la fin de l'antiquité au moyen âge, IIIe–XIIIe siècles*. Paris: Editions du CNRS: 100–128.

Blanchot, Maurice (1986) *Le livre à venir*. Paris: Gallimard/folio essais.

Bohm, David (1965) *The Special Theory of Relativity*. New York: W. A. Benjamin.

Borges, Jorge Luis (1976) *Labyrinths*. Trans. John M. Fein, Dudley Fitts, James E. Irby, Anthony Kerrigan, Julian Palley and Donald A. Yates. Harmondsworth: Penguin.

Bourdieu, Pierre (1977) *Outline of a Theory of Practice*. Trans. Richard Nice. Cambridge: Cambridge University Press.

Bowie, Malcolm (1993) *Psychoanalysis and the Future of Theory*. Oxford: Blackwell.

Bradley, A. C. (1905) *Shakespearean Tragedy: Lectures on Hamlet, Othello, King Lear, Macbeth*. 2nd edn. London: Macmillan.

Braidotti, Rosi (2002) *Metamorphoses: Towards a Materialist Theory of Becoming*. Oxford: Polity.

Bridgeman, Teresa (2007) 'Time and Space', in David Herman, ed. *The Cambridge Companion to Narrative*. Cambridge: Cambridge University Press: 52–65.

Bruner, Jerome (1991) 'The Narrative Construction of Reality.' *Critical Inquiry* 18: 1–21.

Budlender, Debbie, ed. (2010) *Time Use Studies and Unpaid Care Work*. London: Routledge.

Burkhardt, Martin (1997) *Metamorphosen von Zeit und Raum*. Frankfurt am Main: Campus.

Butler, Judith (1990) *Gender Trouble*. New York: Routledge.

——(2005) *Giving an Account of Oneself*. New York: Fordham University Press.

Butter, Michael (2009) 'Zwischen Affirmation und Revision populärer Geschichtsbilder: Das Genre *alternate history*', in Barbara Korte and Sylvia Palatschek, eds *History goes Pop: Zur Repräsentation von Geschichte in populären Medien und Genres*. Bielefeld: Transcript: 65–82.

Butterfield, Herbert (1955) *Man in his Past: The Study of the History of Historical Scholarship*. Cambridge: Cambridge University Press.

Butt, Peter, Robert Eagleson and Patricia Lane (2001) *Mabo, Wik and Native Title*. Canberra, ACT: Federation Press.

Calvino, Italo (1982) *If on a Winter's Night a Traveller*. Trans. William Weaver. London: Picador.

Camden, William (1971) *Camden's Britannia, 1695: A Facsimile of the 1695 Edition Published by Edmund Gibson, Translated from the Latin*. Ed. Stuart Piggott and Gwyn Walters. Newton Abbott: David & Charles.

Canguilhem, Georges (1978) *The Normal and the Pathological*. Trans. Carolyn R. Fawcett. Dordrecht: Reidel.

Capra, Fritjof (1983) *The Turning Point: Science, Society and the Rising Culture*. London: Flamingo.

Carter, Paul (1987) *The Road to Botany Bay: An Essay in Spatial History*. London: Faber & Faber.

Chakrabarty, Dipesh (2000) *Provincializing Europe: Postcolonial Thought and Historical Difference*. Princeton, NJ: Princeton University Press.

——(2002) *Habitations of Modernity: Essays in the Wake of Subaltern Studies*. Chicago: University of Chicago Press.

——(2009) 'The Climate of History: Four Theses.' *Critical Inquiry* 35: 2 (Winter): 197–222.

Chatman, Seymour (1978) *Story and Discourse: Narrative Structure in Fiction and Film*. Ithaca, NY: Cornell University Press.

Chaucer, Geoffrey (1974) *The Complete Works of Geoffrey Chaucer*. ed. N. F. Robinson. 2nd edn. Oxford: Oxford University Press.

Cipolla, Carlo M. (1978) *Clocks and Culture 1300–1700*. New York: Norton.

Clampitt, Amy (1991) *Westward*. London: Faber.

Cockburn, Bruce (1983) 'The Trouble with Normal', Golden Mountain/BMI. Vinyl 1982, digitally remastered 2002. URL: http://cockburnproject.net/albums/thetroublewithnormal.html. Accessed 24 June 2011.

Coetzee, J. M. (1987) *Foe*. Harmondsworth: Penguin.

——(2004) *Dusklands*. London: Vintage.

Cohen, Jeffrey J. (2003) *Medieval Identity Machines*. Minneapolis: University of Minnesota Press.

Colebrook, Claire (2009) 'Stratigraphic Time, Women's Time.' *Australian Feminist Studies* 24.59 (March): 11–16.

Conrad, Joseph (1969) *Joseph Conrad's Letters to R. B. Cunningham Graham*. ed. C. T. Watts. Cambridge: Cambridge University Press.

——(1983) *The Secret Agent: A Simple Tale*. Oxford: Oxford University Press/World's Classics.

——(1990) *Heart of Darkness and Other Tales*. Oxford: Oxford University Press/World's Classics.

——(1991) *Lord Jim*. Oxford: Oxford University Press/World's Classics.

Cowan, Harrison J. (1958) *Time and Its Measurement*. Cleveland, OH: World Publishing Company.

Culler, Jonathan (1981) *The Pursuit of Signs: Semiotics, Literature, Deconstruction*. London: Routledge & Kegan Paul.

Currie, Mark (1998) *Postmodern Narrative Theory*. Basingstoke: Macmillan.

——(2004) *Difference*. London: Routledge.

——(2007) *About Time: Narrative, Fiction and the Philosophy of Time*. Edinburgh: Edinburgh University Press.

Damasio, Antonio R. (1999) *The Feeling of What Happens*. London: Vintage.

Davies, Ben and Jana Funke (2011) 'Introduction: Sexual Temporalities', in Ben Davies and Jana Funke, eds *Sex, Gender and Time in Fiction and Culture*. Basingstoke: Palgrave Macmillan: 1–16.

Davies, Paul (1996) *The Big Questions: Paul Davies in Conversation with Philip Adams*. Camberwell, VIC: Penguin.

De Certeau, Michel (1988) *The Writing of History*. Trans. Tom Conley. New York: Columbia University Press.

Degérando, Joseph (1969) *The Observation of Savage Peoples*. Trans. and ed. F. C. T. More. Berkeley: University of California Press.

De Landa, Manuel (1997) *A Thousand Years of Non-Linear History*. New York: Zone Books/Swerve Editions.

Deleuze, Gilles and Félix Guattari (1983) *Anti-Oedipus*. Trans. Robert Hurley et. al. London: Athlone.

Dening, Greg (1992) *Mr Bligh's Bad Language: Passion, Power and Theatre on the Bounty*. Cambridge: Cambridge University Press.

Derrida, Jacques (1973) *Speech and Phenomena, and Other Essays on Husserl's Theory of Signs*. Trans. David B. Allison. Evanston, IL: Northwestern University Press.

——(1976) *Of Grammatology*. Trans. Gayatri Chakravorty Spivak. Baltimore: Johns Hopkins University Press.

——(1982) *Margins of Philosophy*. Trans. Alan Bass. Chicago: University of Chicago Press.

——(1994) *Specters of Marx: The State of the Debt, the Work of Mourning, and the New International*. Trans. Peggy Kamuf. New York: Routledge.

——(1998) *Archive Fever: A Freudian Impression*. Trans. Eric Prenowitz. Chicago: University of Chicago Press.

Desroche, Henri (1979) *The Sociology of Hope*. Trans. Carol Martin-Sperry. London: Routledge & Kegan Paul.

Dickens, Charles (1985) *Hard Times*. Harmondsworth: Penguin.

Dinshaw, Carolyn, Lee Edelman, Roderick A. Ferguson, Carla Freccero, Elizabeth Freeman, Judith Halberstam, Annamarie Jagose, Christopher Nealon and Nguyen Tan Hoang (2007), 'Theorizing Queer Temporalities: A Roundtable Discussion.' *GLQ: A Journal of Lesbian and Gay Studies* 13.2–3: 177–95.

Donne, John (1964) *The Poems of John Donne*. ed. Herbert Grierson. London: Oxford University Press.

Dostal, Robert J. (1993) 'Time and Phenomenology in Heidegger and Husserl', in Charles Guignon, ed. *The Cambridge Companion to Heidegger*. Cambridge: Cambridge University Press: 141–69.

Duelke, Britta (2008) 'Quoting from the Past or Dealing with Temporality', in Tyrus Miller, ed. *Given World and Time: Temporalities in Context*. Budapest: Central European University Press: 105–29.

Dux, Günter (1989) *Die Zeit in der Geschichte: Ihre Entwicklungslogik vom Mythos zur Weltzeit*. Frankfurt am Main: Suhrkamp.

Eco, Umberto (1995) *The Island of the Day Before*. Trans. William Weaver. Orlando, FL: Harcourt Brace.

Einstein, Albert (1952a) 'The Foundation of the General Theory of Relativity', in H. A. Lorentz, A. Einstein, H. Minkowski and H. Weyl. *The Principle of Relativity: A Selection of Original Memoirs of the Special and General Theory of Relativity*. New York: Dover: 111–64.

——(1952b) 'On the Influence of Gravitation on the Propagation of Light', in H. A. Lorentz, A. Einstein, H. Minkowski and H. Weyl. *The Principle of Relativity: A Selection of Original Memoirs of the Special and General Theory of Relativity*. New York: Dover: 99–108.

——(2001) *Relativity: The Special and the General Theory*. Trans. Robert W. Lawson. London: Routledge.

Elam, Diane (1993) 'Postmodern Romance', in Bill Readings and Bennet Schaber, eds *Postmodernism Across the Ages: Essays for a Postmodernity That Wasn't Born Yesterday*. Syracuse, NY: Syracuse University Press: 216–31.

Elias, Norbert (1993) *Time: An Essay*. Trans. Edmund Jephcott. Oxford: Blackwell.

Eliot, George (1991) *Middlemarch*. Oxford: Oxford University Press/World's Classics.

Eliot, T. S. (1982) *The Complete Poems and Plays of T. S. Eliot*. London: Faber & Faber.

Erlich, Victor (1980) *Russian Formalism: History – Doctrine*. 4th edn. The Hague: Mouton.

Ermath, Elizabeth Deeds (1992) *Sequel to History: Postmodernism and the Crisis of Representational Time*. Princeton, NJ: Princeton University Press.

Eze, Emmanuel Chukuwudi (2008) 'Language and Time in Postcolonial Experience.' *Research in African Literatures* 39.1 (Winter): 24–47.

Fabian, Johannes (1983) *Time and the Other: How Anthropology Makes its Object*. New York: Columbia University Press.

Felski, Rita (2000) *Doing Time: Feminist Theory and Postmodern Culture*. New York: New York University Press.

Ferguson, Arthur B. (1979) *Clio Unbound: Perception of the Social and Cultural Past in Renaissance England*. Durham, NC: Duke University Press.

Ferguson, Niall, ed. (1999) *Virtual History: Alternatives and Counterfactuals*. New York: Basic Books.

Foer, Jonathan Safran (2006) *Extremely Loud and Incredibly Close*. London: Penguin.

Forester, C. S. (1970) *Gold from Crete*. Boston: Little Brown.

Foster, John Bellamy, Brett Clark and Richard York (2010) *The Ecological Rift: Capitalism's War on the Earth*. New York: Monthly Review Press.

Foucault, Michel (1966) *Les Mots et les choses: une archéologie des sciences humaines*. Paris: Gallimard.

——(1990) *Politics, Philosophy, Culture: Interviews and other Writings 1977–84*. ed. Lawrence Kritzman. London: Routledge.

——(1991) *Discipline and Punish: The Birth of the Prison*. Trans. Alan Sheridan. Harmondsworth: Penguin.

——(1994) *Dits et écrits 1954–1988*. ed. Daniel Defert and François Ewald. Paris: Gallimard. 4 volumes.

——(2002) *The Order of Things: An Archaeology of the Human Sciences*. Trans. A. M. Sheridan Smith. London: Routledge.

——(2007) *The Archaeology of Knowledge*. Trans. A. M. Sheridan Smith. London: Routledge.

Francese, Joseph (1997) *Narrating Postmodern Time and Space*. Albany: State University of New York Press.

Frank, Joseph (1963) *The Widening Gyre: Crisis and Mastery in Modern Literature*. New Brunswick, NJ: Rutgers University Press.

Fraser, J. T. (1978) *Time as Conflict: A Scientific and Humanistic Study*. Basel: Birkhäuser.

——(1990) *Of Time, Passion, and Knowledge: Reflections on the Strategy of Existence*. 2nd edn. Princeton, NJ: Princeton University Press.

Freeman, Elizabeth (2007), 'Introduction.' *GLQ: A Journal of Lesbian and Gay Studies* 13.2–3: 159–74.

Freud, Sigmund (1966) *The Standard Edition of the Complete Psychological Works of Sigmund Freud*. Trans. James Strachey. London: Hogarth Press. 24 volumes.

Frow, John (1997) *Time and Commodity Culture: Essays in Cultural Theory and Postmodernity*. Oxford: Clarendon Press/Oxford University Press.

Frye, Northrop (1957) *Anatomy of Criticism: Four Essays*. Princeton, NJ: Princeton University Press.

Fukuyama, Francis (1992) *The End of History and the Last Man*. New York: Avon.

Fussner, F. Smith (1962) *The Historical Revolution: English Historical Writing and Thought, 158–1640*. New York: Columbia University Press.

Gadamer, Hans-Georg (1965) *Wahrheit und Methode: Grundzüge einer philosophischen Hermeneutik*. Tübingen: J. C. Mohr (Paul Siebeck).

——(2004) *Truth and Method*. 2nd rev. edn. Trans. Joel Weinsheimer and Donald G. Marshall. London: Continuum.

Galison, Peter (2003) *Einstein's Clocks and Poincaré's Maps: Empires of Time*. New York: W. W. Norton.

Ganguly, Keya (2004) 'Temporality and Postcolonial Critique', in Neil Lazarus, ed. *The Cambridge Companion to Postcolonial Literary Studies*. Cambridge: Cambridge University Press: 162–79.

Gann, Kyle (2010) *No Such Thing as Silence: John Cage's 4'33"*. New Haven, CT: Yale University Press.

Gaonkar, Dilip Parameshwar, ed. (2001) *Alternative Modernities*. Durham, NC: Duke University Press.

Gaylard, Gerald (2005) *After Colonialism: African Postmodernism and Magical Realism*. Johannesburg: Wits University Press.

Gelder, Ken and Jane M. Jacobs (1998) *Uncanny Australia: Sacredness and Identity in Postcolonial Australia*. Melbourne: Melbourne University Press.

Genette, Gérard (1980) *Narrative Discourse*. Trans. Jane E. Lewin. Oxford: Blackwell.

Gibbon, Edward (1994) *The Decline and Fall of the Roman Empire*. London: Random House/Everyman. 6 volumes.

Giddens, Anthony (1982) *Profiles and Critiques in Social Theory*. London/Basingstoke: Macmillan.

——(1990) *The Consequences of Modernity*. Stanford, CA: Stanford University Press.

Gide, André (2000) *The Immoralist*. Trans. David Watson. Penguin: Harmondsworth.

Gleick, James (1988) *Chaos: Making a New Science*. London: Cardinal/Sphere.

Glennie, P. and Thrift, Nigel (1996) 'Reworking E. P. Thompson's "Time, Work-discipline and industrial capitalism" '. *Time and Society* 5.3: 275–99.

Glissant, Edouard (1989) *Caribbean Discourse: Selected Essays*. Trans. J. Michael Dash. Charlottesville: University Press of Virginia.

——(1987) *Mahogany*. Paris: Seuil.

——(1981) *Le Discours antillais*. Paris: Seuil.

Grafton, Anthony (2007) *What Was History? The Art of History in Early Modern Europe*. Cambridge: Cambridge University Press.

Gray, Jeremy (1989) *Ideas of Space: Euclidean, Non-Euclidean and Relativistic*. 2nd edn. Oxford: Clarendon Press.

Green, André (2002) *Time in Psychoanalysis: Some Contradictory Aspects*. London: Free Association Books.

Greer, Germaine (2003) *Whitefella Jump Up: The Shortest Way to Nationhood. Quarterly Essay* 11. Melbourne: Black Inc.

Grosz, Elizabeth (2004) *The Nick of Time: Politics, Evolution and the Untimely.* Durham, NC: Duke University Press.

——(1999) 'Thinking the New: Of Futures Yet Unthought', in Elizabeth Grosz, ed. *Becomings: Explorations in Time, Memory, and Futures.* Ithaca, NY: Cornell University Press: 15–28.

——(2005) *Time Travels: Feminism, Nature, Power.* Durham, NC: Duke University Press.

Guha, Ranajit and Gayatri Chakravorty Spivak, eds (1988) *Selected Subaltern Studies.* New York: Oxford University Press.

Guha, Ranajit, ed. (1997) *A Subaltern Studies Reader 1986–1995.* Minneapolis: University of Minnesota Press.

Gurvitch, Georges (1964) *The Spectrum of Social Time.* Trans. Myrtle Korenbaum. Dordrecht: Riedel.

Haebich, Anna (2000) *Broken Circles: Fragmenting Indigenous Families 1800–2000.* Fremantle, WA: Fremantle Arts Centre Press.

Hamilton, Paul (2002) *Historicism.* 2nd edition. London: Routledge.

Hall, Stuart (1996) 'When Was "The Postcolonial"? Thinking at the Limit', in Iain Chambers and Lidia Curti, eds *The Post-Colonial Question: Common Skies, DiviDed Horizons.* London: Routledge: 242–60.

Hanley, R., ed. (2004) *Moving Goods, People and Information in the 21st Century: The Cutting-Edge Infrastructures of Networked Cities.* London: Routledge.

Harper, Kenneth E. (1954) 'A Russian Critic and *Tristram Shandy.*' *Modern Philology* 52 (November): 92–99.

Harris, Jonathan Gil (2009) *Untimely Matter in the Time of Shakespeare.* Philadelphia: University of Pennsylvania Press.

Harris, Robert (1993) *Fatherland.* London: Arrow.

Harvey, David (1989) *The Condition of Postmodernity: An Enquiry into the Origins of Cultural Change.* Oxford: Basil Blackwell.

——(2006) *The Limits to Capital.* 2nd rev. edn. London: Verso.

——(2010) *The Enigma of Capital and the Crises of Capitalism.* London: Profile.

Hayles, N. Katherine (1990) *Chaos Bound: Orderly Disorder in Contemporary Literature and science.* Ithaca, NY: Cornell University Press.

Hegel, G. W. F. (1956) *The Philosophy of History.* Trans. J. Sibree. New York: Dover.

——(1961) *Philosophie der Geschichte.* ed. Theodor Litt. Stuttgart: Reclam.

Heidegger, Martin (1953). *Sein und Zeit.* New edn. Tübingen: Niemeyer.

——(1962) *Being and Time.* Trans. John Macquarie and Edward Robinson. Oxford: Blackwell.

Heise, Ursula K. (1997) *Chronoschisms: Time, Narrative, and Postmodernism.* Cambridge: Cambridge University Press.

Herodotus (1961) *The Histories.* Trans. Aubrey de Sélincourt. Penguin: Hamondsworth.

Hesiod (2006) *Theogony – Works and Days – Testimonia.* Trans. Glenn W. Most. Cambridge, MA: Harvard University Press.

Hill, Christopher (1972) *The World Turned Upside Down: Radical Ideas During the English Revolution.* London: Temple Smith.

Hobsbawm, Eric (1992) 'Introduction: Inventing Traditions', in Eric Hobsbawm and Terence Ranger, eds *The Invention of Tradition*. Cambridge: Cambridge University Press/Canto: 1–14.

Hodge, Bob and Vijay Mishra (1993) 'What is Post(-)Colonialism?', in Patrick Williams and Laura Chrisman, eds *Colonial Discourse and Post-Colonial Theory: A Reader*. Brighton: Harvester Wheatsheaf: 276–90.

Hofstadter, Douglas R. (1980) *Gödel, Escher, Bach: An Eternal Golden Braid*. Harmondsworth: Penguin.

Holford-Strevens, Leofranc (2005) *The History of Time: A Very Short Introduction*. Oxford: Oxford University Press.

Holt, Albert (2001) *Forcibly Removed*. Broome, WA: Magabala.

Horkheimer, Max and Theodor W. Adorno (2002) *Dialectic of Enlightenment*. Trans. Edmund Jephcott. Stanford, CA: Stanford University Press.

Hospital, Janette Turner (1990) *Charades*. London: Virago.

——(1993) *The Last Magician*. London: Virago.

Hoy, David Couzens (2008) 'The Politics of Temporality: Heidegger, Bourdieu, Benjamin, Derrida', in Tyrus Miller, ed. *Given World and Time: Temporalities in Context*. Budapest: Central European University Press: 261–76.

HREOC (Human Rights and Equal Opportunities Commission) (1997) *Bringing Them Home: Report of the National Inquiry on the Removal of Aboriginal and Torres Strait Islander Children from their Families*. Canberra: AGPS.

Huggan, Graham and Helen Tiffin (2010) *Postcolonial Ecocriticism: Literature, Animals, Environment*. London: Routledge.

Hume, David (1961) *A Treatise of Human Nature*. London: Dent. 2 volumes.

Husserl, Edmund (1991) *On the Phenomenology of the Consciousness of Internal Time (1893–1917)*. [*Edmund Husserl – Collected Works*, Vol. 4]. Trans. John Barnett Brough. The Hague: Nijhoff.

Huyssen, Andreas (1995) *Twilight Memories: Marking Time in a Culture of Amnesia*. New York: Routledge.

Iweala, Uzodinma (2006) *Beasts of No Nation*. New York: Harper Perennial.

Jagose, Annemarie (2002) *Inconsequence: Lesbian Representation and the Logic of Sexual Sequence*. Ithaca, NY: Cornell University Press.

Jakobson, Roman (1971) *Selected Writings*. The Hague: Mouton. 8 volumes.

James, William (1890) *The Principles of Psychology*. New York: Henry Holt. 2 volumes.

Jameson, Fredric (1972) *The Prison-House of Language: A Critical Account of Structuralism and Russian Formalism*. Princeton, NJ: Princeton University Press.

——(1992) *Postmodernism, or, The Cultural Logic of Late Capitalism*. London: Verso.

——(2003a) *A Singular Modernity: Essays on the Ontology of the Present*. London: Verso.

——(2003b) 'The End of Temporality.' *Critical Inquiry* 29.4 (Summer): 695–718.

Jardine, Alice A. (1985) *Gynesis: Configurations of Woman and Modernity*. Ithaca, NY: Cornell University Press.

Jay, Martin (1984) *Marxism and Totality: The Adventures of a Concept from Lukács to Habermas*. Cambridge: Polity.

Johnston, Andrew James (2008) *Performing the Middle Ages from Beowulf to Othello*. Turnhout, Belgium: Brepols.

Joyce, James (1969) *Ulysses*. Penguin: Harmondsworth.

——(1975) *Finnegan's Wake*. London: Faber.

Kant, Immanuel (2003) *Critique of Pure Reason*. Trans. Norman Kemp Smith. London: Palgrave.

Kermode, Frank (1967) *The Sense of an Ending: Studies in the Theory of Fiction*. New York: Oxford University Press.

Kern, Stephen (1983) *The Culture of Time and Space 1880–1918*. London: Weidenfeld & Nicolson.

Kerr, Heather and Amanda Nettelbeck, eds (1998) *The Space Between: Australian Women Writing Fictocriticism*. Nedlands, WA: University of Western Australia Press.

King-Smith, Leah (1994) 'Patterns of Connection', in Gabrielle Pizi, ed. and cur. *Voices of the Earth: Paintings, Photography and Sculpture from Aboriginal Australia*. Exhibition Catalogue, 'Voices of the Earth' Exhibition in Seoul. Melbourne: Gabrielle Pizzi Gallery: 61–75.

Kishlansky, Mark (2011) 'Madd Men'. *London Review of Books* 33.4 (17 February): 20–21.

Kirk, G. S., J. E. Raven and M. Schofield (1983) *The Presocratic Philosophers: A Critical History with a Selection of Texts*. 2nd edn. Cambridge: Cambridge University Press.

Knorr Cetina, Karin (2004) 'How are Global Markets Global? The Architecture of a Flow World.', in Karin Knorr Cetina and Alex Preda, eds *The Sociology of Financial Markets*. Oxford: Oxford University Press: 38–61.

König, Kaspar, Emily Joyce Evans and Falk Wolf, eds (2011) *Remembering Forward: Australian Aboriginal Painting since 1960*. Cologne: Museum Ludwig/London: Paul Holberton.

Kristeva, Julia (1980) *Desire in Language: A Semiotic Approach to Literature and Art*. Ed. Leon Roudiez. Trans. Thomas Gora, Alice Jardine and Leon Roudiez. New York: Columbia University Press.

——(1984) *Revolution in Poetic Language*. Trans. Margaret Waller. New York: Columbia University Press.

——(1986) 'Women's Time', in Toril Moi, ed. *The Kristeva Reader*. Oxford: Blackwell: 187–213.

——(1987) *Tales of Love*. Trans. Leon S. Roudiez. New York: Columbia University Press.

——(2001) *Au risque de la pensée*. Paris: L'Aube.

Kunkel, Benjamin (2011) 'How Much is Too Much?' *London Review of Books* 33: 3 (3 February): 9–14.

Kwinter, Sanford (2003) *Architectures of Time: Toward a Theory of the Event in Modernist Culture*. Cambridge, MA: MIT Press.

Kwong, Luke S. K. (2001) 'The Rise of Linear Perspective on Time and History in Late Qing China c.1860–1911.' *Past and Present* 173: 157–90.

Labov, William (1972) *Language in the Inner City*. Philadelphia: University of Pennsylvania Press.

LaCapra, Dominick (2001) *Writing History, Writing Trauma*. Baltimore: Johns Hopkins University Press.

Lamb, Jonathan (2009) 'Introduction to Settlers, Creoles and Historical Reenactment', in Vanessa Agnew and Jonathan Lamb, eds *Settler and Creole Re-enactment.* Basingstoke: Palgrave: 1–18.

Lanchester, John (2011) 'The Non-Scenic Route to the Place We're Going Anyway.' *London Review of Books* 33.17 (8 September): 3–5.

Landes, David S. (2000) *Revolution in Time: Clocks and the Making of the Modern World.* Rev. edn. Cambridge, MA: Belknap Press of Harvard University Press.

Langford, Rachael (1999) 'Revolutionary Times: The Use of the Diary Form to Contest the French Third Republic in the *Jacques Vingtras* Trilogy by Jules Vallès', in Rachael Langford and Russell West, eds *Marginal Voices, Marginal Forms: Diaries in European Literature and History.* Amsterdam/Atlanta GA: Rodopi: 90–106.

Laplanchle, Jean and J.-B. Pontalis (1998) *Vocabulaire de la psychoanalyse.* Paris: PUF/Quadrige.

Larkin, Philip (1988) *Collected Poems.* Ed. Anthony Thwaite. London: Faber.

Latour, Bruno (1993) *We Have Never Been Modern.* Trans. Catherine Porter. Cambridge, MA: Harvard University Press.

——(2004) 'Why Has Critique Run Out of Steam? From Matters of Fact to Matters of Concern.' *Critical Inquiry* 30.2 (Winter): 225–48.

Le Goff, Jacques (1980) *Time, Work and Culture in the Middle Ages.* Trans. Arthur Goldhammer. Chicago: University of Chicago Press.

Le Lionnais, François (1959) *Le Temps.* Paris: Depire.

L'Engle, Madeleine (1962) *A Wrinkle in Time.* New York: Farrar, Straus and Giroux.

Lévinas, Emmanuel (1987) *Time and the Other: And Additional Essays.* Trans. Richard A. Cohen. Pittsburgh: Dusquesne University Press.

——(2006) *Humanism of the Other.* Trans. Nidra Poller. Urbana, IL: University of Illinois Press.

Lingis, Alphonso (1998) *The Imperative.* Bloomington: University of Indiana Press.

Lloyd, David (2008) *Irish Times: Temporalities of Modernity.* Dublin: Field Day Publications.

Lotman, Jurij (1977) *The Structure of the Artistic Text.* Trans. Gail Lenhoff and Ronald Vroon. Ann Arbor: University of Michigan – Department of Slavic Languages and Literatures.

Lovejoy, Arthur O. (1957) *The Great Chain of Being: A Study of the History of an Idea.* Cambridge, MA: Harvard University Press.

Lucas, Gavin (2005) *The Archaeology of Time.* London: Routledge.

Luckhurst, Roger (2008) *The Trauma Question.* London: Routledge.

Luhmann, Niklas (1976) 'The Future Cannot Begin: Temporal Structures in Modern Society.' *Social Research* 43: 130–52.

Lukács, Georg (1970) *History and Class Consciousness.* Trans. Rodney Livingstone. Cambridge, MA: MIT Press.

——(1978) *The Theory of the Novel: A Historico-Philosophical Essay on the Forms of Literature.* Trans. Anna Bostock. London: Merlin.

Lyotard, Jean-François (1984) *The Postmodern Condition: A Report on Knowledge.* Trans. Geoff Bennington and Brian Mussumi. Minneapolis: University of Minnesota Press.

McCrone, John (1999) *Going Inside: A Tour Round a Single Moment of Consciousness*. London: Faber & Faber.

Macintyre, Stuart and Anna Clark (2003) *The History Wars*. Carlton, VIC: Melbourne University Press.

Mainzer, Klaus (2002) *Zeit*. 4th edn. Munich: C. H. Beck.

Mann, Thomas (1975) *The Magic Mountain*. Trans. Helen Lowe-Porte. Harmondsworth: Penguin.

——(1991) *Der Zauberberg*. Munich: Fischer.

Marais, Hein (2011) *South Africa Pushed to the Limit: The Political Economy of Change*. Cape Town: University of Cape Town Press.

Marlowe, Christopher (1985) *The Complete Plays*. ed. J. B. Steane. Harmondsworth: Penguin.

Marvell, Andrew (1969) *The Poems of Andrew Marvell*. ed. Hugh MacDonald. London: Routledge Kegan Paul.

Marx, Karl (1969) *Karl Marx on Colonization and Modernization*. ed. Shlomo Avineri. New York: Doubleday Anchor.

——(1970) *Grundrisse der Kritik der politischen Ökonomie*. Frankfurt am Main: Europäische Verlagsanstalt.

——(1975) *Das Kapital*, Vols I–III. Berlin: Dietz. [*Marx-Engels Werke*, vols 23–25].

——(1976) *Capital: A Critique of Political Economy, Volume One*. Trans. Ben Fowkes. Harmondsworth: Penguin.

——(1993) *Grundrisse: Foundations of the Critique of Political Economy*. Trans. Martin Nicolaus. Penguin: Harmondsworth.

Marx, Karl and Friedrich Engels (1983) *The Communist Manifesto*. Trans. Samuel More. Harmondsworth: Penguin.

Massey, Doreen (1996) 'Masculinity, Dualisms and High Technology', in Nancy Duncan, ed. *BodySpace: Destabilizing Geographies of Gender and Sexuality*. London: Routledge: 109–26.

Matchinske, Megan (2009) *Women Writing History in Early Modern England*. Cambridge: Cambridge University Press.

May, Jon and Nigel Thrift (2001), 'Introduction', in May and Thrift, eds (2001) *TimeSpace: Geographies of Temporality*. London: Routledge: 1–46.

Mbembe, Achille (2001) *On the Postcolony*. Berkeley: University of California Press.

——(2008) 'Aesthetics of Superfluity', in Sarah Nuttal and Achille Membe, eds *Johannesburg: The Elusive Metropolis*. Durham, NC: Duke University Press: 37–67.

Mellor, Doreen and Anna Haebich, eds (2002) *Many Voices: Reflections on Experiences of Indigenous Child Separation*. Canberra, ACT: National Library of Australia.

Merleau-Ponty, Maurice (2002) *Phenomenology of Perception*. Trans. Colin Smith. London: Routledge.

Meyerhoff, Hans (1955) *Time in Literature*. Berkeley: University of California Press.

Michaels, Anne (1998) *Fugitive Pieces*. London: Bloomsbury.

Middleton, Thomas (1988) *Five Plays*. ed. Bryan Loughrey and Neil Taylor. Harmondsworth: Penguin.

Minkowski, H. (1952) 'Space and Time', in H. A. Lorentz, A. Einstein, H. Minkowski and H. Weyl. *The Principle of Relativity: A Selection of Original Memoirs of the Special and General Theory of Relativity*. New York: Dover: 75–96.

Mishra, Vijay and Bob Hodge (2005) 'What Was Postcolonialism?' *New Literary History* 36.3: 375–402.

Muecke, Stephen (2002) 'The Fall: Fictocritical Writing.' *Parallax* 8.4: 108–12.

——(2004) *Ancient and Modern: Time, Culture and Indigenous Philosophy*. Sydney: UNSW Press.

——(2012) 'Motorcycles, Snails, Latour: Criticism without Judgement.' *Cultural Studies Review* 18.1, forthcoming.

Müller, A. M. Klaus (1972) *Die präparierte Zeit: Der Mensch in der Krise seiner eigenen Zielsetzung*. Stuttgart: Radius.

Mumford, Lewis (1963) *Technics and Civilization*. New edn. New York: Harcourt, Brace and World.

Murray, Noëleen, Nick Shepherd and Martin Hall, eds (2007) *Desire Lines: Space, Memory and Identity in the Post-Apartheid City*. London: Routledge.

Naipaul, V. S. (2002) *A Bend in the River*. London: Picador.

Nancy, Jean-Luc (2007) *Listening*. Trans. Charlotte Mandell. New York: Fordham University Press.

Newton, Isaac (1966) *Principia*. Trans. Andrew Motte and Florian Cajori. Berkeley: University of California Press. 2 volumes.

Norretranders, Tor (1998) *The User Illusion: Cutting Consciousness Down to Size*. New York: Viking.

Nowotny, Helga (1989) *Eigenzeit: Entstehung und Strukturierung eines Zeitgefühls*. 2nd edn. Frankfurt am Main: Suhrkamp.

Nuttall, Sarah (2009) *Entanglement: Literary and Cultural Reflections on Post-Apartheid*. Johannesburg: Wits University Press.

Ondaatje, Michael (1993) *The English Patient*. London: Picador.

Osborne, Peter (1995) *The Politics of Time: Modernity and Avant-Garde*. London: Verso.

Osterhammel, Jürgen (2009) *Die Verwandlung der Welt: Eine Geschichte des 19. Jahrhunderts*. Munich: C. H. Beck.

Parry, Graham (1995) *Trophies of Time: English Antiquarians of the Seventeenth Century*. Oxford: Oxford University Press.

Paulson, William (2001) *Literary Culture in a World Transformed: A Future for the Humanities*. Ithaca, NY: Cornell University Press.

Perlin, Ross (2011) *Intern Nation: How to Earn Nothing and Learn Little in the Brave New Economy*. London: Verso.

Piggot, Stuart (1989) *Ancient Britons and the Antiquarian Imagination*. London: Thames & Hudson.

Plato (1952) *Timaeus – Critias – Cleitophon – Menexenus – Epistles*. Trans. R. G. Bury. London: Heinemann/Cambridge, MA: Harvard University Press. 2 volumes.

Plotnitsky, Arkady (1994) *Complementarity: Anti-Epistemology after Bohr and Derrida*. Durham, NC: Duke University Press.

Povinelli, Elizabeth A. (2005) 'A Flight from Freedom', in Ania Loomba et al. eds *Postcolonial Studies and Beyond*. Durham, NC: Duke University Press: 145–65.

Prigogine, Ilya and Isabelle Stengers (1984) *Order Out of Chaos: Man's New Dialogue with Nature*. London: Heinemann.

Prigogine, Ilya (2003) *Is Future Given?* River Edge, NJ: World Scientific Publishers.

Pusch, Luisa (1990) *Alle Menschen warden Schwestern*. Frankfurt am Main: Suhrkamp.

Quinones, Ricardo J. (1972) *The Renaissance Discovery of Time*. Cambridge, MA: Harvard University Press.

Rabinowitz, Peter (2002) 'Reading Beginnings and Endings', in Brian Richardson, ed. *Narrative Dynamics: Essays on Time, Plot, Closure, and Frames*. Columbus, OH: Ohio State University Press: 300–313.

Racin, John (1974) *Sir Walter Raleigh as Historian: An Analysis of the History of the World*. Salzburg: Institut für Englische Sprache und Literatur, Universität Salzburg.

Radstone, Susannah (2007) *The Sexual Politics of Time: Confession, Nostalgia, Memory*. London: Routledge.

Raleigh, Sir Walter (1964) *The Works of Sir Walter Raleigh*. New York: Burt Franklin. 8 volumes.

Reichenbach, Hans (1951) *The Rise of Scientific Philosophy*. Berkeley: University of California Press.

Reichert, Klaus (1985) *Fortuna oder die Beständigkeit des Wechsels*. Frankfurt am Main: Suhrkamp.

Rhys, Jean (1968) *Wide Sargasso Sea*. Harmondsworth: Penguin.

Richardson, Brian (2002) 'Beyond Story and Discourse: Narrative Time in Postmodern and Nonmimetic Fiction', in Brian Richardson, ed. *Narrative Dynamics: Essays on Time, Plot, Closure, and Frames*. Columbus, OH: Ohio State University Press: 47–63.

Rickard, John (1996) *Australia: A Cultural History*. 2nd edn. London: Longman.

Ricoeur, Paul (1983–85) *Temps et récit*. Paris: Seuil. 3 volumes.

——(1984–88) *Time and Narrative*. Trans. Kathleen McLaughlin and David Pellauer. Chicago: University of Chicago Press. 3 volumes.

Rose, Deborah Bird (1996) *Nourishing Terrains: Australian Aboriginal Views of Wilderness and Landscape*. Canberra, ACT: Australian Heritage Commission.

Rosenberg, Daniel and Anthony Grafton (2010) *Cartographies of Time: A History of the Timeline*. Princeton, NJ: Princeton Architectural Press.

Rosset, Clément (1971) *La logique du pire*. Paris: PUF.

——(1977) *Le Réel: Traité de l'idiotie*. Paris: Minuit.

Rothschild, Babette (2000) *The Body Remembers: The Psychophysiology of Trauma and Trauma Treatment*. New York: W. W. Norton.

Rushdie, Salman (1984) *Shame*. London: Picador.

——(1991) *Imaginary Homelands: Essays and Criticism 1981–1991*. London: Granta.

——(1995) *Midnight's Children*. London: Vintage.

Russell, Bertrand (1962) *Human Knowledge: Its Scope and Limits*. New York: Simon & Shuster.

Ryan, Joanna, with Frank Thomas (1980) *The Politics of Mental Handicap*. Harmondsworth: Penguin.

Rysman, Alexander (1977) 'How the "Gossip" Became a Woman.' *Journal of Communication* 27.1: 176–80.

Safranski, Rüdiger (1994) *Ein Meister aus Deutschland: Heidegger und seine Zeit*. Munich: Hanser.

Said, Edward (1985) 'Orientalism Reconsidered', in Francis Barker et. al. eds *Europe and Its Others, Volume I: Proceedings of the Essex Conference on the Sociology of Literature July 1984*. Colchester: University of Essex: 14–27.

——(1997) *Beginnings: Intention and Method*. New ed. London: Granta.

Sartre, Jean-Paul (1970) *Qu'est ce que la littérature?* Paris: Gallimard/Idées.

——(2001) *What is Literature?* Trans. Bernard Frechtman. London: Routledge.

——(2003) *Being and Nothingness: An Essay on Phenomenological Ontology*. Trans. Hazel E. Barnes. London: Routledge.

Saussure, Ferdinand de (1974) *Course in General Linguistics*. Trans. Wade Baskin. London: Fontana.

Schlunke, Katrina (2005) *Bluff Rock: Autobiography of a Massacre*. Perth, WA: Curtin University Press.

Scott, Kim (1999) *Benang*. Fremantle, WA: Fremantle Arts Centre Press.

——(2009) 'Apologies, Agency and Resilience', Address at 'The Australian History Wars Revisited' Conference, Free University of Berlin, October 2009.

——(2010) 'Apologies, Agency and Resilience', in Russell West-Pavlov and Jennifer Wawrzinek, eds *Frontier Skirmishes: Literary and Cultural Debates in Australia after 1992*. Heidelberg: Winter, 2010: 57–68.

Scott, Kim and Hazel Brown (2005) *Kayang and Me*. Fremantle, WA: Fremantle Arts Centre Press.

Self, Will and Martin Amis (1993) 'An Interview with Martin Amis.' *Mississippi Review* 21.3 (Spring): 143–69.

Shelton, Beth Ann (1992) *Women, Men and Time: Gender Differences in Paid Work, Housework and Leisure*. Westport, CT: Greenwood Press.

Shklovsky, Viktor (1990) *Theory of Prose*. Trans. Benjamin Sher. Elmswood Park, IL: Dalkey Archive Press.

Shohat, Ella (1992) 'Notes on the "Post-Colonial".' *Social Text* 31/32: 99–113.

Siegel, Jerrold (2005) *The Idea of the Self: Thought and Experience in Western Europe since the Seventeenth Century*. Cambridge: Cambridge University Press.

Smil, Vaclav (1994) *Energy in World History*. Boulder, CO: Westview.

Sohmer, Steve (2002) 'The "Double Time" Crux in *Othello* Solved.' *English Literary Renaissance* 32:2 (Spring): 214–38.

Spinoza, Benedict de (1996) *Ethics*. Trans. Edwin Curley. Harmondsworth: Penguin.

Spivak, Gayatri Chakravorty (1999) *A Critique of Postcolonial Reason: Towards a History of the Vanishing Present*. Cambridge, MA: Harvard University Press.

Sterne, Laurence (1985) *The Life and Opinions of Tristram Shandy*. Harmondsworth: Penguin.

Stevenson, Randall (1992) *Modernist Fiction: An Introduction*. Hemel Hempstead: Harvester Wheatsheaf.

Stürzl, Erwin (1965) *Der Zeitbegriff der Elisabethaner: The Lackey of Eternity*. Vienna: Braunmüller.

Swain, Tony (1993) *A Place for Strangers: Towards a History of Australian Aboriginal Being*. Cambridge: Cambridge University Press.

Tawney, R. H. (1964) *Religion and the Rise of Capitalism*. Harmondsworth: Penguin.

Terdiman, Richard (1993) *Present Past: Modernity and the Memory Crisis*. Ithaca, NY: Cornell University Press.

——(2008) 'Taking Time: Temporal Representation and Cultural Politics', in Tyrus Miller, ed. *Given World and Time: Temporalities in Context*. Budapest: Central European University Press: 131–44.

Thom, René (1983) *Mathematical Models of Morphogenesis*. Chichester: Horwood.

Thompson, E. P. (1967) 'Time, Work-Discipline and Industrial Capitalism.' *Past & Present* 38 (December): 56–97.

——(1968) *The Making of the English Working Class*. Harmondsworth: Penguin.

Thoreau, Henry David (1906) *Walden or Life in the Woods*. London: J. M. Dent.

Thrift, Nigel (1988) '"Vivos Voco": Ringing the Changes in Historical Geography of Time Consciousness', in M. Young and T. Schuller, eds *The Rhythms of Society*. London: Routledge: 53–94.

——(2008) *Non-Representational Theory: Space | Politics | Affect*. London: Routledge.

Thucydides (1978) *The Peloponnesian War*. Trans. Rex Warner. Harmondsworth: Penguin.

Tillyard, E. M. W. (1978) *The Elizabethan World Picture*. Harmondsworth: Penguin.

Toulmin, Stephen and Jane Goodfield (1965) *The Discovery of Time*. Chicago: University of Chicago Press.

Trevor-Roper, Hugh (1992) 'The Invention of Tradition: The Highland Tradition of Scotland', in Eric Hobsbawm and Terence Ranger, eds *The Invention of Tradition*. Cambridge: Cambridge University Press/Canto: 15–41.

Vasse, Denis (1969) *Le Temps du désir: Essai sur le corps et la parole*. Paris: Seuil.

Virilio, Paul (1986) *Speed and Politics: An Essay on Dromology*. Trans. Mark Polizotti. New York: Semiotext(e).

——(1991) *The Lost Dimension*. Trans. Daniel Moshenberg. New York: Semiotext(e).

——(1994) *Bunker Archaeology: Texts and Photos*. Trans. George Collins. New York: Princeton Architectural Press.

Vonnegurt, Kurt (1968) *Slaughterhouse-Five*. New York: Bantam.

Waldenfels, Bernhard (2004) *Phänomenologie der Aufmerksamkeit*. Frankfurt am Main: Suhrkamp.

Watt, Ian (1981) *Conrad in the Nineteenth Century*. Berkeley: University of California Press.

Weber, Eugene (1979) *Peasants into Frenchmen: The Modernisation of Rural France 1870–1914*. London: Chatto & Windus.

Weizäcker, Carl Friedrich von (1977) *Im Garten des Menschlichen: Beiträge zur geschichtlichen Anthropologie*. Munich: Hanser.

Wenz, Karin (1997) *Raum, Raumsprache und Sprachräume: Zur Textsemiotik der Raumbeschreibung*. Tübingen: Gunter Narr.

West-Pavlov, Russell (2010) *Spaces of Fiction/Fictions of Space: Postcolonial Place and Literary DeiXis*. Basingstoke: Palgrave Macmillan.

——(2011) 'The Time of Biopolitics in the Settler Colony.' *Australian Literary Studies* 26.2 (June): 1–19.

West-Pavlov, Russell and Jennifer Wawrzinek, eds (2010) *Frontier Skirmishes: Literary and Cultural Debates in Australia after 1992*. Heidelberg: Winter.

White, Hayden (1973) *Metahistory: The Historical Imagination in Nineteenth-Century Europe.* Baltimore: Johns Hopkins University Press.

——(1978) *The Tropics of Discourse: Essays in Cultural Criticism.* Baltimore: Johns Hopkins University Press.

White, Hayden and Frank E. Manuel (1978) *Theories of History: Papers read at a Clark Library Seminar, March 6, 1976.* Los Angeles: William Andrews Clark Memorial Library.

Whitehead, Alfred North (1920) *The Concept of Nature: Tanner Lectures Delivered in Trinity College November 1919.* Cambridge: Cambridge University Press.

Whitrow, C. J. (1988) *Time in History: The Evolution of Our General Awareness of Time and Temporal Perspective.* New York: Oxford University Press.

Wilcox, Donald J. (1987) *The Measure of Time Past: Pre-Newtonian Chronologies and the Rhetoric of Relative Time.* Chicago: University of Chicago Press.

Williams, Raymond (1977) *Marxism and Literature.* Oxford: Oxford University Press.

Wittgenstein, Ludwig (1974) *Tractatus Logico Philosophicus.* Trans. D. F. Pears and B. F. McGuinness. London: Routledge & Kegan Paul.

Wolf, Eric (1982) *Europe and the People without History.* Berkeley: University of California Press.

Wood, David (2001) *The Deconstruction of Time.* Evanston, IL: Northwestern University Press.

Wood, David Houston (2009) *Time, Narrative and Emotion in Early Modern England.* Farnham: Ashgate.

Woolf, Virginia (1980) *The Letters of Virginia Woolf.* ed. Nigel Nicolson and Joanne Trautmann. London: Chatto & Windus. 5 volumes.

——(1984) *Mrs Dalloway.* London: Grafton.

——(2000) *To the Lighthouse.* Harmondsworth: Penguin.

——(2008) *Orlando: A Biography.* Oxford: Oxford University Press/World's Classics.

Wordsworth, William (1990) *William Wordsworth: The Oxford Authors.* ed. Stephen Gill. Oxford: Oxford University Press.

Young, Robert (1990) *White Mythologies: Writing, History and the West.* London: Routledge.

——(2001) *Postcolonialism: An Historical Introduction.* Oxford: Blackwell.

Zoll, Rainer, ed. (1988) *Zerstörung und Wiederaneignung von Zeit.* Frankfurt am Main: Suhrkamp.

Index